"A clear and accessible account of the early church coming to terms with what happened in the life, death, resurrection, and ascension of Jesus (what do we believe?) and the impact those events had on daily life (how do we live differently because of what we believe?). The early church lived as faithful Christ-followers in an empire hostile to their beliefs and behaviors, and as traditionally 'Christian' countries become more hostile to Christian faith, contemporary Christians would do well to go back to these early sources of faith. Sittser's book takes an enormity of information about the early church and presents it in an inviting way. You will learn doctrine, church history, and formation practices, but most of all you'll come away inspired by these first Christians and challenged to follow Jesus with the same level of devotion and sacrifice that they did."

—**Mary S. Hulst**, college chaplain, Calvin College

"I wish I could make this exceptional new book by Gerald L. Sittser required reading for all contemporary Christians. With questions swirling about the relevance and contributions of the Christian faith today, Sittser presents a winsome picture of the many ways that the earliest Christians contributed to the world around them through their distinctive way of life. In the face of a crisis of discipleship and formation in the contemporary church, Sittser reminds us of all that we can learn from the ways the earliest Christians were formed into 'improvisational disciples' who could seek God's kingdom every day, right where they were. Exploring the formative role of worship and the intentional process of formation that developed in the early church, Sittser helps us look back so that we can more faithfully move forward in our complex cultural moment, embodying our faith in ways that eschew both accommodation and separation. If you have appreciated the works of Alexander Schmemann, Jamie Smith, Kevin Vanhoozer, or Sam Wells, you will love this book."

—**Kristen Deede Johnson**, Western Theological Seminary

"I have the privilege of knowing Jerry Sittser up close. For most of the past twenty years we have co-led reading groups for pastors. We met for lively discussion around applying the insights of ancient Christian sources to our lives and ministries. Jerry is a first-rate scholar who cares deeply about the church and its leaders. His passion is to reconnect the academy and the church. This book is a beautiful example of that synergy of scholarship and ministry application. Pastors will find it not only educational but helpful and practical as they consider how to make disciples in our post-Christendom setting. Jerry has done us a great favor, pointing us forward by helping us look back."

—**Joe Wittwer**, lead pastor of Life Center, Spokane, Washington, and sending pastor of seventeen daughter and granddaughter churches

"In this stimulating book Gerald Sittser powerfully argues that the gospel message can reverse the continued decline and superficiality of Western Christianity. His constructive analysis demonstrates that the Christian faith is most resilient against culture when it is most deeply grounded in Jesus Christ. To counter current trends Sittser recovers the ancient practice of the catechumenate to transform stagnant believers into dynamic disciples. Anyone concerned about the contemporary health of the Western church will profit from this insightful study. This deeply researched and highly readable book is enriched by a wisely annotated collection of sources that can guide interested readers in further study. For weary and frustrated Christians, I highly recommend it!"

—**Tom Schwanda**, Wheaton College

"The mainline and evangelical church needs the refreshing hope Jerry Sittser's book *Resilient Faith* provides. Historical. Applicable. Mind stretching. Christ centered."

—**Bob Bouwer**, author, church coach, and senior pastor of Faith Church (RCA), a multiplying movement of six-plus churches

"Rather than surrender to gloom and pessimism about the future of the church, Sittser fills this book with hope. Sittser uses the early church as the model, and he enthusiastically describes their ability to thrive, flourish, and expand in a hostile culture by thoroughly inculcating the tenets of the Christian faith into new believers."

—**Kay Warren**, bestselling author and cofounder of Saddleback Church

"It's hard to find a book that is both scholarly and accessible to a general reading audience. Gerald Sittser believes his vocation is to write this kind of book, and he's done so in *Resilient Faith*."

—**Chris Hall**, president of Renovaré

RESILIENT
FAITH

RESILIENT FAITH

How the Early Christian
"Third Way" Changed the World

GERALD L. SITTSER

Brazos Press
a division of Baker Publishing Group
Grand Rapids, Michigan

© 2019 by Gerald L. Sittser

Published by Brazos Press
a division of Baker Publishing Group
PO Box 6287, Grand Rapids, MI 49516-6287
www.brazospress.com

Printed in the United States of America

Library of Congress Cataloging-in-Publication Data
Names: Sittser, Gerald Lawson, 1950– author.
Title: Resilient faith : how the early Christian "third way" changed the world / Gerald L. Sittser.
Description: Grand Rapids : Brazos Press, a division of Baker Publishing Group, 2019. | Includes index.
Identifiers: LCCN 2019006893 | ISBN 9781587434082 (pbk.)
Subjects: LCSH: Church history—Primitive and early church, ca. 30–600. | Christianity—Influence.
Classification: LCC BR162.3 .S58 2019 | DDC 270.1—dc23
LC record available at https://lccn.loc.gov/2019006893

ISBN 978-1-5874-3454-9 (casebound)

19 20 21 22 23 24 25   7 6 5 4 3 2 1

In keeping with biblical principles of creation stewardship, Baker Publishing Group advocates the responsible use of our natural resources. As a member of the Green Press Initiative, our company uses recycled paper when possible. The text paper of this book is composed in part of post-consumer waste.

To James R. Edwards

Contents

Acknowledgments

Usually the name of only one person appears on the cover of a book as its author. It is, of course, misleading, for many people contribute to the writing of it. I am deeply indebted to a community of people who encouraged me to write *Resilient Faith* and provided critical comments to improve it.

My wife, Patricia, never stopped championing this project. She believes in my calling—to serve as a bridge between the academy and the church—and reminds me often of its importance. She read the first draft and offered just the right comments. "Wordy!" "Boring!" "Tedious!" But also "Winsome!" "Lucid!" "Convicting!" This book is leaner and cleaner because of her sensibilities.

Two pastors, Scot Rees and Brian Keepers, read the manuscript with the church in mind, and three scholars, Jim Edwards, Adam Neder, and Rick Steele, with the academy in mind. This book is sharper and deeper because of their academic prowess, critical eye, and attention to detail.

A group of friends—Sarah Butler, Myra Watts, Krisi Sonneland, Krista Lack, Leslie McAuley, Julie Jones, Josh Bingle, Bob Brewster, Carter Hudson, John Carter—read a draft, too. We enjoyed an extraordinary evening of conversation about it. My brother-in-law, Jack Veltkamp, suggested that his small group read and discuss the manuscript during their weekly meetings. I joined them one Saturday and benefited from their comments. These friends remind me that professors and pastors should never forget that there are a lot of smart and serious Christians sitting in the pews every Sunday. They deserve our best.

Anna Irwin Applebach, Lilly Davis, Adam Blyckert, and Christopher Pieper served as research fellows for me while they were undergraduate students at Whitworth. Their research introduced me to literature I would have otherwise not had time to discover. This book is broader because of their careful work.

This is my first book with Brazos Press. A few years ago I met Robert Hosack over coffee when I was speaking at Calvin College. He invited me to submit a book proposal. Since that first encounter, Robert, James Korsmo, Jeremy Wells, and the rest of the team have operated according to the highest personal and professional standards. My relationship with them has been positive from beginning to end.

I am dedicating this book to my dear friend and colleague James R. Edwards, a scholar and teacher of unusual competence.

I arrived at Whitworth in 1989, a fresh University of Chicago PhD in hand. I spent the next two years teaching what seemed like an endless stream of new courses. Still, I found time to deliver two papers and revise my dissertation for publication (*A Cautious Patriotism: The American Churches and the Second World War*). My aspiration was to continue to specialize in twentieth-century American religion, focusing on the postwar era.

In 1991, tragedy changed those plans. I spent the next decade occupied not only with my academic responsibilities but also with domestic duties, which were far more important to me. Thrust into the role of being a single parent, I began to think more about the needs of people who do not make their living in the rarified world of higher education. I wrote three popular books, one on loss (*A Grace Disguised*), another on the will of God (*The Will of God as a Way of Life*), and a third on the mutuality commands (*Love One Another*). I assumed that I would never again return to serious academic research and writing.

Jim Edwards did not share that sentiment. He encouraged me to pursue my calling as a scholar, though in the meantime my interests and instincts had changed considerably. Eventually I resumed more academic writing (book reviews, lectures, chapters, articles), which led to the publication of *Water from a Deep Well*. Along the way I discovered that I could best use my gifts as a scholar in service to the larger public. In fact, I wondered why I had not thought of it sooner. Physicians do not provide medical care only to fellow physicians. Why should scholars speak only to the members of the guild? This calling has been very meaningful to me, but it has not been easy. I am not exactly a pure academic, nor a popular writer, but something in between, a kind of hybrid that eludes convenient classification—too light for some, too heavy for others. Still, it is where I belong, where my gifts are most needed, and where I find the greatest joy.

Jim has read and critiqued almost everything I have written over the past fifteen years, including this manuscript. He holds me to high standards, to be sure; but he also celebrates my calling as an academic who writes to a broader audience. I dedicate this book to him with a deep sense of gratitude for his investment in my success, and even more so for his friendship.

Abbreviations

ANF *Ante-Nicene Fathers.* Edited by Alexander Roberts and James Donaldson. 10 vols. Peabody, MA: Hendrickson, 1994.

Bettenson, ECF Bettenson, Henry, ed. *The Early Christian Fathers: A Selection from the Writings of the Fathers from Clement of Rome to St. Athanasius.* New York: Oxford University Press, 1956.

Eusebius, *Hist.* Eusebius. *The History of the Church from Christ to Constantine.* Revised and edited by Andrew Louth. Translated by G. A. Williamson. New York: Penguin, 1989.

Hippolytus, *Ap. Trad.* Hippolytus. *On the Apostolic Tradition.* Translated by Alistair Stewart-Sykes. Crestwood, NY: St. Vladimir's Seminary Press, 2001.

NPNF² *Nicene and Post-Nicene Fathers.* 2nd series. Edited by Philip Schaff and Henry Wace. 14 vols. Peabody, MA: Hendrickson, 1994.

Richardson, ECF Richardson, Cyril C., ed. *Early Christian Fathers.* New York: Touchstone, 1996.

1

Then and Now

It was known as the "Third Way."

The phrase comes from the early Christian period. To my knowledge it first appeared in a second-century letter written to a Roman official, a certain Diognetus.[1] The author—we don't know his name or identity—wanted to describe the peculiar nature of Christianity to a member of the Roman elite. He commended Diognetus's curiosity and assured him that he would do his best to answer his questions about Christianity. He then referred to the Christian movement as a "new race" or "third race," which I have chosen to identify as the Third Way.

The Greek word the author uses—*genos*—is difficult to translate. It could be rendered "race," "tribe," "clan," "stock," "family," "life," or even "people." It implied a deep kinship connection, a sense of belonging to a people and, as a people, living in a distinct way, which Diognetus and other Roman officials had observed to be true of Christians. The Christian movement was forming a new community of people who claimed to believe in a new kind of God and to follow a new way of life.

I have chosen to use "Third Way" for two reasons: first, because it strikes me as less charged than "race" or "clan" or "tribe"; and second, because early on, Christians were known as followers of "the way." This translation fits well enough, but only if we understand it as conveying a larger meaning than merely following a new and trendy way of life

1

that is here today and gone tomorrow.[2] The early Christian movement was anything but that.

Diognetus was familiar with the phrase, implying that it might have been coined by the Romans themselves to categorize three distinct and different religious ways of life: Roman, Jewish, and Christian. The author warned Diognetus that he was going to be surprised by what he learned. He exhorted him to clear out his old thoughts about religion. "You must become like a new man from the beginning, since, as you yourself admit, you are going to listen to a really new message."[3]

Of course a third way implies a first and second way. The first, as Diognetus would have known, was the Roman way, which organized life around Greco-Roman civil religion and was the most ubiquitous and popular of the three. Civic life and religious life were virtually inseparable in the Roman world. Public officials were responsible for managing the religious affairs of a community, including maintenance of temples and performance of various rituals. People worshiped and sacrificed to the gods; they visited temples, shrines, and monuments; they participated in pagan feasts and festivals; they kept and cared for household deities at the family altar; they experimented with and sometimes joined mystery cults. Above all, they swore allegiance to the emperor as a god. They observed these and other rituals largely to secure Rome's prosperity, and their own as well.[4]

Rome's religious system was largely transactional. Romans honored the gods and goddesses, and they expected those gods and goddesses to respond in kind. Their religion was based on ritual observance more than doctrinal belief and ethical behavior. Worship was supposed to bring benefits, especially to the empire. Rome was tolerant, pluralistic, and syncretistic. It exhibited an amazing capacity to absorb new religions into its pantheon, assuming that adherents, whatever they believed and however they lived, would be subservient to Rome and swear allegiance to the divine status of the emperor. It had the most trouble with the religions that demanded exclusive commitment to one God and to one way of life. Most religions of this kind, especially Christianity, were considered by definition anti-Roman.

In the end, Rome's religion was Rome itself.

The second was the Jewish way. Rome respected Judaism because the religion was ancient and enduring. Jews had survived opposition for over a thousand years and, in spite of that opposition, had spread throughout the Roman Empire and beyond. Rome even showed favor to the Jews. For example, Roman authorities did not require Jews to venerate the gods (say, through sacrificial offerings in local temples) or to serve in the military, and Romans viewed and used at least some local synagogues as civic centers, which implies that Judaism served the larger Roman public, however modestly. Jews were far more integrated into Roman society than it might at first appear.

Still, there were reasons why Judaism was known as the second way, distinct from the first way. Jews worshiped one God, Yahweh, to whom they were exclusively devoted; followed a rigorous set of ethical and religious practices; and refused to participate in pagan rituals and festivals. They observed a way of life that set them culturally apart. The Jewish rite of circumcision kept Romans who were attracted to Judaism from wholesale conversion. Jewish kosher laws required that Jews shop in their own stores, their dress codes made them noticeable, and their commitment to marry only fellow Jews prevented them from assimilating into Roman culture. Such relative cultural isolation made it easy for Roman officials to identify Jews, thereby diminishing the threat or, short of that, allowing Romans to keep an eye on them, as sports enthusiasts might when eyeing fans wearing the jersey of a rival team.

However respected by the Romans and integrated into the larger Roman society, Jews were different enough to be classified as the second way.

And then there was Christianity, the Third Way. Christians appeared to live like everyone else. They spoke the local language, lived in local neighborhoods, wore local styles of clothing, ate local food, shopped in local markets, and followed local customs. "For Christians cannot be distinguished from the rest of the human race by country or language or custom. They do not live in cities of their own; they do not use a peculiar form of speech; they do not follow an eccentric manner of life."[5] At a surface level Christians appeared to blend in to Roman society quite seamlessly.

Yet they were different, too, embodying not simply a different religion but a different—and new—way of life. "They live in their own countries, but only as aliens. They have a share in everything as citizens, and endure everything as foreigners. Every foreign land is their fatherland, and yet for them every fatherland is a foreign land." They functioned as if they were a nation within a nation, culturally assimilated yet distinct at the same time. "Yet, although they live in Greek and barbarian cities alike, as each man's lot has been cast, and follow the customs of the country in clothing and food and other matters of daily living, at the same time they give proof of the remarkable and admittedly extraordinary constitution of their own commonwealth." They constituted a new race of people—hence the Third Way. Rome could not so easily monitor and control this group.[6]

What made Christians different? What was this Third Way?

Christians believed in the reality of another and greater kingdom over which God ruled. It was a spiritual kingdom—not *of* this world, but certainly *over* this world as superior and supreme, *for* this world's redemption, and *in* this world as a force for ultimate and eternal good. Far from being "resident aliens," Christians thus viewed themselves as "alien residents," members of the true and universal commonwealth, but still living within the Roman commonwealth. They believed that God's kingdom, though transcendent over all, impinged on this world and would someday subsume it, as the rising sun overwhelms the light of moon and stars.

Early Christians confessed that this kingdom was concealed, seen only through the eyes of faith, though that faith was both informed and formed by God's involvement in human history, a history that culminated in the coming of Jesus. But what was concealed would someday be gloriously revealed, and God would rule in mercy and justice over the entire created order. The Third Way was like a resistance movement, both subversive and peaceful, bearing witness to God's coming kingdom. But rather than following a strategy of violent revolution, as, say, the zealots did, Christians immersed themselves in the culture as agents of the kingdom. Christians aspired to follow another way, Jesus' way. They prayed for the emperor but refused to worship him.

The Centrality of Jesus

Jesus was at the center of this vision of the kingdom. Surprisingly so, for he was not what anyone, whether Jew or Roman, expected or wanted. As the author of this unusual letter to Diognetus argued, humanity wants—and sometimes creates—gods in its own image, gods to reinforce its idols and idolatries, gods to disguise its egoism, gods who serve the interests of the elites, gods who rule by power, but not gods who love, and especially who love the poor and powerless. But the God of the early Christians did not follow that script, because they believed God revealed himself as Jesus Christ—not as a wise man like Socrates, not as a strong man like Hercules, not as a powerful man like Augustus, not as a military commander like Alexander the Great, and not even as a Messiah, at least according to the claims and intentions of someone like Simon Bar Kokhba.

Instead, Jesus appeared to be a humble, foolish, weak man who was born in a stable and who suffered on a cross. No one expected a divine appearance (or "incarnation") of this kind. Why would they? As Paul writes, both Greeks and Jews assumed that God is by definition bigger, stronger, and wiser than the biggest, strongest, and wisest on earth. The incarnation surprised and baffled everyone because it departed from traditional expectations of the divine. "For the foolishness of God is wiser than human wisdom, and the weakness of God is stronger than human strength" (1 Cor. 1:25 NIV).

Christians strived to live according to their master, Jesus. They wanted their way of life to align with his, which was *the* way. Jesus modeled this true way *of* life because he was first and foremost the way *to* true life. The discipline of Christians was born out of devotion to Jesus as Savior and Lord. Jesus was both center and substance of the Third Way—God come as a human, the kingdom appearing in a person.

Christians faced the unimaginable challenge of bearing witness to the kingdom in the massive expanse of the Roman Empire, and eventually beyond, functioning as suspect outsiders—or on occasion as outright enemies—for some 250 years. As Christianity began to get a foothold in the Mediterranean world, Rome altered its response to the movement. At first it largely ignored and dismissed it, critical of its (often exaggerated and misunderstood) peculiarities. Then it ramped up opposition, which included mostly local or regional persecution of various kinds. In the end, it turned on it violently, as if blasting shrill music to drown out the new song of Christianity, only to change its mind and accept it, which led to the mutual transformation of both empire and church.

What made it so successful in spite of these inhospitable conditions?[7]

Christians had to guard the newness of the message without isolating themselves from the culture or accommodating themselves to the culture, which required them to form people in the faith and thus grow a movement of genuine disciples who could survive, and even thrive, in such a world. Rome would have ignored Christianity if Christians had been too isolated; it would have absorbed it if they had become too accommodating.[8] For the most part it did neither.

This Third Way movement grew steadily, though unevenly, for some 250 years under Rome's watchful and sometimes hostile eye. It is impossible to calculate exact figures. But it is safe to say that Christians numbered roughly five thousand in the year AD 40 and five million by the year 300, worshiping in some sixty-five thousand house churches of varying sizes.[9] Such an impressive growth rate would seem to require some level of state support and cultural privilege. Yet Christians enjoyed few of the benefits that Christians take for granted today, at least in the West. They did not worship in official church buildings (as we would understand them today), send their children to Christian schools, enjoy the benefits of cultural power and visibility, or flex their Christian political muscles. The Christian movement embodied a new and different way of knowing God and living in the world. It was so new and different, in fact, that it developed a process of formation to move people, slowly and deliberately, from participation in Greco-Roman religion or Judaism into the Christian fold. That was one major reason for its success. This process, as we will see, enabled the movement to adapt to many different cultural settings without losing its essential identity.[10]

Christendom

With the accession of Constantine to the throne of the Roman Empire in 312, the status of Christianity was forever changed. He set in motion a long process that led, first, to the legalization of Christianity *in* the Roman Empire; then, under the emperor Theodosius, to the official establishment of Christianity as the religion *of* the empire; and finally, during the Middle Ages, to Christianity's overwhelming cultural dominance *over* the empire. This arrangement shaped the entire history and identity of Europe, and later of North America. It took hundreds of years, of course. And it was never complete. Not every person living in the Middle Ages was a serious and sincere Christian, nor every institution good and just. Still, the movement was successful enough to justify the claim that the West had become Christian, and would presumably remain so.

Over time the designation "Third Way" faded as Christianity became the *only* way—that is, the dominant religion in the West. The emergence of Christendom—the symbiotic relationship between church and state, Christianity and culture—made the Third Way irrelevant. There was no need for it as long as Christianity, having no major rivals, ruled the culture. No wonder the phrase itself was largely lost to historical memory. It was forgotten because the Third Way was no longer needed. If there was an exception to this, it was the rise of the monastic movement, which kept alive the Third Way in reaction to Christianity's dominant—and compromised—role in the empire. The vision of the Third Way never died, but it certainly moved to the margins of the church as a kind of memory of an earlier, and presumably better, age.

If we could travel back in time to the year 1200 or the year 1600, we would be hard-pressed to find a person living in the West who did not claim to be Christian (except for Jews and Muslims), and we would observe the visible and concrete presence of Christianity everywhere. We would see church buildings, monasteries, schools and universities, hospitals, law courts, pilgrimage sites, religious art and texts, feasts and festivals, priests and liturgical pageantry, monks and nuns, and rites

7

and relics and rituals, all reflecting the dominance of Christianity as a religion and the centrality of the church as an institution.

Not that Christianity was uniform or the church united. Arguments often divided the church, sometimes irreparably. East and West split in 1054, the former becoming the Orthodox Church, the latter the Roman Catholic Church. The Western church broke apart in the wake of the Reformation, which set in motion a series of divisions that have continued to this day. Nor did Christians always conduct themselves as they should have, as the Crusades, the wars of religion, and persecution of Jews illustrate. Still, Christianity continued to dominate in the West for many centuries, with hardly a dissenting voice, except for Jews, Muslims, and a few elite deists and atheists, who functioned as an alternative to the Christian majority—influential, to be sure, but never large and dominant enough to threaten Christianity's hegemony. The arguments that divided the church were about family matters, involving clashes of doctrine, practice, politics, and personality.

America tells a different story, though only slightly. Christendom took a peculiar turn in our nation's history. Observing the problem of the state-established church in Europe, the founders and framers decided to create a different kind of church-state relationship. We know it as the official separation of church and state. As the First Amendment states, "Congress shall make no law respecting an establishment of religion, or prohibiting the free exercise thereof." Cut loose from state support and control, the churches in America learned to function more independently, becoming entrepreneurial and competitive.

The essential difference in the American experiment—including many of its successes—captured the attention of Alexis de Tocqueville, a French aristocrat. In the 1830s he traveled to America to discover why democracy in America was flourishing, much to the surprise of many Europeans. He observed that it was due, at least in part, to the "habits of the heart" of the American people, which kept them from exploiting and abusing the freedoms that the Bill of Rights granted to them. These habits were largely the result of Christianity's influence.

How did it exercise so much influence? According to Tocqueville, Christianity worked at the grassroots level—in homes, public schools and private colleges, churches, and voluntary societies (nonprofits), which served the needs of the country beyond what government was capable of doing. It functioned as a restraining influence, preventing the American people from taking advantage of the freedom they had. "Thus, while the law allows the American people to do everything, there are things which religion prevents them from imagining and forbids them to dare."[11]

Tocqueville believed that democracy, more than any other political system, needed religion, but only if religion remained separate from the state, independent of outside interference, resistant to control, and thus free to operate on its own term. "Despotism may be able to do without faith, but freedom cannot. Religion is much more needed in the republic they advocate than in the monarchy they attack, and in democratic republics most of all. How could society escape destruction if, when political ties are relaxed, moral ties are not tightened? And what can be done with a people master of itself if it is not subject to God?"[12]

Thus America became a *cultural*—though unofficial—Christendom. Observers took notice of this arrangement, mostly with approval. Abraham Lincoln called America "the almost chosen people."[13] G. K. Chesterton referred to America as "the nation with the soul of a church," which the church historian Sidney Mead later used in the title of an essay.[14]

We carry this idea of Christendom in our cultural memory, almost as if it were cellular.[15] It is so deeply rooted in us that we hardly think about it. We simply assume it. It is like a wedding band that never comes off, like a license carried in wallet or purse, like basic knowledge of arithmetic. We might not darken the door of churches very often; we might not read much theology; we might not know the Bible very well. Still, we know enough about Christianity to feel comfortable around it, like the home we grew up in. We attend Christian weddings and funerals, worship on Christmas and Easter (or more often), sing the first verse of "Amazing Grace" by memory, and assume—whether with pleasure or with shame—that the president will conclude major speeches with "God bless America." Nearly 70 percent of Americans say they are Christian. The majority of those belong to a church of some kind.[16]

9

Our cultural memory reminds us that we are a Christian people living in a Christian nation.[17]

Post-Christendom

But is that claim still accurate? Was it ever?

First, it should be obvious that, even during the heyday of American Christendom, there were many people excluded. The postwar period marked the epitome of American cultural Christianity. I was a child then. I believed—or, better to say, assumed—that being Christian, being middle class, being white, and being American were roughly the same thing. Almost weekly I attended worship ("went to church," as we put it back then), ate brunch after worship at the downtown men's club, and played golf at a local country club. Our family prayed before meals, dressed up for church (I started wearing a sport coat in late elementary school), put money in the offering plate every Sunday, and celebrated holidays, both liturgical (e.g., Christmas) and patriotic (e.g., Memorial Day), as if they were all Christian events. It was the good life, the Christian life, the American way of life. It was a seamless whole, or so it appeared.[18]

But the "we" and "I" sprinkled throughout the last paragraph is misleading. There never was a "we" in the first place. Christendom might have existed, after a manner of speaking. It clearly made positive contributions to our society (higher education, Christian nonprofits, and the like). It no doubt brought benefits to many Americans (higher literacy)—but not to all. African Americans would tell a very different story, first of slavery and then of racism. So would some immigrant groups, many women, and other outsiders, to say nothing of Native Americans, who suffered loss of land and near genocide. The "we" did not include everyone; it often excluded large segments of the population, and did so knowingly.

Second, cultural Christianity was probably not as healthy as it seemed to be at the time, however dominant its influence in American society, for it tended to produce nominal—"in name only"—Christians who claimed Christianity as their religion for reasons other than the inherent value and truthfulness of Christianity itself. It was good for business; it left a favorable impression on people; it was socially respectable; it established one's place in the community. In many cases it was simply what Americans were supposed to do, a matter of social habit. They "did" religion in much the same way they practiced a profession or enjoyed a hobby. Many Americans confined it to a distinct and separate sphere of life. Christendom made being Christian relatively normal, easy, and convenient.

Third, however enduring over the centuries, Christendom has more recently become fragile. Christianity in America is losing ground, no longer exercising the dominance it once did. Not that it has disappeared, of course. There are signs of vitality and creativity in many places. If anything, groups demonstrating intense and serious devotion to Christianity are holding their own, and in some cases even growing and attracting people who want more than nominal faith, though much of that growth is at the expense of other religious groups, like mainline Protestants and Catholics.[19] That Christians in America are attending more conservative churches in greater numbers and with greater frequency is not in and of itself a good sign. It could mean that they are only attracting members from other churches and isolating themselves from the larger culture, not learning how to engage and win it.

The fact is: Christianity in America is declining, in both numbers and influence. The culture is changing, and we must therefore recognize that we live in a world very different from the one that existed even half a century ago during what appeared to be the "golden age" of American Christianity.

You probably sense the change and observe the trends, too. You know about the decline of mainline churches; the lack of growth in evangelical churches; the rise of "dones" (Christian dropouts) and "nones" (those people who refuse to identify with any religious tradition); the ideological division between liberal and conservative Christians, often accompanied by an unconscionable level of vitriol; the obsession with political power; the rise of Christian nationalism; the creeping loss of religious freedom; the growing dominance of secularity in the public square; the deterioration of traditional morality in the entertainment

11

industry.[20] My own profession illustrates the point. Only a century ago (even half a century ago) Christianity played a significant role in shaping the ethos and curriculum of most colleges and universities across the country, which is hardly the case anymore.[21]

Many of us have read reports and experienced the changes. We *feel* it, too, like the stuffiness and headache that warns of an oncoming cold.

At this point I probably sound like a political conservative, longing for better days. It appears to be a growing sentiment. Many conservative Christians argue that America once played a special, even divinely appointed, role in history, as if it were a "chosen nation," and they advocate that America should step into that role once again, which leads them to impose their brand of conservative morality and politics on the nation, sometimes as brashly and bellicosely as the opponents they detest. It will not work, at least not anymore. It has probably never worked, or if it has, under terms in which the cost was probably too high, sacrificing genuine Christian influence for the sake of political power.

I am not advocating that Christians follow this strategy, any more than I would argue that Christians make common cause with left-wing politics. Either way, it is not the right way, nor the Third Way. And it is not the best way to influence society. Power at the expense of the gospel is not a power the church should ever seek. The problem we currently face is not primarily political or ideological. The problem is the compromised identity of the church itself and the compromised message of the gospel. The role of Christianity in the West has changed. It is no longer culturally dominant. A political strategy to hold on to or to regain power will only set the church back even further. It would be like a boxer swinging aimlessly at an opponent to prolong time in the ring, even though the match is nearly over and clearly lost.[22]

I write this not to lament lost identity and influence, which was far more superficial than once thought, but to embrace a new challenge; not to pine for the past, which was hardly ideal anyway, but to plot a course for the future. Christian belief is far less familiar, pervasive, and persuasive than it once was, and Christian institutions and practices far less visible and dominant or, in the few cases where they still are, often tainted with a bad reputation. Our cultural memory of the past might actually be keeping us from seeing the changes happening before our very eyes and from adapting creatively to them. The best hours of Western Christianity might be ahead of us, not behind us, assuming we dare to think differently about what it means to be Christian and to live as Christians in a culture that is changing. But our worst days could be ahead of us, too. There is no guarantee that Christianity in America will regain its strength or, even better, discover and follow a better way forward. There are other examples in history of the irreversible decline of Christianity in regions where it was once strong (e.g., the Orthodox Church in modern Turkey).

The World of Millennials

Let me attempt to put a human face on the essential situation before us.

It goes something like this: I hear from former students a few years after graduating from the university at which I teach. They tell me they are no longer Christian, which is always disheartening to hear. But it is the reason behind it that I find especially disturbing. "I can't for the life of me think of one good reason to believe in Christianity anymore, or even God. It has become entirely irrelevant to my life."

It seems less a choice and more a default, as if reason and debate have given way to inertia. Students these days are not usually won over to secularity by argument, as sometimes happened a generation or two ago when they read the likes of Nietzsche, Darwin, Marx, Freud, and Russell. After moving to cities like Seattle, Portland, and San Francisco (it could be many others as well), they begin to breathe a different air, the air of unbelief and secularity. They step into a world in which Christianity seems unnecessary and obsolete, like floppy disks, VCRs, and slide rules. They don't reject faith, as if won over to unbelief through reasoned argument. They simply and slowly drift away. Indifference—and even intellectual laziness—plays a bigger role than argument, though millennials still exhibit concern for the common good of society, as evidenced by the number of hours they devote to volunteerism.

It is the result, I think, of living in a *post-Christendom* society, where much of the cultural power, privilege, and influence of Christianity has been eroded, leaving little more than a thin layer of topsoil. Belief has become not only intellectually implausible, if that even matters anymore, but also personally irrelevant.

Such is the new state of affairs in the Western world. Which means that we as Christians can no longer do business the old way. The cultural Christianity that once had few rivals has been dethroned. During the many centuries of Christendom, belief in Christianity seemed as natural, familiar, and inevitable as immediate marriage and employment after college used to be. It was simply what people in the West did. Faith might not have been genuine or deep, but it was still widespread and established. It was a cultural habit, like wearing robes for a graduation ceremony.

That phase of history in the West is drawing to a close, as I have already argued. We see ample evidence of this erosion in Europe and on the coasts in the United States.[23] It has left the church concerned, confused, and sobered—but also curious and teachable, which is one reason why Christians are looking for new resources, movements, and models that might help us, as Christians living in the West, respond faithfully and winsomely to this new state of affairs.[24]

Backward First

I believe one of those resources is knowledge of early Christian history. We must look backward before we can move forward. The church has been around for some two thousand years. Surely it has something to teach us. We just might find models and movements that could guide us through the troubled times in which we live and provide historical analogues that could illumine the pathway down which we should travel.[25]

I attended seminary in the 1970s. I had to take several classes in the history of Christianity, though in those days it was called "church history." My professor was learned and famous. He taught the course largely as a history of Christian thought. We studied orthodoxy and heresy in the early Christian period, monastic and scholastic theology in the medieval period, the Reformation controversies of the sixteenth and seventeenth centuries, the evangelical awakenings of the eighteenth century, and the liberal theology of the nineteenth and twentieth centuries, as well as its major twentieth-century critics (Barth and Bonhoeffer). In general, we learned church history from a Christendom perspective. Questions of correct belief loomed largest, at least as I remember it. We studied it as a kind of history of the Christian family, which was *our* family.

In the beginning of my teaching career I taught the history of Christianity in much the same way. My primary interest was Reformation theology and the evangelical awakenings, though I never totally neglected to tell the larger story. Students seemed interested enough, at least for a while.

But then they began to change. Their interests have clearly shifted over the years. They question the excessive attention to doctrinal precision that emerged during the Reformation period. How, they ask, could the great Reformer Martin Luther split a movement over the meaning of four words: "This is my body"? They wonder about the excessive emotion of the evangelical awakenings. How, they inquire, could a person become a Christian so quickly and easily? Doctrinal faith seems too abstract and narrow, emotive faith too fragile and insecure. I was teaching a Christendom course. My students were asking for something different. I discovered that they *needed* something different because they are growing up in a world very different from the one that existed only a generation ago.

Together we—professor and students—found it in early Christianity. They began to pepper me with questions. How did early Christians start and sustain a movement over such a long period of time (some 250 years), *before* Christendom began to emerge? How did the church maintain a steady rate of growth under such difficult circumstances? How did Christian leaders make disciples without the religious benefits and privileges we take for granted today, such as the massive availability of Christian literature, the use of technology to spread the message and nurture faith, the influence of high-profile Christian leaders, and the dominance of large-scale Christian institutions like megachurches and big nonprofits? How did this minority movement influence the larger culture, even though the vast majority of people living in the Roman

Empire did *not* assume Christianity was the one true religion, Christian ethics were the best way to live, and Christian institutions were worthy of special privilege? Christians back then had every reason to fail. But they succeeded. Students wanted to know why, and how.

The success of the early church was certainly not inevitable. Christians could have accommodated to the culture to win recognition and, most likely, approval, which would have undermined the uniqueness of their belief system and way of life. In some cases they did exactly that. But for the most part they chose not to. This would have fit well with the first way, the Roman way. Christians could have isolated themselves from the culture to hide and survive, which would have kept them on the margins—safe, to be sure, but also irrelevant. In some cases, of course, they did follow this strategy. But, once again, for the most part they chose not to. This would have matched the second way, the Jewish way. Instead, Christians engaged the culture without excessive compromise, remained separate from the culture without excessive isolation. Christians figured out how to be both faithful and winsome. They followed a Third Way, living for the unseen reality of the kingdom as they saw and believed it in Christ. They immersed themselves in the culture and over time transformed it from within, though never aiming to directly.

We might be tempted at this point to idealize early Christianity, as if it epitomizes the golden age of Christianity. But such is not the case. There has never been a golden age of Christianity, not even during the apostolic period. A perusal of Paul's first letter to the church in Corinth will disabuse us of that idea. Our churches look healthy and vital in comparison to that church! It is therefore not that early Christianity was better; the church had troubles then, as it does today. But the church was different. We can learn from that difference as we begin to share more in common with that early Christian period.[26]

Forming Christians

Here is my essential argument: the early Christian movement became known as the Third Way because Jesus himself was a new way, which in turn spawned a new movement—new in theology, in story, in authority, in community, in worship, and in behavior. Christian belief was so new, in fact, that it required Christians to develop a process of formation in the Third Way to move new believers from conversion to discipleship, from outsider to insider, from observer to full-fledged member, which produced generation after generation of believers who, established firmly in the faith, were able to grow the movement over a long period of time. Rejecting both accommodation and isolation, early Christians immersed themselves in the culture as followers of Jesus and servants of the kingdom of God.

Not that all Christians were serious about discipleship, any more than all Yankee fans are fanatics or all French people are foodies or all South Americans are nominal Catholics—or even Catholics at all. Nor, for that matter, were all ancient Romans "pagans" (a pejorative term that I will try my best to avoid). At this point I want to sound a clear note of caution. I am stating generalities. There were exceptions—and plenty of them, as scholars are quick to identify. Early Christians were different, to be sure; but they were not *that* different. All people have needs, hopes, and longings. And many turn to religion for answers, which of course includes Christianity. Still, Christianity was unique and compelling enough in the ancient world for the Romans themselves to notice—and then ignore, reject, persecute, or embrace.

Could it be that we are entering a period of Western history in which Christians will no longer be able to rely on the favor of the state, the popularity of Christianity, and the power of being the dominant majority? The premise of this book is that we, witnessing the end of Christendom, might have much to learn from Christians who lived before Christendom began. They could not rely on the kinds of cultural props that make being Christian normal, natural, and convenient. They had to choose for Christ; they had to live by conviction; they had to count the cost. Of course nominal Christians lived back then, as they do now. But on the whole, Christians living in the first few centuries were serious about discipleship. They had to be.

Of course our circumstances are clearly *not* the same as those of the early Christian period, at least not entirely. Christians once lived in an ancient pre-Christendom world; we now live in a modern post-Christendom world. They faced the challenge of introducing Christianity as a new—and radically different—religion; we face the problem of trying to reclaim and restore a faith that is plagued by lukewarmness, division, worldliness, nationalism, and ignorance. But there is enough similarity between then and now to provide us with a model for consideration.[27]

The ancient might not be as far removed from the modern as we think. Traveling back in time might be our best course of action as we move into the future with renewed energy, creativity, and courage.

2

Old World and New World

Christianity was noticeably new and different in the ancient world, so different that it developed the reputation of being a "Third Way."

But difference in and of itself is not necessarily a significant designation. It can be and often is vacuous, even meaningless. Many things can be different—novel perhaps, but also innocuous, like a strange food or a new style of clothing. Even a new religion can be innocuous.

What was it about Christianity that made it not just different but unsettlingly, menacingly, threateningly so? There is an easy answer to the question. It was Jesus Christ, at least as the apostles understood him. We have their witness to contend with.

Two ancient documents help us explore this question from the Roman perspective. A Greco-Roman official wrote the first; a group of Christian leaders wrote the second. Both explain why Christianity was considered both different and threatening.

Pliny and Polycarp

Pliny the Younger (AD 61–113) was a member of Rome's elite, similar to our Ivy League elite, only more exclusive. He was born into the wealth, privilege, and status of the equestrian order, which ranked second only to the senatorial. Typical for a person of his rank, he was educated at home and then in schools until a single teacher—the well-known Quintilian—completed his education in Rome, instructing him in philosophy and rhetoric. His famous uncle, Pliny the Elder, served as his mentor; the Younger also received the Elder's entire and extensive estate after the Elder died in the eruption of Mt. Vesuvius in AD 79.

The Younger's formal career began at the age of eighteen. He rose quickly through the ranks, entering the senatorial order in his late twenties. He served as both prosecutor and defender in Rome's legal system; as a member of the official senate in Rome and then of the emperor's staff; as tribune and prefect of the treasury; as a superintendent of Tiber River banks; and finally as imperial governor.

He conducted a vast correspondence, 247 letters of which are still available to us. They depict the life of an influential Roman. One letter in particular is relevant for our purposes. In AD 111 the emperor Trajan appointed Pliny to serve as governor of the province of Bithynia, located in north-central Asia Minor (modern Turkey). It proved to be a difficult assignment, for Bithynia had been notoriously mismanaged by local authorities. Trajan wanted Pliny to clear up the mess.[1]

As any competent governor would do, Pliny toured the province to study its needs and problems. During his travels he heard complaints about the disruptive influence of a new religion, Christianity. He did not know quite how to manage the problem, which prompted him to write to the emperor to seek his advice. As he noted in the letter, Christians did not appear to be guilty of any crime worthy of punishment. Pliny mentioned accusations of "secret crimes," but these proved to be baseless. Were Christians guilty only of the "crime of a name," not "the name of a crime," as Tertullian, the famous apologist, declared with obvious cynicism some sixty years later?[2]

Pliny followed imperial protocol. He asked suspected Christians if they were in fact Christian. If they confessed, he asked them a second and then a third time. If they refused to deny the charge, he ordered their execution, unless they were Roman citizens, in which case he sent them to Rome for trial. Pliny's charge against the Christians, which he cited as sufficient justification for capital punishment, seems pathetic

20

and cowardly to us now, as if he were searching for an excuse to rid the province of them. Christians, he said, were guilty of "stubbornness." They would not buckle under Roman pressure. It was not as if they were naturally incorrigible, as a child might be. They were stubborn for a very specific reason.

Of course news spread of the charges, which invited an avalanche of accusations, many anonymous. Pliny applied a test that seemed to work. He ordered the accused to recite a prayer to the gods, make supplication with incense before a statue of the emperor, and curse Christ, things that, as Pliny wrote, "those who are really Christians cannot be made to do."[3] In short, Christians were stubborn because they refused to yield to the demands of Rome and offer a sacrifice to the imperial cult.

Meanwhile, Pliny learned a few notable facts about the new faith. His sources included two women—he called them "deaconesses"—whom he tortured for information. Christians, they said, met for worship on a "fixed day" and before sunrise, reciting or singing "by turns a form of words to Christ as a god." At these gatherings they would swear an oath not to commit any "crimes," such as theft and adultery, nor to break their word, nor to withhold money if asked or demanded. After worship, they would meet for a meal. Pliny found nothing explicitly illegal in their rituals and conduct. He concluded that Christianity was only "a perverse and extravagant superstition."[4]

The new religion proved to be disruptive all the same. It attracted a large following, becoming popular enough to affect the local economy. Christianity was bad for business because converts to the new religion refused to participate in Roman rituals, visit shrines and temples, buy merchandise used in Roman religious rituals, and offer sacrifices, which reduced the profits that local merchants and farmers hoped to pocket.[5] Pliny was pleased to announce, however, that the measures he had taken were showing signs of success. People were beginning to return to the temples. He was confident "a multitude could be reclaimed."[6]

Trajan approved Pliny's basic policy. Pliny was to continue to demand sacrifices and prayers to the gods as a test of loyalty. "They are not to be sought out; but if they are accused and convicted, they must be punished—yet on this condition, that whoso denies himself to be a

Christian and makes the fact plain by his action, that is, by worshipping our gods, shall obtain pardon on his repentance, however suspicious his past conduct may be."[7] He cautioned Pliny, however, not to accept anonymous accusations, which he deemed unworthy of Roman law.

The second document—another letter—comes from the hand of church leaders in Smyrna (modern Izmir, located on the western coast of Turkey). It tells the story of the martyrdom of a beloved bishop of Smyrna, Polycarp, who was executed in AD 155 at the age of eighty-six. The letter extols Polycarp as a Christian witness, magnifies his courage, and shows that true martyrdom is a calling, not a choice. It lifts up Polycarp's death as a standard against which other martyrdoms should be measured.

As the story goes, a mob, whose thirst for Christian blood had already been whetted, demanded the death of the leader of the church in Smyrna. Polycarp's friends advised him to withdraw from the city, as if to test whether or not martyrdom was his divinely appointed destiny. So Polycarp withdrew to a farm for a few days, "doing nothing else night and day but pray for all men and for the churches throughout the world, as was his constant habit."[8]

Officials tracked him down. Before surrendering, Polycarp welcomed them, offered them food, and prayed for them. Only then did he allow them to transport him to the city. Upon arrival, Polycarp was ushered into the arena, where a proconsul and an angry mob awaited him. The proconsul ordered Polycarp to deny Christ and swear to Caesar, which shows that Pliny's policy had become official. Polycarp refused, confessing that, as Christ had been faithful to him for so many years, he would be faithful to Christ. "If you imagine that I will swear by Caesar's fortune, as you put it, pretending not to know who I am, I will tell you plainly, I am a Christian." The proconsul threatened to throw Polycarp to the beasts, but Polycarp retorted, "Call them. . . . Do what you want."[9] Meanwhile, Polycarp remained serene and calm, full of courage and joy.

A crier then walked to the middle of the arena and announced three times over, "Polycarp has confessed that he is a Christian." And the crowd, boiling with anger, charged, "This fellow is the teacher of Asia, the father of the Christians, the destroyer of our gods, who teaches numbers of people not to sacrifice or even worship."[10]

The enraged crowd demanded his death. Soldiers bound Polycarp to the stake, stacked wood around it, and set it on fire. Encircling him, the flames did not and—according to the account—could not consume him, as if held back by a protective curtain. Meanwhile, Polycarp prayed, "I bless Thee, because thou hast deemed me worthy of this day and hour, to take my part in the number of the martyrs, in the cup of thy Christ, for 'resurrection to eternal life' of soul and body." The proconsul then ordered execution by sword.

After Polycarp's death, a public official requested that his body be disposed of secretly so that Christians would be prevented from turning it into an object of veneration, "being ignorant that we can never forsake Christ, who suffered for the salvation of the whole world of those who are saved, the faultless for the sinners, nor can we ever worship any other." Polycarp's death bore witness to Christ's. There was an infinite difference between the two—one a martyr's death, the other a savior's. The story concludes by offering praise to Jesus, the one for whom Polycarp died. "For we worship this One as Son of God, but we love the martyrs as disciples and imitators of the Lord, deservedly so, because of their unsurpassable devotion to their own King and Teacher."[11]

The Destroyer of Our Gods!

These two accounts share much in common. Both indicate that Christianity was spreading and the church growing, that it was undermining traditional religious rituals, and that it was challenging the Greco-Roman way of life. Pliny could not name an actual crime, nor was the proconsul able to level a concrete charge of wrongdoing against Polycarp.

Yet for some reason Rome considered Christianity a menace and a threat.

Two comments stand out as significant. First, Pliny stated that Christians worshiped Jesus "as a god," indicating that Christians viewed Jesus as divine. This observation was not in and of itself unusual. If anything, it fit Rome's religious categories, for Romans worshiped many gods, including humans elevated to divine or semidivine status, though in this case the word Pliny used referred to the highest kind of god in the Roman pantheon.

But that was not all. The proconsul's comment reveals why Christianity was not only different but also offensive. Christians did not worship Jesus in the same way Romans worshiped their gods and goddesses. The proconsul accused Polycarp of being "the destroyer of our gods."[12] Christians worshiped Jesus *to the exclusion* of all other gods, thus rejecting Rome's pantheon. Christians might have honored martyrs like Polycarp, but they did not confuse them with Jesus, whom they called Savior and Lord. This Jesus was truly *the* Son of God; he alone was worthy of worship.

Rome would not accept such exclusivity. Its pantheon was fluid, expansive, and absorptive. It included the ancient gods of Olympus, only changing their names from Greek to Latin (e.g., Zeus becoming Jupiter; Hera, Juno; and Ares, Mars). It also adopted gods personifying an ideal, like Victory; gods associated with a natural phenomenon, like the Tiber River; and gods who performed good deeds for humanity, like Aesculapius (Greek *Asclepius*), the god of healing. Humans could become gods, too, provided that they accomplished heroic feats worthy of the gods, as Hercules did.[13] As we shall see, the best example—and most relevant for our purposes—is Caesar Augustus, who was widely proclaimed during the imperial era as "divine Augustus" because his spirit was godlike, thus deserving of promotion to Rome's pantheon.

Rome also added gods and goddesses from other cultures, sometimes grudgingly, as in the case of Mithras, and sometimes willingly, as in the case of Isis. These gods and goddesses brought with them their own stories—of creation and fertility, of death and rebirth. Rome was like an art museum that kept adding works to the collection and wings to the building, filling its galleries with portraits and sculptures of gods and goddesses from around the known world. Rome's pantheon became crowded with beings accorded veneration, if not worship.[14]

Emperors became gods, too, and early on in the history of the empire. The senate named a month after Julius Caesar and proclaimed him a god, which made Octavian (or Augustus), his adopted son, the "son of god." The Greek east was more amenable to such deification than the Roman west, having inherited this proclivity and practice from the Egyptians, Persians, and Greeks. The Roman west was more cautious because the memory and customs of the period of the republic lingered even after emperors began to rule.

In short, Rome approached religion one way, Christians another—and very different—way. Rome integrated many gods and goddesses into its pantheon, assuming that in the end Rome itself would thereby prosper and dominate. Christians worshiped the one whom they considered the true God, but they worshiped Jesus, too (a subject to which we will return in chap. 4). There was no possibility of reconciling or integrating the two. They were rival faiths.[15]

We can trace the dramatic difference between these two religions—Greco-Roman and Christian—by comparing the biographies of Augustus, the first emperor, and Jesus, whom Christians called "the Christ." Both were known by the title "Son of God." Though the title was the same, the meaning was profoundly different.

Augustus, Son of God

Augustus served as emperor from 31 BC to AD 14. His birth name was Octavian. He stepped into a power vacuum after Cassius and Brutus assassinated Julius Caesar in 44 BC. He formed a triumvirate of leadership with Mark Antony, Caesar's chief lieutenant; and Lepidus, governor of Spain and Gaul. After defeating Brutus and Cassius, they took control of Rome and gradually won the support of Rome's ruling class. They also defeated armies in the Balkans and Syria still loyal to Brutus and Cassius. Then Octavian moved against Antony because his affair and alliance with Cleopatra appeared to threaten Rome's dominance of the Mediterranean world. He defeated Antony at the naval battle at Actium in 31 BC and extinguished Egypt as an independent empire. He also marginalized Lepidus, finally pushing him out of power. He became the sole ruler of the empire until his death in AD 14 and was given the name Augustus.

Augustus proved to be remarkably able not only in accumulating power but also in wielding it effectively. He faced complicated circumstances. He needed to assert command over a sprawling empire without offending those who represented the vestiges and defended the interests of the old republican order, which was characterized by the rule of the senate. His strategy was largely successful. He became a dictator by universal consent. He secured election as consul every year, assumed authority over the military, and claimed the right to intervene in the affairs of the provinces. Gradually he squeezed out the competition, turning even the old order to his advantage. He was known as the *princeps*, the chief citizen, who exceeded everyone in authority. He assumed the religious office of *pontifex maximus* (the head of the principal college of priests), too, in his effort to renew the traditional religion of ancient Rome. Thus through senatorial support, careful diplomacy, and raw assertion of power, his rule became nearly absolute.[16]

Augustus's accomplishments reinforced his power. He ushered in the Pax Romana ("peace of Rome"), dispatched the military to protect borders and maintain order, used Rome's patronage system to win the loyalty of citizens and cities, and initiated so many building projects in Rome that "he found it a city of brick and left it a city of marble," as the historian Suetonius observed.[17] He also provided various forms of entertainment for the masses (games, horse races, and the like) and donated massive funds in times of crisis. He made both land routes and waterways safer for travel and transportation of goods, which increased trade and contributed to the economic development of the empire. As many contemporaries noted, Augustus presided over a Roman renaissance.

He was well aware of his achievements. In a lengthy document written a year before his death, which was inscribed on two temple columns, Augustus stated, "In my sixth and seventh consulates [28–27 BC], after putting out the civil wars, having obtained all things by universal consent, I handed over the state from my power to the dominion of the senate and Roman people. And for this merit of mine, by a senate decree, I was called Augustus and the doors of my temple were publicly clothed with laurel and a civic crown was fixed over my doors." He concluded that he "exceeded all in influence,"[18] though, as he claims, he had no more power than his fellow rulers.

That claim was palpably false. The title "Augustus" connoted the numinous and conveyed mystery and power. People called him "son of god." His statue stood in temples, his image appeared on coins, his greatness was proclaimed at feasts and festivals, his name was associated with the dawn of a new age. His presence as an emperor—and as a god—was ubiquitous.[19]

Not that Augustus claimed to be a god, at least not in Rome, where conservative elements would have resented and resisted it. But he did not disavow the title either, when people from the east, especially those living in Asia Minor, honored him as such. The famous Priene Inscription illustrates this. It states that Augustus, a man of virtue, became a "savior" for the Romans, secured peace, and surpassed all in accomplishments. It thus proposed that the New Year begin with his nativity, September 23, because "the birthday of this God has become through him a beginning of the good tidings."[20] A year later the senate decided that the month of Sextilis should be renamed August. Augustus thus became a constant in the annual calendar.

Rome did not separate the spheres of religion and politics, as the West does today. Augustus was emperor; Augustus was military commander; Augustus was chief priest; Augustus was a god. He traced his ancestry back to the founder of Rome, implying his rule carried forward and embodied the divine origin and destiny of the city and empire. He enjoyed all the trappings of earthly and heavenly authority.[21] Like Alexander the Great, he epitomized the best that humanity could produce. If Jews demanded signs and Greeks sought wisdom, as the apostle Paul wrote, then Rome loved power. Augustus was the embodiment of that power, the perfect symbol of empire, the glorious incarnation of divinity.[22] It was therefore impossible to separate the greatness of the empire from the greatness of its first emperor.[23]

Jesus, Son of God

It was under Augustus's reign as emperor that another Son of God was born. Augustus in fact played a role in how that birth occurred.[24] We are not entirely sure of all the facts, but the outline is clear enough.

Augustus ordered that a census be taken in the east to number and tax everyone living in that region of the empire, which forced Joseph and his betrothed, Mary, to travel from Nazareth, their hometown, to Bethlehem, their ancestral home, to register for the census. In Bethlehem Mary gave birth to Jesus. Luke claims that angels appeared at this birth, announcing to shepherds that this baby was the Son of God and Savior of the world.

Augustus ruled in Rome, a city of such size (perhaps one million people), wealth, and splendor that it ought to be classified as a Wonder of the Ancient World. If *Time* or *People* magazine had been published back then, Augustus and his court would have dominated the front cover and news of every issue. If he had hosted a party to announce the census, every person of note would have wanted to attend, except for observant Jews. Augustus stood at the apex of power.

Yet Luke mentioned Augustus only in passing, as if to relegate his reign to a mere historical footnote. His reign provided background information to the more important story, the birth of another Son of God and Savior, who would become a major rival to emperor, empire, and all things Roman, as Pliny's letter and the account of Polycarp's martyrdom illustrate.

Jesus hardly seems worthy of the title. If Augustus excelled in greatness, Jesus lived in obscurity; if Augustus wielded absolute military and political power, Jesus attracted only a small following of mostly common people; if Augustus ruled an empire, Jesus saw even his closest friends abandon him. Jesus left nothing in print or in stone to announce his accomplishments and to demonstrate his greatness, as Augustus had done. The small movement he started was left in shambles when he died. How could this man ever be considered a rival?

Our main source of information comes from the four canonical Gospels, which were written by Jesus' followers or their friends. The writers claimed to derive their accounts from eyewitnesses of events that none of them could have imagined (e.g., the crucifixion of Jesus) and nothing in their cultural background predisposed them to believe (e.g., the bodily resurrection of Jesus *within* history and not at the end of history, as the Pharisees expected). Yet what they did finally come to believe transformed their lives. According to their testimony, the story demanded not only a hearing but also absolute commitment, for they simply spoke and then wrote what they had "seen and heard," proclaiming it good news for the entire world.[25] They claimed that the Jesus they knew and followed was truly the Son of God and Savior of the world.

Their writing is peculiar. It is clear that they were telling stories about events that they understood one way when experiencing them firsthand and another way when looking back on them. This radical change of perspective is not entirely foreign to our own experience. A season-ending injury might look one way at the time of its occurrence and another way years later when, looking back, the person who suffered the injury recognizes that it led her to become an orthopedic surgeon.

How did the disciples understand Jesus during his earthly life? What caused them to change their mind?

Growing up in obscurity, Jesus emerged as a figure of note when he was about the age of thirty. His disciples called him a rabbi. Rabbis would gather a circle of disciples and teach them how to interpret and obey the law of Moses. They gained their authority by attending a rabbinic school and learning from a recognized rabbi, who would always teach from within the framework of a particular rabbinic tradition. Jesus was unusual because he did not follow that conventional pathway. He never attended a school, never studied under an established rabbi, and never taught his followers a rabbinic tradition. He never once even quoted a rabbi. If anything, he accused rabbis of failing to teach the real meaning of the law of Moses.

But that was not all. At times he even challenged Moses. No rabbi would have dared to do such a thing; it was tantamount to disobeying God himself. In the Sermon on the Mount, Jesus taught, "You have heard that it was said . . . ," which was followed by a quote from the law of Moses. But he continued, "But I say to you . . . ," as if his authority surpassed even Moses.

It became clear that Jesus claimed to have divine authority. The Gospel accounts tell stories to show how and why. For example, Jesus was teaching at a home. Crowds clamored to listen. Then four men arrived, carrying a paralytic on a stretcher. Realizing that they would not be able to reach Jesus through the door, they ascended stairs to the rooftop and made an opening big enough to lower their friend on his stretcher. They wanted Jesus to heal him. But Jesus failed to perform on cue. Instead, he forgave the man. Shocked by his audacity, the Pharisees asked how this man could presume to speak as God. Jesus overheard their grumbling and asked them which is easier: to heal the man or to forgive him? The Pharisees, masters of the law of Moses, knew the right answer. It was far easier to heal the man, they said, for healing would prove that *God had already forgiven him*. Demonstrating that he had the authority to forgive sins and in fact had forgiven the paralytic's sin, Jesus turned to the man and commanded him to stand up, pick up his bed, and walk home. The man did exactly as he was told. The onlookers were shocked, wondering what kind of person could exercise an authority that belongs only to God (Mark 2:1–12).

They were right to call him rabbi. But he seemed to be so much more.

Jesus performed miracles. Other Jewish leaders did the same. When the Pharisees accused him of being in league with Satan, Jesus asked them if their sons were, too, for they also performed miracles. Like them, Jesus received power from God to do the work of God. But there was a difference in his healing all the same. For one, he healed through his word alone. As God spoke creation into existence, Jesus spoke healing. "Be healed," he said, and it was so. For another, he wielded a power that no one had seen before. He could heal the blind, resuscitate the dead, calm storms—all by a simple command. He exercised absolute power—over sickness, the natural world, and death—but only in a benevolent way. As both followers and enemies alike kept repeating, they had never seen anything like it before.

They were right to call him a miracle worker. But he seemed to be so much more.

Jesus taught with authority, just as the prophets did. "Thus says the Lord." The crowds wondered if Jesus was a prophet—say, John the Baptist raised from the dead, or Elijah returned to earth, or Jeremiah, or someone else. Jesus seemed to fit the profile of a prophet, too, for many prophets lived on the margins, denounced corrupt political and religious rulers, and called the people of Israel to repent and return to God. But Jesus spoke as no prophet ever had before. Never once did he say, "Thus says the Lord," as the prophets of old had done. He simply spoke. Far from speaking on behalf of God, he spoke *as if he were God*.

They were right to call him a prophet. But he seemed to be so much more.

There was one more title they had at their disposal. It was the most sacred of all. Did this title fit Jesus? The first disciples were all Jews. They studied torah in the synagogue, confessed the Shema, and recited the psalms in worship. They sat at the feet of the rabbis and strived to obey the law of Moses in ritual and ordinary life, in work and leisure, in marriage and family. They knew their history, too. They recalled with longing the years of independence under the Maccabees, and they hated the Romans whose political domination and military presence were palpably, brutally evident. They prayed for the Messiah to come. They believed he would amass a popular following, march on Jerusalem, incite a revolution, drive out the Romans, and usher in a golden age.

Was Jesus the Messiah? His ministry said so. He formed what appeared to be a new Israel, appointing twelve disciples as leaders after the precedent of the twelve tribes of Israel. He challenged the religious status quo. He wielded unusual authority and demanded absolute allegiance. When he asked his disciples what others thought of him, they said that they thought him a prophet. When he asked them their own opinion, they proclaimed him the Messiah.

He never denied it, either. He did, however, redefine it. That was the problem.

Jesus predicted that as Messiah he would suffer and die at the hands of the Romans. This prediction made no sense to them. They rejected it as a total betrayal of the true calling of the Messiah, as contrary to the character of a Messiah as a hero fleeing from a battle. A true Messiah could not suffer defeat and death. A true Messiah could only win.[26]

This clash of expectations hovered over them as Jesus and his followers marched into Jerusalem. The disciples viewed this triumphal

31

entry as a virtual coronation; Jesus understood it as a step toward defeat and death. They were ready to lead an armed revolt; Jesus knew that the leaders of the Sanhedrin would seek to destroy him, that Roman soldiers would arrest him, and that his followers would desert and deny him. During their final meal together, his disciples debated who would assume the most honored positions in the new kingdom; Jesus announced his impending sacrificial death. In Gethsemane his followers rested to get ready for battle; Jesus prayed in agony, asking his Father if there was another way. In the end he submitted himself to his Father's will.

Then it all unraveled, at least in the minds of his followers. Within a matter of hours their Messiah was crucified. The one they hoped was the Messiah had failed. There had been failed Messiahs in the past; there would probably be others in the future. But a failed Messiah was a contradiction; it was no Messiah at all.

At that point, if his death had been the end of the story, as they assumed it was, then Jesus would have become a footnote in history rather than Augustus.

But that is not how the story ended, at least according to his disciples, who claimed that this Messiah, crucified under Pontius Pilate during the reign of Tiberius Caesar, was raised from the dead—not resuscitated, only to die again, but resurrected from death to life. His resurrection was unlike anything anyone had witnessed before. Jesus had died. Alive once again, he would never die again. The entire world of the disciples had been swallowed up by light, life, and glory. They had been exposed to a new dimension of reality, as if eternity had invaded time. Jesus was the resurrected Lord. However offensive to modern sensibilities—and ancient, too—the disciples believed and proclaimed it because they claimed to have met the risen Jesus.

The resurrection forced the disciples to revisit and reconsider their entire experience of Jesus, including his death. Their memories were flooded with new insights. The resurrection changed the way they viewed the entire story. They understood his identity, teaching, and ministry in a whole new light, as if emerging from an endless night. They saw his death no longer as a defeat but as a victory, not as the end of the story but as the key turning point in the story. They became witnesses to Jesus' sacrificial death and glorious resurrection. Jesus was not a martyr, as they had once thought, but the Savior.

Eventually they scattered "to the ends of the earth" (Acts 1:8 NRSV) to announce that Jesus, the Son of God, had visited earth to redeem all people and to renew and restore the entire created order. The kingdom of God had come in Jesus. Their experience of the resurrection allowed for no other response. It transformed their lives and, they believed, would transform the entire course of history, as if what appeared to be a dead end turned out to be the only way through.[27]

Jesus became other than what they had thought, and so much more than what they had expected. Thomas spoke for everyone. Bowing before Jesus, he proclaimed, "My Lord and my God!" (John 20:28). A devout Jew, Thomas proclaimed that God had entered history as a human being, Jesus of Nazareth. He came not to coerce but to serve, not to intimidate but to woo, not to win but to lose (or to win by losing). Jesus, they confessed, became sacrifice and priest, victim and victor, suffering servant and Lord of all.[28] Even his resurrection did not reverse the trajectory of the story. Jesus did not visit revenge on his enemies, invade Rome with an army of angels, assume the throne of an earthly kingdom, and recruit the best and the brightest to do his bidding and conquer the world. Instead, he commissioned his disciples, most of them ordinary people, to proclaim the gospel, follow his example of service and sacrifice, and invite all people, both near and far, insider and outsider, into the kingdom.[29]

Jesus died. That is a fact. And death is unrelenting. It simply cannot be ignored or denied forever.[30] History has witnessed the deaths of many great men and women through the ages. Never once did their followers proclaim a resurrection in the wake of their death. They might have honored them as martyrs and heroes; they might even have elevated them to a godlike status postmortem. But they did not call them the Lord God—yet the disciples, witnesses to the resurrection, called Jesus Lord.

It was this witness to Jesus as Lord that Rome considered a menace and a threat.

Porphyry

One Roman intellectual had a solution to the problem. The third-century Neoplatonic philosopher Porphyry, a member of Rome's elite, actually viewed Christianity in a spirit of openness and generosity.[31] Surprising his intellectual peers, he announced that Jesus did in fact merit admiration and respect as a pious figure, and he suggested Rome invite Jesus into its pantheon. He gave a positive appraisal of Jesus within the framework of traditional religion. "What I am about to say may seem surprising to some, namely that the gods have proclaimed Christ to be most pious and immortal, and that they remember him in a laudatory way."[32]

But he rejected the *Christian* view of Jesus as Son of God and Savior of the world, which he considered presumptuous and arrogant. "No doctrine has yet been established to form the teaching of a philosophical sect which offers a universal way for the liberation of the soul; no such way has been produced by any philosophy (in the truest sense of the word), nor by the moral teachings and disciplines of the Indians, nor by the magical spells of the Chaldeans, nor in any other way."[33]

Which leads us back to the beginning of the chapter. Rome recognized that Christians believed in Jesus "as a god." But that was not the real problem. As we have already observed, Rome's religion was expansive and absorptive, making room in its pantheon for additions. Jesus, as such, was not, nor has ever been, the real problem. Over the past two millennia many of his followers and admirers, such as they are, have found reasons to follow and admire him, *but only on their own terms*. Gnostics believed in a disembodied Jesus, Marcionites a historically rootless Jesus. Others have turned Jesus into a remote judge (the Pantocrator), a powerful warrior (the crusading Christ), an enlightened philosopher, the epitome of Aryan supremacy, a radical revolutionary.[34] In our own day we find people believing in a capitalist Jesus, a positive-thinking Jesus, a liberationist Jesus, a mystical Jesus, a manly Jesus, an American nationalist Jesus. Jesus has always been malleable to human whims and wishes.[35]

If Jesus wasn't the real problem, what was? Porphyry studied Christianity but rejected it. Why? Because he understood what the central problem was. It was Jesus, Son of God, Savior of the world, Lord over all. It was the Jesus whom the apostles knew and loved and followed, and to whom they bore witness in their testimonies and martyrdoms. They called this Jesus Lord. It was *this* Jesus who gave rise to the Third Way.[36] Porphyry would have nothing to do with this Jesus. Neither would Rome.

It was Augustus or Jesus; it was Rome or Christianity. It could not be both.[37]

3

Fulfillment

Was Christianity a new religion when it first appeared on the stage of history some two thousand years ago?

The Roman intellectual Celsus thought so. He argued that Christianity departed sharply from its family of origin, the religion of Israel, like a rebellious child who denounces his ancestry, choosing to sever all ties and go his own way. Celsus believed Christianity violated the essential teachings of Israel. "Who is wrong? Moses or Jesus? Or when the Father sent Jesus had he forgotten what commands he gave to Moses? Or did he condemn his own laws and change his mind, and send his messenger for quite the opposite purposes?"[1] Christianity, he concluded, was in fact a new religion. And Rome was suspicious of all things new, especially religion.

But was Christianity *really* new? What did the first disciples believe?

The Old Story Made New

The first disciples were devout Jews, every one of them. They never repudiated their Jewish background, nor did they neglect Jewish rituals and ceremonies, such as Sabbath observance. They studied and worshiped in synagogues, visited the temple on holy days, and circumcised their children. They followed the torah. They continued to identify themselves as Jews even when Jewish leaders spurned them or persecuted them. They claimed that Jesus came not to start a new religion but to continue and complete an old one. Jesus, they proclaimed, was the fulfillment of the religion of Israel, not a departure from it.[2]

They believed that Jesus fit into a larger narrative of creation, fall, and redemption. The history of God's people, going all the way back to Abraham, told a story that looked to the future for fulfillment. Jesus came to fulfill that story. The ancient stories of Israel pointed to Jesus. Without him those stories seemed to go nowhere; with him they all made sense. Such was the message the apostles proclaimed.

The New Testament makes this quite clear. It is not possible to read these texts without observing the important role the Old Testament and the story of Israel play. The apostolic writings show that Jesus did not suddenly appear out of nowhere, like some phantom. He was born and raised a Jew; he lived as a Jew. Far from breaking with the religion of Israel, his mission was to fulfill the very faith he believed and practiced.

Thus Peter interpreted the life, death, and resurrection of Jesus in light of Jewish history (Acts 2:14–36). The Gospel of Luke shows that Jesus understood his own mission according to the message of Isaiah (Luke 4:18–19) and his death and resurrection according to the law and the prophets (Luke 24). The Gospel of Matthew quotes many passages from the Old Testament to explain the origin, identity, and ministry of Jesus. The apostle Paul cites the story of Abraham to explore the significance of Christ's redemptive work (Rom. 4), and the book of Hebrews situates Jesus in torah—for example, the tabernacle, the Aaronic priesthood, and the sacrificial system. The story of Israel and the life of Jesus are as closely connected as seed and plant, sowing and harvesting. The first followers of Jesus believed that the former leads inevitably to the latter; the latter gives meaning and purpose to the former. The entire history of Israel culminates in Jesus. He fulfills it.

Still, the disciples came to this conviction slowly. They grew up hearing the ancient stories of their people and carried them in their memory, like adults remembering every square inch of their childhood home and backyard. They had to figure out how to integrate Jesus into that story, and how to interpret that story in light of Jesus. It proved to be difficult because Jesus did not turn out to be the kind of Messiah they were expecting (as we observed in chap. 2). We can only imagine what they discovered—and how they must have felt—when recalling, for example, Isaiah 53 in the wake of Jesus' death and resurrection. They shed tears, I am sure, realizing that Jesus, their Messiah, was *that* man, the suffering servant.

The disciples chose to make Israel's Bible the Christians' Bible. They believed the ministry of Jesus fulfilled Israel's story and the church became the new Israel. They used the Jewish Bible—what Christians call the Old Testament—in worship, preached it in sermons, and quoted it in their writings. They affirmed that the story of redemption stretched all the way back to creation and would end in the new heavens and new earth. They proclaimed that it is one glorious narrative, and Jesus is at the center of it all.

It seems that these apostolic decisions about the continuity between Israel and Jesus should have sufficed. At least it might seem clear to us now. But to the generations that followed the apostles it was less clear. Why?

New Problems

There are at least three reasons why the connection between Israel and Jesus seemed fragile and tenuous. First, gentiles began entering the church, first as a trickle and then as a river. Even within Paul's lifetime, gentiles probably outnumbered Jews in many Christian congregations and in the Christian movement as a whole, to say nothing about the generations that followed.

The influx of gentiles posed a problem. They were certainly open to the gospel and responded to the good news with enthusiasm. The book of Acts makes that abundantly clear. The first gentile converts were familiar with and attracted to Judaism, too. They studied and admired it. They knew the story; believed in Jewish teachings about God, salvation, and the world; and followed a Jewish way of life as best they could, though they rarely converted to Judaism. Many of these "God-fearing" gentiles responded with enthusiasm to the gospel message.

The decision of the Jerusalem Council (Acts 15) only reinforced the attractiveness of Christianity to outsiders. Gentiles could become full-fledged Christians without having to convert to Judaism first. In short, they could have the best of both worlds—old and new, the religion of Israel and Christianity—without having to submit to every Jewish practice, such as kosher laws and circumcision. It seemed a relatively easy task to explain how old and new fit together, the former setting the stage for the latter, at least for gentiles who were already familiar with and attracted to the Judaism of their day.

Over time, however, the Christian movement attracted an increasing number of gentiles who did not know the larger story of salvation. They were outsiders and aliens to Israel and its faith. They knew little or nothing of the account of creation and fall, the covenant with Abraham, the revelation of the divine name to Moses and the events of the exodus, the conquest of Canaan, the monarchy and divided kingdom, the promise to David, or the message of the prophets. Christian teachers faced the daunting task of telling and explaining this history to gentiles who had grown up in a Greco-Roman culture. There was much in it that was hard to explain. Was it worth it?

There was a second reason, too. Christians disputed with Jews over the right interpretation of the story. Rabbis explained the story of Israel to the Jewish faithful one way, but Christian teachers thought there was a better way, claiming that the ancient story pointed to Jesus. Rabbis required Jews to obey a strict and elaborate interpretation of the law of Moses, but Christian teachers thought there was a better way, the Sermon on the Mount. Jews gathered in synagogues; Christians met in house churches. Jews observed the Sabbath; Christians worshiped on the Lord's Day. Though *Jewish* converts to Christianity continued to attend the synagogue and observe the Sabbath, *gentile* converts did not. Neither did gentile Christians practice circumcision or eat kosher. The "better way" to which Christian teachers referred was Jesus as fulfillment, which changed how both law and prophets functioned in the Christian community.

Christians contended that the Jews of Jesus' day rejected him because they misunderstood and distorted the religion of Israel. Where,

Christians asked, was their commitment to being a "light to the nations"? Why did they fail to recognize Jesus as the suffering servant of Israel who proved at the same time to be the Messiah? How could they miss the priority of justice over strict religious observance? Thus Christians made a clear distinction between the religion of Israel, which Jesus came to fulfill, and the religion of the Jews, or Judaism, which had departed from that ancient faith. They embraced the former and rejected the latter.[3]

Some Christian leaders plainly encouraged such rejection. Ignatius of Antioch warned Christians to avoid Judaism, claiming that it distorted the true teachings of the Old Testament. Christians were right, Jews were wrong, proving themselves unfaithful to their own heritage. "If any one preaches the one God of the law and the prophets, but denies Christ to be the Son of God, he is a liar, even as also is his father the devil, and is a Jew falsely so called, being possessed of mere carnal knowledge."[4] But such criticism raised questions about the relevance of the religion of Israel for Christianity. Could the church stay committed to Israel's faith, considering how Judaism—*as the rabbis taught it*—departed from it? How could the church adopt the ancient story as its own? It seemed a complicated business.

There was also a third reason. The New Testament as we know it today—that is, a collection of Christian canonical texts—did not yet exist. The emergence of the book of Christians took time. To be sure, many of the books now included in the New Testament achieved *functional* authority when the church was still in infancy. Christians read from those books in worship, as if they were authoritative; pastors preached on them; writers quoted and copied and circulated them. Thus Polycarp's letter to the church in Philippi cites verses from a number of books in the New Testament, treating them as sacred Scripture.[5] Still, the New Testament *as officially canonical* was still two centuries away, which means the church lacked an official authoritative guide to help Christians interpret the Old Testament in the light of the coming of Jesus.[6]

Sooner or later it was bound to happen. Someone was going to raise questions about the legitimacy of the religion of Israel, the usefulness of its practices, and the truthfulness of its Bible, someone who cared about gentile converts and considered Judaism perverse, obsolete, invalid, burdensome, and even dangerous, and who refused at the same time to make a distinction, as the apostles clearly did, between ancient Israel and rabbinic Judaism. Should Christians even *try* to maintain a connection with Israel and its sacred book, as complicated as it appeared to be? Would it not be far better to sever ties with it so that Christianity could go its own way, free from the burden of having to teach its scandalous story and demanding religion to converts?

Why even bother?

The time was ripe for a radical proposal, especially when, by the middle of the second century, the church comprised mostly gentiles. Many were unfamiliar with both the Old Testament and the Jewish community and its traditions. Was it time to set a new course for the gentile church? Should distance give way to official separation, even divorce?

Marcion's Proposal

Marcion of Sinope grew up in Pontus, a province in Asia Minor on the southern coast of the Black Sea. He was born into a Christian home. His father, in fact, served as bishop of Sinope. Marcion became a businessman and acquired vast wealth in the shipping industry.

Around the year 140 he moved to Rome. He became a major philanthropist for the church, donating some two hundred thousand sesterces ($4 million in today's dollars). After he was expelled from the church as a heretic, the church in Rome returned the money to him.[7]

Marcion studied the Old Testament, and it horrified him. He saw nothing but brutality and crudity. How could a Christian take the religion and god of Israel seriously? He viewed the Hebrew god as nasty, vindictive, and petty, a kind of tribal deity unworthy of worship. This lesser god created the physical world, a grave error, Marcion thought, because the physical world was prone to deterioration and doomed for destruction. The Jewish god was hostile to human beings and kept them from discovering true spiritual knowledge. He wanted to keep them enslaved and ignorant, trapped in materiality. The moral law of this god was legalistic; it promised a good life in this world but ended up punishing and enslaving people, not enlightening them. The ceremonial law was equally appalling, requiring the people of Israel to appease a wrathful god. Marcion read the Old Testament literally. He believed the text was trustworthy; but he considered it wrong, contrary to true religion.

How could Christians consider this god and his story worthy of confidence and belief, especially in light of the simple and loving message of Jesus?

Marcion became a teacher in the church in Rome, which comprised many house churches scattered throughout the city. It took time for his ideas to spread. Eventually he met with church leaders to explain himself and his ideas. He was clearly on a mission. He proposed to draw a firm line between the religion of the Jews and the religion of Jesus, between the god of Israel and the God who sent Jesus.

What *was* the religion of Jesus? And how did Marcion know? According to Marcion, it was *not* what the original apostles taught. They were simply too Jewish to understand the real Jesus, and thus they were unreliable as sources of information about him. That they kept quoting the Old Testament provided evidence enough in Marcion's mind of their failure to grasp the true identity and mission of Jesus.

If the original followers of Jesus could not be trusted, then who could be? As it turns out, Marcion proclaimed that Paul could be trusted, as could one of Paul's companions, Luke, the physician. As the main architect of the mission to the gentiles, Paul was far more reliable than the other apostles. But even his writings, as well as Luke's, were questionable at points because Judaizers (Jewish Christians who made Christianity subservient to Judaism) amended them to fit their Jewish vision of Jesus. Marcion had to complete what Paul had started, purging Christianity of the poison and perversion of Judaism. He edited Paul and Luke, eliminating all references to the teachings of the Old Testament.

According to Marcion, Jesus came to start a new story, not to complete an old one. Thus Marcion's Bible—parts of Paul and Luke—told the true story of Jesus and the mysterious God he came to reveal. In the end, Marcion rejected not only the Old Testament but also most of the New Testament. He compiled a different Bible to reveal a very different religion.[8]

His Jesus bore little resemblance to the Jesus we meet in the Gospels. Marcion believed that Jesus only assumed a body, as if putting on a costume, so that he could communicate with humans and explain true religion. But he was not truly human. Ignorant and enslaved people—the Jews—crucified him in order to silence him. But they did not realize that it is impossible to kill a purely spiritual being. His work of teaching continued even after his body died.

In Marcion's religion there was no divine creation, no divine judgment, no redemption of the body, no salvation story, no need to care for the world. Christ came to enlighten, not to suffer and die. There was forgiveness for all and eternal life for all, except for those who follow the creator god of the Jews. The church was a spiritual fellowship that proclaimed a spiritual message. Still living in this evil world, however, true Christians had to wean themselves from all earthly attachments. Marcion thus rejected marriage and required married people to abstain from sex, even for the purpose of procreation. He also spurned all physical pleasures. How could true disciples enjoy things that are inherently sinful?

Church leaders in Rome excommunicated him, as his own father had done years earlier when Marcion was still living in Pontus, and two important late second-century theologians—Irenaeus of Lyon (d. 200) and Tertullian of Carthage (d. 220)—wrote books against him. They believed that Marcion had invented a new religion, and they branded him a heretic.

In their minds there was good reason to do so.

Tertullian, for example, set out to prove that Jesus Christ, the incarnate Son of God, came to redeem fallen creation. He challenged what he believed was Marcion's superficial and simplistic view of God, and he asserted that God created all things visible and invisible and that Christ fulfilled the ancient prophesies. Tertullian also explained how the very authors to whom Marcion appealed—namely, Luke and Paul—taught a message that was the very opposite of Marcion's religion. Marcion could not edit them enough to obfuscate their real message.

Tertullian believed that Marcion's religion lacked clarity and cogency. His god was unknowable; his Christ rootless, groundless, and insubstantial; his view of salvation superficial. If there is no sin and judgment, how can there be salvation? If there is no creation, how can there be redemption? If there is no story, why did Jesus appear how he did and when he did? Why at all? "What would your opinion be of a physician who by delaying treatment should strengthen the disease, and by deferring remedy should prolong the danger, so that his services might command a larger fee and enhance his own repute?"[9]

Why the strong reaction? Because Tertullian believed that nothing less than salvation was at stake. According to Tertullian, Marcion's Jesus came to earth unannounced: he had no history and people, no ancestry, no parentage, no cultural background, and hence *no humanness*. How, Tertullian asked, could there be an incarnation and resurrection if Christ was not a real person? How could there be salvation apart from a larger story? Marcion stripped Jesus of particularity and concreteness, making him like a ghost.

Without the story of Israel, Tertullian argued, there could be no Jesus.[10] "We have set forth Jesus Christ as none other than the Christ of the Creator. Our proofs have drawn from His doctrines, maxims, affections, feelings, miracles, sufferings, and even resurrection—as foretold by the prophets. . . . Marcion, I pity you; your labor has been in vain. For the Jesus Christ who appears in your Gospel is mine."[11]

Why this extensive exploration of Marcion's ideas, which appears so obscure and irrelevant to us now? The debate with Marcion, as technical as it is, seems appropriate for experts to study, but not ordinary Christians. Tertullian's long and complex rebuttal demands much from readers. It is a heady work, tedious to read and hard to understand.

But the controversy was not—and is not—as abstract and irrelevant as it might at first appear. Marcion's proposal had far-reaching consequences, and it ended up accomplishing the opposite of what he intended. His ideas awakened a sense of urgency to assert that Jesus came *from* God—and *as* God—to fulfill and complete the redemptive

45

story of Israel, as the apostles proclaimed. There were three significant outcomes to the controversy, all of which have shaped the Christian movement to this day.

The first was the Bible. The church chose—or better, recognized—an official canon, which we now call the New Testament. The second was the biblical story. The church planted Jesus firmly in the history of Israel, believing that Jesus came to fulfill it. The third was the biblical story as it unfolded in and shaped the larger story of human history. The church explored how the history of salvation, culminating in Jesus Christ, illuminates all of human history. The first concerns how the Bible came to be, the second how the Bible tells one story, and the third how the Bible makes sense of human history.

The Bible

Early Christian leaders—the vast majority of whom were Jews—carried the Old Testament with them into Christianity. The reaction to Marcion was severe largely because he challenged what they simply assumed and practiced. Jesus came to fulfill the story. How could they understand Jesus apart from that story? Thus the Old Testament set the stage for the New. Augustine summarized it about as succinctly as anyone could. "Therefore, in the Old Testament the New is concealed; in the New the Old is revealed."[12] Both canonical texts (e.g., the Gospels, Paul) and post-apostolic writings (e.g., 1 Clement, Didache) treat the story of Israel as essential preparation for the coming of Jesus. Jesus makes no sense apart from it. The first Christians decided the Hebrew Bible had to be their Bible, too. Hence the title: Old Testament.

The writings of the apostles emerged as equally authoritative and took their place alongside the Old Testament as sacred texts. These "accepted" texts included the four Gospels, the Acts of the Apostles, and the apostolic letters. Churches used them as if they were canonical, like unwritten rules that govern a sport before the rules become official. The names of these texts appeared everywhere in second-century writings: Matthew, Mark, Luke, John, Acts, Romans, 1 and 2 Corinthians,

Galatians, Ephesians, Philippians, Colossians, 1 John, 1 Peter. They carried weight because they bore witness to Jesus as fulfillment of the story.

The church also rejected a number of other texts. These texts focused on Jesus, to be sure, but in a way that appeared to contradict the teachings of the apostles. A good example is the Gospel of Thomas. It tells the story of a very different Jesus. Thomas's Jesus does not have a background and parentage, work miracles, befriend strangers, walk dusty roads, travel from town to town, nap in a boat, feed five thousand people, teach his disciples to carry on his mission, nor suffer and die for the sins of the world and conquer death through his bodily resurrection. He talked with only *one* disciple, revealing the secrets that would lead to enlightenment and liberation, because the others were too stupid to grasp his esoteric message.

A third group of texts faced a different kind of scrutiny. These were "disputed" texts. There was nothing inherently objectionable about them. They belonged in the same world as the Gospels and the writings of Paul, John, and Peter. But questions remained all the same. In some cases it was unclear who wrote them (e.g., the book of Hebrews). In other cases it was unclear when they were written (e.g., Jude). In still other cases it was unclear how to interpret them (e.g., Revelation). The church debated the status of these disputed texts for some time. In the end, consensus prevailed. Most of the disputed texts were included in the canon (e.g., Hebrews, Jude, 2 Peter, 2 and 3 John, Revelation); some were excluded (the Didache, the Epistle of Barnabas). None were considered so objectionable to be labeled as heretical and dangerous.[13] Reflecting on the process of canonization in the early fourth century, the historian Eusebius never made a sharp distinction between how the church functioned to "recognize" these texts and how the Holy Spirit guided the process, as if human agency and divine intervention worked seamlessly together.[14]

Eventually the time came to close the canon. The process was more organic than organizational, more consensual than coercive, more natural than artificial. Athanasius (d. 373), bishop of the church in Alexandria, identified the twenty-seven books now included in the New Testament and, in a festal letter to his Alexandrian diocese (367), acknowledged that this list was—and had been for some time—functionally canonical, and should therefore be recognized as the final canonical standard for the church. Other bishops and churches (Rome, for example, in 382) followed his recommendation with little argument.[15]

Thus the Bible as we know it today—the Old Testament and the New Testament—became the book of Christians. What had long been viewed as having functional authority became officially authoritative.

The Biblical Story

But there was a second implication to Marcion's radical proposal, which addresses how the church *reads and interprets* the Bible. How exactly did Jesus fulfill the story? Early Christians explored various ways of understanding this idea.[16]

In the early second century, Ignatius, bishop of Antioch, wrote a series of letters to churches while he was being transported as a prisoner from Antioch to Rome. Ignatius saw Christ everywhere in the Old Testament, so much so that he asserted that the true "archives" of the Old Testament are not written words at all but Jesus himself. In a sense, Jesus *is* the story, though it takes knowing the redemptive story to understand him. "My authentic archives are His cross, and death, and resurrection, and the faith which bears on these things, by which I desire, through your prayers, to be justified."[17]

The teachings and stories of Israel point to Christ, and they are fulfilled in Christ. Priests, Ignatius argued, were good, but the High Priest—Jesus—is better. The powers of the ancient story were good, but the comforting work of the Holy Spirit is better. "This is the way, which leads to the Father, the Rock, the Defence, the Key, the Shepherd, the Sacrifice, the Door of knowledge, through which all Old Testament figures of faith entered." Thus "the Gospel possesses something transcendent . . . , the appearing of our Savior Jesus Christ, His passion and resurrection."[18] It is as if Jesus were the final movement of a symphony that integrates earlier themes into a glorious and climactic finale.

48

Ignatius was not the only Christian teacher who argued this way. Writing around the year 150 in Rome, Justin Martyr, perhaps the first Christian philosopher, saw Jesus foreshadowed and foretold in the Old Testament. "In these books, then, of the prophets we found Jesus our Christ foretold as coming, born of a virgin, growing up to man's estate, and healing every disease and every sickness, and raising the dead, and being hated, and unrecognized, and crucified, and dying, and rising again, and ascending into heaven, and being, and being called, the Son of God."[19]

Perhaps the best example is Irenaeus, bishop of Lyon from 180 to around 200. In addition to writing a very long book to expose the fallacy of various heresies, he also wrote a short book of instruction to explain how Jesus fulfilled the ancient story of Israel. Irenaeus viewed Marcion and his supporters as a major threat to the gospel. He said they were like people who take the precious stones of a beautiful mosaic—say, of a king—and rearrange the stones to depict a dog, thus destroying the features of the original subject.

Irenaeus quoted from virtually every book now included in the New Testament. He skillfully wove together passages from Old Testament and New to show that there is one God; one plan of salvation; one redemptive story; one final revelation of God in his Son, Jesus Christ; one Holy Spirit; one human race that desperately needs salvation; all told in one grand narrative.

How did Irenaeus make his point? First, he argued that the stories of the Old Testament point forward, as if providing clues for some big event yet to happen. Jesus is that event; his life and ministry became the "recapitulation" of the story. He is thus the second Adam; the cross is the second tree. Second, he showed that the prophets foretold it all. "That all those things would thus come to pass was foretold by the Spirit of God through the prophets, that . . . we might know that it was God who previously proclaimed to us our salvation."[20]

Thus Old Testament stories and prophecies look ahead. Christ's life, death, and resurrection look back. Jesus is the final piece of evidence that makes sense out of it all. He is the answer to the mystery. Irenaeus concluded, "This, beloved, is the preaching of the truth, and this is the character of our salvation, and this is the way of life, which the prophets announced and Christ confirmed and the apostles handed over and the Church, in the whole world, hands down to her children."[21] Jesus should not and could not be severed from the very root system from which he came. Irenaeus argued that we do not have the liberty to make of him whatever we want. Jesus entered the story to fulfill it, not abrogate it.

The Biblical Story in History

The story of Israel, however, was not a story unto itself but was situated in a larger history involving many of the great empires that dominated the ancient world, among them the Egyptians, Assyrians, Babylonians, Persians, and Greeks. Likewise, the story of Jesus and the church unfolded under the shadow of Rome, a Mediterranean empire numbering some fifty to sixty million people. These empires had their own religions and their own stories to tell. How does the biblical story of redemption fit into the larger story of humanity?

The answer to this question addresses the third consequence of Marcion's idea.

The first historian of the church, Eusebius, believed that Acts 28 did not end the redemptive story. It continued long after the last of the apostles died. It would not end, he implied, until Jesus returned to establish a new heavens and a new earth, bringing history to a close. In the meantime, the church had kingdom work to do.

Eusebius set out to tell the story of what happened from the death of the apostles all the way to the rise of the first Christian Roman emperor, Constantine, who died in AD 337. During this period the church started as a Jewish sect but turned into a formidable movement that infiltrated the Mediterranean world. It grew from some five thousand Christians in AD 40 to some five million by AD 300 and some thirty million by AD 360. Eventually Christianity became *the* religion of Rome.

Eusebius saw the hand of God in all of it.

We learn much from him about this early period: for example, how Paul and Peter and many of the other apostles died; how early Christians suffered persecution and martyrdom; how the teachings of the apostles were passed on from one generation to the next, especially through the office of bishop; how the process of canonization of the Bible occurred; how the church combated heresies; and how Roman rulers failed to snuff out Christianity.

Behind this history is a clear point of view. It was inevitable, Eusebius argued, that Christianity and church would triumph over their enemies. It was bound to happen because Christianity is true. Christianity reveals who God truly is in the face of Jesus Christ, God's Son, who visited earth to redeem it. In Jesus truth triumphed, once and for all.

Constantine's victories both symbolized and epitomized this triumph. In the year 312 he waged war against Maxentius, the other major contender for control of the western half of the empire. On the night before battle, Constantine saw a vision of the Chi-Rho, a symbol for Christ. A voice from heaven said to him, "By this sign conquer." He marched into battle under this symbol and, facing an army quadruple the size of his own, won. A year later Constantine gave legal recognition to Christianity and over the next twenty-five years granted it increasing privileges.

In AD 323 Constantine fought another battle, this time against Licinius, emperor of the east. Again Constantine defeated the foe, and he thus became the sole ruler of the empire. Eusebius could no longer contain his enthusiasm. He saw this as the work of God. "Men had now lost all fear of their former [pagan] oppressors; day after day they kept dazzling festival; light was everywhere, and men who once dared not look up greeted each other with smiling faces and shining eyes. They danced and sang in city and country alike, giving honor first of all to God our Sovereign Lord, as they had been instructed, and then to the pious emperor and his sons, so dear to God." Eusebius understood Constantine's victory as the final triumph of Christianity and the culmination of history. "Old troubles were forgotten, and all irreligion passed into oblivion; good things present were enjoyed, those yet to come eagerly awaited."[22]

Eusebius honored God for his goodness. But he honored Constantine, too, as God's good and godly leader. "In every city the victorious emperor published decrees full of humanity and laws that gave proof of munificence and true piety." It was a new day for Christianity and empire, for the two had become one. God had established his rule within history; Constantine was his chosen servant. "Thus all tyranny had been purged away, and the kingdom that was theirs was preserved securely and without question for Constantine and his sons alone. They, having made it their first task to wipe the world clean from hatred of God, rejoiced in the blessings that He had conferred upon them, and, by the things they did for all men to see, displayed love of virtue and love of God, devotion and thankfulness to the Almighty."[23]

We can hardly fault Eusebius for his euphoria, considering the terrible persecution Christians suffered under Constantine's predecessor, Diocletian.

Still, there is a problem with Eusebius's view of history all the same. It is easy to write history in light of the winners, especially if Christians attribute the victory to God. But what happens if, a generation or two later, they lose? Eusebius did not live long enough to witness the demise of the empire: the rise of Arian emperors who closed down orthodox churches and exiled orthodox bishops; the invasion of tribal groups that overran the western half of the empire; the massive decline of cities; the rise of the Arabs (and their new religion, Islam), who conquered more than half of the Mediterranean world; the strain between eastern and western churches, which later divided into Orthodox and Roman.

What would Eusebius have written in the light of these tragic events? Surely he would have been less sanguine about Constantine, less confident in easy victory, less certain about a simple story of persecution leading to privilege and triumph. God's people are not always on the "winning" side. Perhaps they never are, or at least never should be. Someone had to develop a more nuanced philosophy of history that would take into account decline, failure, and defeat, even of the church.

That person was Augustine of Hippo. Augustine grew up in North Africa and rejected Christianity as a young teenager but gradually returned to Christianity during early adulthood, finally committing his life to Christ at the age of thirty. By then he was teaching rhetoric and philosophy in Milan. After his conversion under the influence of Ambrose, the bishop of Milan, he returned to North Africa and served as a bishop in the city of Hippo for some thirty-five years. He died in the year 430. Much happened during the one hundred years between Eusebius and Augustine, including a number of tribal invasions that overwhelmed the western empire.

One event in particular stood out. In the year 410 a Germanic tribe, the Visigoths, attacked, sacked, and ravaged the city of Rome. It was a devastating event. How could this city, the center of civilization for centuries, fall to an army of "barbarians"? Some Roman intellectuals blamed Christianity, saying that the gods and goddesses of Rome had punished the city (and empire) because a large number of Romans—too many, as it turns out—had abandoned traditional religion for Christianity. Augustine wrote *The City of God* to challenge that argument. It outlines a Christian philosophy of history far more nuanced than what Eusebius presented.[24]

Augustine was profoundly learned. He read his opponents and knew Rome's history. He studied Greco-Roman mythology, philosophers, and historians. Irenaeus wrote to Christians. Augustine had the knowledge to write to the world.

He argued that it was too simple to blame Christianity for the fall of Rome. Rome was to blame for its own fall, as even Roman historians—Tacitus and Suetonius, for example—had already argued. Its entire history—including its greatest accomplishments (and Augustine could name them)—was full of corruption, violence, and idolatry. Rome did not fall because the gods turned against it. It fell because it failed.

Augustine countered by explaining history from a Christian perspective. In his view the Triune God of Christianity—Father, Son, and Holy Spirit—rules over history, though it is often difficult, if not impossible, to see how. If anything, it seemed the traditional gods of Rome exercised more power than the Christian God, Greco-Roman religion more power than the Christian religion, ancient empires more power than the Christian church.

But there is more going on than meets the eye. Augustine wrote that there are really two histories—he called them "two cities"—unfolding at the same time. One is the history of fallen angels and of a proud humanity in rebellion against God, the other the history of God's people

53

who are pilgrims on earth. The former worships the self, the latter worships the only true God. The former treats this world alone as the end, which always leads to idolatry and perversion; the latter sees the kingdom as the end. The former tells the story of earthly empires—say, Assyria and Rome, the two civilizations that Augustine considered the greatest on earth; the latter tells the story of God's people.

These two histories are not separate, as if they were two plays being acted out on separate stages, using different props and involving different actors. They unfold on one stage, using the same set of props and involving the same actors, like wheat and tares sown in the same field. But there are two scripts all the same, one telling the story of lost humanity, the other of the people of God. "Accordingly, two cities have been formed by two loves: the earthly by the love of self, even to the contempt of God; the heavenly by the love of God, even to the contempt of self. The former, in a word, glories in itself, the latter in the Lord. For the one seeks glory from men; but the greatest glory of the other is God, the witness of conscience. The one lifts up its head in its own glory; the other says to its God, 'Thou are my glory, and the lifter of mine head.'"[25]

Sharing the same stage, the citizens of both cities experience pleasure and face suffering, choose good and pursue evil, achieve greatness and fail miserably. But the citizens of the heavenly city always in the end turn toward God in repentance and faith. The good they experience on earth awakens greater longing for God, "for the best of this world is simply not enough," and the suffering they face in this world inspires them to seek for a better country, God's kingdom.[26] Thus the citizens of the earthly city seek earthly prosperity alone; to them this world is all there is. But the citizens of the heavenly city "look for those eternal blessings which are promised, and use as pilgrims such advantages of time and of earth as do not fascinate and divert them from God."[27]

God is central and supreme in the City of God, for all good comes from God. His people thank him for his gifts, steward those gifts under his rightful rule, and always seek God as the ultimate good. "In this, too, is the origin, the enlightenment, the blessedness of the holy city which is above among the holy angels. For if we inquire whence it is,

God created it; or whence its wisdom, God illumined it; or whence its blessedness, God is its bliss. It has its form by subsisting in Him; its enlightenment by contemplating Him; its joy by abiding in Him. It is; it sees; it loves. In God's eternity is its life; in God's truth its light; in God's goodness its joy."[28]

Augustine took his cue from the Bible. He traced the two cities through the entire biblical story. Thus God called Moses to lead his people out of bondage, which took place against the backdrop of the Egyptian Empire. God sent his people into exile in Babylon, but later used Persia to allow them to return to the promised land. The birth of Jesus occurred in Bethlehem, fulfilling the ancient prophecy, which was set in motion by Augustus and the census. Jesus was crucified under the rule of the procurator, Pontius Pilate, who presided over his bogus trial.

One stage, one set of props, one cast. But two scripts. Only those living by faith know and follow the second script, which tells the story of the City of God, for they believe that God is working to redeem the world. Those living for themselves play a role in the redemptive story, too, though they are oblivious to it. Thus Augustus acted out of self-interest when he called for a census. Little did he know that this decision set in motion events that culminated in the birth of the Son of God in Bethlehem.

Augustine believed that this is God's story, not ours. God chose to reveal himself in human history, beginning with Abraham. The story moved through the patriarchs and Joseph, Moses and Joshua, the judges and Ruth, the kings and Esther. Jesus came at the right time to fulfill the story. Marcion wanted to uproot Jesus from this story, to strip Jesus of background and context. But once he uprooted Jesus from the story of Israel, it was inevitable that he would plant him in another story and thereby change the very nature of Jesus and his mission. In short, he would make Jesus a main character in the story of the City of Man, not the City of God.

Marcion might seem remote to us now, separated as we are from him by over eighteen hundred years, and thus hard to take seriously. But we should never overlook his appeal. Then as now, Marcion's Jesus was flexible and adaptable because he had no history, family, and humanity, which made him subject to whatever cultural values dominated at the time, to ideology and fashion, to whim and wish.

But then what power does he have to redeem? Early Christians rejected Marcion because they believed Jesus came to fulfill a larger story: God created a good world; humans rebelled, driving the world into ruin; God set in motion a story of redemption, which culminated in the coming of Jesus. Jesus came to fulfill this ancient story. They taught converts that story, too, which is probably why Irenaeus wrote his book in the first place. He wanted to help converts read the Bible as a single story. He invited them to learn, enter into, and act out a new script, as Augustine later outlined. They became citizens of the City of God.

Augustine argued that the real and true story was not the story of Roman triumph but the redemptive work of Jesus and the birth of the church. The setting was not a palace but a stable, not a glittering city but a hill of execution, not majestic temples but tiny house churches. The plot involved mostly unknown and unimportant people who trusted and honored God, "choosing rather to share ill-treatment with the people of God than to enjoy the fleeting pleasures of sin," for they considered "abuse suffered for Christ to be greater wealth than the treasures of Egypt" (Heb. 11:26 NET). They took courage and found comfort, believing that history will look very different in the coming kingdom. To them there really is more going on than meets the eye.[29]

4

Map

During the years my children were at home, our family always went on summer vacations to national parks. We developed the habit of consulting maps before visiting the parks because we wanted to discover the best hikes to take and the best places to camp. The maps beckoned us to explore the parks in person. They were no substitute for the parks themselves, of course. My children would have been sorely disappointed had we stayed at home and been content simply to study maps.

Christian theology is like a map that charts a landscape—the landscape of who God is and what God does in the world. The first to draw these maps—the apostles—claimed that God took the initiative to reveal himself to humanity, which in turn inspired them to proclaim what they had "seen and heard."

But that posed a problem for them, for their experience of God was unusual—in fact, not just unusual but unique. No one had ever had the same experience of God; consequently, no one had ever drawn the same map. The problem centered on Jesus. He shattered all previous categories and conceptions of how God can be known, which required them to chart a new landscape. No one had ever seen or heard anything like it before. Where they landed surprised them; it came through difficult struggle and deep reflection. They believed, however, that their actual experience of Jesus allowed for no other conclusion.

This chapter is about the uniqueness of Christian belief. The ancients were critical of Christianity, especially its view of God. Jews accused Christians of blasphemy because their worship of Jesus undermined monotheism, and Roman elites scoffed because Christian belief in the incarnation and resurrection violated the unknowable and immutable nature of God. Their opposition illustrates just how peculiar Christian belief was.

Celsus on Christianity

Take, for example, Celsus, whom I mentioned in the previous chapter. A member of Rome's intellectual elite and a friend of Marcus Aurelius (who ruled as emperor from AD 161–80), Celsus wrote a book critiquing Christianity around 170. Christianity had few followers then, perhaps one hundred thousand in an empire of sixty million, and it had very little cultural power. It attracted mostly urban dwellers— former slaves, merchants, artisans, household servants, freemen, and the like.[1] It had no schools and few buildings of any size and architectural significance. Why would a member of Rome's elite even bother to take notice?[2]

But Celsus did. In his *On the True Doctrine* he skewered the new faith because it attracted lowly people, "wool-workers and cobblers" and others of similar status, and told a fanciful story about some obscure man's death on a cross. "By the fact that they themselves admit that these people are worthy of their God, they show that they want and are able to convince only the foolish, dishonorable and stupid, and only slaves, women and little children." He noted that Christians won converts not through public debate among elites—as Celsus would have wished—but through quiet witness in their homes and places of work, which he found disconcerting.[3]

Celsus charged that the elevation of Jesus made him a rival of the one High God who, according to Celsus, is known by many names. There were lesser gods, to be sure. Christians could have treated Jesus as a lesser god, of which there were many in Rome's pantheon. Celsus even conceded that if Christians "worshipped no other God but one, perhaps they would have had a valid argument against others." But he was alarmed by how Christians viewed Jesus. "But in fact they worship *to an extravagant degree* this man who appeared recently, and yet think it does not offend God if they also worship his servant."[4] By adoring Jesus *as if he were God*, Christians had undermined devotion to the only true God. "If you taught them [Christians] that Jesus is not [God's] Son, but that God is father of all, and that we really ought to worship him alone, they would no longer be willing to listen to you unless you included Jesus as well, who is the author of their sedition. Indeed, when they call him Son of God, it is not because they are paying very great reverence to God, but because they are *exalting Jesus greatly*."[5]

He considered the incarnation preposterous. How, Celsus asked, could God become a human being? It was impossible because it violated the nature of God, at least the Greco-Roman understanding of it. God might on occasion make forays into the human world, but he would surely not identify with humans, especially human weakness and frailty, for that would require God to undergo change, something humans do but God never does, or even can. "God is good and beautiful and happy, and exists in a most beautiful state. If then he comes down to men, he must undergo a change, a change from good to bad, from beautiful to shameful, from happiness to misfortune, and from what is best to what is most wicked. . . . It is the nature only of a mortal being to undergo change and remolding, whereas it is the nature of an immortal being to remain the same without alteration. Accordingly, God could not be capable of undergoing this change."[6]

The resurrection was equally preposterous because it would require God to reverse the natural process of disintegration. "For what sort of body, after being entirely corrupted, could return to its original nature and that same condition which it had before it was dissolved? . . . But, indeed, neither can God do what is shameful nor does He desire what is contrary to nature."[7] Celsus believed that God is subject to the laws of nature, not transcendent over them. God, he argued, cannot do something contrary to reason and nature.

Celsus concluded that the whole story was pure invention—and a complete scandal. He speculated that Jesus learned magic in Egypt and made up the virgin birth to hide his mother's affair. He was a sorcerer, not the Son of God. Besides, the writers of the Gospels were hardly reliable, because they had a vested interest. As predisposed as they were to believe in Jesus, they could not be trusted as witnesses.[8] They simply made up most of the stories to save face because Jesus was really a fraud. "How many others produce wonders like this to convince simple hearers whom they exploit by deceit?"[9]

Celsus could have made a very different argument. He had evidence at his disposal to do so, which makes it surprising that he overlooked it. There were alternative views of Jesus circulating in his day, and these fit more naturally into Roman religion. There was Gnosticism, which rejected the incarnation and resurrection of Jesus; Ebionism, which rejected the divinity of Jesus; and Marcionism, which rejected the story of Israel that Jesus came to fulfill. All three postured as genuine Christianity. Their leaders claimed to be Christian, started churches, sent missionaries, produced texts, and often referred and appealed to Jesus as a significant figure. Celsus could have claimed that *these* represented true Christianity, and he could have done so without offense. But he ignored these alternative movements. For whatever reason, he focused his attention—and criticism—on the one that was truly different. The others were not a problem. The apostolic witness to Jesus was.

How did early Christians arrive at this unique view of Jesus? And how did this view of Jesus change their understanding of God?

My purpose in this chapter is not to provide an exhaustive explanation of incarnation and resurrection, nor of the Trinity, nor of the divine and human natures of Jesus Christ, nor of the identity and work of the Holy Spirit. I will touch on them, to be sure, but more as if I were sketching a map rather than drawing a detailed one. What matters most to me is the *process* by which the first disciples developed basic Christian belief, not the intricacies of the doctrines they spelled out.

The writings of the early Christians about this issue might at first seem contradictory and confusing. But how could it be otherwise, considering the new territory they were exploring?

But appearances can be deceiving.

If my children and I had drawn maps of the parks after we had visited them, we would have drawn ones that looked different from each other, at least at first glance. My daughter's maps would have appeared artsy, emphasizing the beauty of the places we discovered; my two sons' would have looked dramatic, highlighting the big sites we saw and the adventures we had along the way; mine would have been the most technically accurate. But it would become apparent soon enough that we were all drawing maps of the same places. And the reason is obvious. We visited those places together and thus drew maps that, however different, depicted the same reality.

This is what happened to the first disciples. They had a common experience, one that was completely unexpected and unimaginable. They explored the place first; then they drew the maps. Their experience of the place surprised them, which created difficulties as they tried to draw maps that were true to their experience. It is important to keep this in mind. The theological maps we now study might look different—for example, the Gospel of John and the Gospel of Luke tell different stories and make different points. But it is obvious that they are pointing to the same reality; they tell stories about the same person; they affirm he has the same essential identity. Thus the "I am" of John is the same Jesus who assumed the divine prerogative to forgive sins, as we read in Luke.

The Experience of the Disciples

To understand the uniqueness of Christian belief, we must start where the disciples did, at the very beginning, long before they came to know who Jesus truly was. As I mentioned in chapter 2, the first followers of Jesus were all Jews. They had been educated in the synagogue, trained by the rabbis, taught to obey the law of Moses, and expected to practice Jewish rituals. They recited the Shema: "Hear, O Israel: The LORD our God, the LORD is one" (Deut. 6:4 NIV). They believed that God is the great I Am, transcendent, sovereign, and holy. There is no other God but this God, as Isaiah proclaimed to the exiles (Isa. 46:8–11).

Then Jesus showed up in the rural setting of Galilee.

Intrigued, the disciples began to follow him. At first they thought him a rabbi; then a miracle worker, a sage, and a prophet; and finally the Messiah. In the end these titles fell short, especially the title of "Messiah," not because the titles were wrong but because they were either misleading or incomplete. Jesus died, failing in his mission. There had been other failed Messiahs in the past, as Gamaliel mentioned in his speech before the Sanhedrin (Acts 5). The disciples fell into profound disillusionment and despair, as anyone would in the wake of such a brutal and irreversible loss.

But a few days later those same disciples were wild with joy. They proclaimed that the crucified one had been raised from the dead, not as a resuscitated corpse but as a resurrected being. Death itself had been utterly defeated. The disciples were overcome with both disbelief and wonder.

In the months that followed, they revisited their entire experience of Jesus. They remembered it differently in the light of the resurrection. They also reviewed their entire understanding of the Old Testament story. Again, they understood it differently in the light of the resurrection. They realized that the coming of Jesus marked the turning point in all of human history. Something new had happened; and they were eyewitnesses to it. Thomas's confession symbolized this massive change of perspective. Bowing in worship, he said to Jesus, "My Lord and my God!" (John 20:28). As a strict Jew, Thomas used the divine name of the man Jesus, the man he had known as a friend and followed as a teacher for three years. Yet he did not think this confession conflicted with his belief in Yahweh, the one God. How could a human being be God? It was unthinkable.

Over time the disciples settled on the conviction that Jesus made it possible to know God in a new way because this man, Jesus Christ, came to reveal God, not merely by teaching about God but by *being God*. They claimed that in seeing Jesus, you see God; in hearing Jesus, you hear God; in knowing Jesus, you know God; in believing in Jesus, you believe in God. Judaism considered it blasphemous to confuse the creator God with the creation. Yet as observant Jews, the disciples worshiped Jesus, called him Savior and Lord, and prayed in his name. They wrote Gospels to tell the story and letters to strengthen, encourage, and instruct the church. They began to chart a new territory never seen or explored before.

The generations of Christians that followed continued on this trajectory, convinced that what the apostles experienced was true, their witness reliable. They reflected on what it might mean that God had come to earth as a human being. They used language—abstract terms, stories, metaphors, and the like—to draw a new map of God. Their writing has a breathtaking quality to it, much like the writing of a scientist trying to describe a supernova or a young artist her first visit to the Sistine Chapel. They were overwhelmed with wonder, and they refused to hold back. God chose to become human for the sake of the world's salvation! They simply had to proclaim it and try their best to explain it.

That God would come at all was strange enough to them; that he came *as he did*, stranger still. God could have used muscle to bully people into belief, power to intimidate people into submission, knowledge to make people feel like fools. That way he could have proven just how great he was, how *divine* he was. But Jesus Christ chose another way—humility, foolishness, and weakness. Though Christ was in the "form" of God, as the apostle Paul wrote, he "did not count equality with God a thing to be grasped, but emptied himself, taking the form of a servant, being born in the likeness of men. And being found in human form he humbled himself and became obedient unto death, even death on a cross" (Phil. 2:6–8). What humans fail to do when at their best, God accomplished when at his weakest and worst, or so it seemed at the time. "For God's foolishness is wiser than human wisdom, and God's weakness is stronger than human strength" (1 Cor. 1:25 NRSV).

The Search for Language

Early Christian writers searched for words and images to explain this great mystery. It is apparent that they were trying to describe a new reality. In a letter written in AD 95, only thirty years after the apostle

Paul was martyred, Clement, the bishop of Rome, confessed that God came as a human in the least expected way. "Our Lord Jesus Christ, the Scepter of the majesty of God, did not come in the pomp of pride or arrogance, although He might have done so, but in a lowly condition, as the Holy Spirit had declared regarding him."[10] He could hardly fathom that, when seeing the man Jesus Christ, his followers were gazing into the very face of God. "By Him we look up to the heights of heaven. By Him we behold, as in a glass, his immaculate and most excellent visage. By Him are the eyes of our hearts opened. By Him our foolish and darkened understanding blossoms up anew towards His marvelous light."[11]

Ignatius, bishop of Antioch, who most likely died as a martyr sometime in the early second century, expressed astonishment that Jesus Christ was as human as he was. Surely the Son of God would maintain some measure of greatness when entering the world and manifest his divine nature while being in the world. He is, after all, God. But God chose otherwise. Ignatius testified that Jesus was truly human in every way. He did "truly assume a body," he "did in reality both eat and drink," he "really, and not merely in appearance, was crucified, and died, in the sight of beings in heaven, and on earth, and under the earth."[12]

The unknown author of *The So-Called Letter to Diognetus* could hardly contain his sense of wonder over the surprising way God came as Jesus Christ. He was not only human; he was also humble. God, humble? How could this be? "Now, did God send [his son], as a human mind might assume, to rule by tyranny, fear, and terror? Far from it! He sent him out of kindness and gentleness, like a king sending his son who is himself a king. He sent him as God; he sent him as man to men. He willed to save man by persuasion, not by compulsion, for compulsion is not God's way of working."[13]

Bishop of Lyon for over twenty years, Irenaeus (d. 202) believed that Jesus Christ served as the perfect mediator between God and humanity because he was both divine and human, "for the Father is the invisible of the Son, and the Son the visible of the Father."[14] As a human, Jesus passed through every stage through which every human passes, "restoring to all communion with God." Thus the "mediator between God and man, by his relationship to both," brought "both to friendship and concord."[15]

Tertullian (d. 220), a lawyer and an apologist living in Carthage, North Africa, affirmed that the very impossibility of the incarnation was reason to believe it. It was utter and complete humiliation for humanity's sake. Could God actually do this? Would he? A master rhetorician, Tertullian asked one question after another, each one adding to the sense of wonder that it was no less than the Son of God who chose to visit earth and to die for the sins of the world. Was he not crucified? Did he not really die? But did he not also conquer death? "The Son of God was born shameful, therefore there is no shame. The Son of God died: absurd, and therefore utterly credible. He was buried and rose again: impossible, and therefore a fact." Tertullian saw in Christ one who was perfectly divine, but also perfectly human. "Thus the quality of the two modes of being displayed the humanity and the divinity: born as man, unborn as God; in one respect material, in the other spiritual; in one respect weak, in the other exceedingly strong; in one respect dying, in the other living."[16]

The first great biblical scholar in the history of the church, Origen (d. 254), confessed Jesus Christ as the first and only manifestation of the divine splendor that human eyes could actually see without going blind. "This brightness falls softly and gently on the tender and weak eyes of mortal man and little by little trains and accustoms them, as it were, to bear the light in its clearness." Origen speculated that Christ was like an identical copy of the incomprehensible God, only made smaller so that Christ could be comprehended. In this way "those who were unable to perceive and behold the immense one could yet be confident that they had seen it when they saw the small one, because this preserved every line of limbs and features and the very form and material with an absolutely indistinguishable similarity."[17]

Athanasius (d. 373), the intrepid bishop of Alexandria, understood Christ to be the solution to what he called the "divine dilemma." As he stated, God "saw" humans wasting away, "saw" human corruption getting worse, "saw" the law being violated time and again, "saw" death reigning supreme over sinful humans. In a final flourish of rhetorical brilliance, he concluded, "*All this He saw* and, pitying our race, moved with compassion for our limitation, unable to endure that death should have the mastery, rather than that His creatures should perish and the work of His Father for us men come to nought, He took to Himself a body, a human body even as our own."[18]

Why the incarnation? It was not simply to make God known—Jesus Christ being the divine self-portrait in human flesh. It was also to suffer and die for the sins of humanity. In fact, it was the incarnation that made suffering and death redemptive. The author of *The So-Called Letter to Diognetus* echoed the apostle Paul when describing this act of self-surrender and self-sacrifice. "In his mercy, he took up the burden of our sins. He himself gave up his own Son as a ransom for us—the holy one for the unjust, the innocent for the guilty, the righteous one for the unrighteous, the incorruptible for the corruptible, the immortal for the mortal. For what else could cover our sins except his righteousness? In whom could we, lawless and impious as we were, be made righteous except in the Son of God alone?" Becoming poetic with praise, he exclaimed, "O sweetest exchange! O unfathomable work of God. O blessings beyond all expectation!"[19]

In my mind no one captured the mystery and beauty of the incarnation more profoundly than Gregory of Nazianzus (d. 390). Known as "the Theologian" in Eastern Orthodoxy, this fourth-century bishop and theologian spelled out the irony of the incarnation, how Christ's degradation resulted in human exaltation. Impossible to summarize and yet preserve the eloquence, this passage deserves to be quoted at length.

> He hungered—yet he fed thousands. . . . He thirsted—yet he explained, "Whosoever thirsts, let him come to me and drink." . . . He was tired—yet he is the "rest" of the weary and the burdened. . . . He prays, yet he hears prayer. He weeps, yet he puts an end to weeping. . . . He is sold, and cheap was the price—thirty pieces of silver; yet he buys back the world at the mighty cost of his own blood. A sheep, he is led to the slaughter—yet he shepherds Israel and now the whole world as well. A lamb, he is dumb—yet he is [the] "Word." . . . He is weakened, wounded—yet he cures every disease and every weakness. He is brought up to the tree and nailed to it—yet by the tree of life he restores us. . . . He is given vinegar to drink, gall to eat—and who is he? Why, one who turned water into wine, who took away the taste of bitterness, who is all sweetness and desire.

He surrenders his life, yet he has power to take it again. He dies, but he vivifies and by death destroys death. He is buried, yet he rises again.[20]

These early Christian writers believed that they were witnessing the glorious condescension of the divine splendor and greatness. As they expressed it, big became little; strength, weakness; rich, poor; and wise, foolish. Providence chose personhood; power embraced pain; sovereignty gave way to suffering. It was as if all the light of the universe—galaxy upon galaxy of blazing brightness—was reduced to the flicker of one candle without suffering any diminution, without becoming less radiant than it was before. It was as if all the weight of the universe was reduced to the lightness of a feather, light enough to tickle the palm of your hand, without becoming less heavy than it was before. The divine light and weight became hidden and concealed. The Son of God became an embryo and nine months later was born in a stable, perfectly, bloodily, painfully human. But no less divine than before.

Perhaps I have cited too many sources, almost drowning you with quotations. It reflects my deep appreciation for these early Christian writers. What better way to capture their utter astonishment and awe than by using their own words? Reading them is like feeling the full force of cascading water as it rushes down a mountainside. Their words wash over us. Such was their passion about the incarnation.

No wonder Christianity seemed alien and strange to the ancients, a complete reversal of what people thought God was supposed to be and do. Celsus claimed God could do no such a thing. Why would God descend to earth when the goal of spiritual knowledge was to escape the world and ascend to God? Why would God bother to save a world that is decaying, corrupt, and destined for destruction? Ancients did not—and could not—imagine a God who would choose to become human to redeem humanity and renew creation.

The Triune God

Belief in the incarnation permeated the world of early Christians. It is impossible to ignore or dismiss. But their reflection did not—*and could not*—stop there. Like an intriguing and compelling first chapter in a novel, the incarnation beckoned early Christians to proceed further and explore deeper questions about the very identity of God and the person of Jesus Christ. Two questions in particular demanded the church's attention and reflection.[21]

The first concerned God. If Jesus Christ really was God, as Thomas confessed in his first encounter with Christ after the resurrection, then what does that say about God? Was Jesus Christ a window into the very being of God? Is God a God of both unity and distinction? Is God one in relationship? Early Christians assumed such was the case. They read a Bible that spoke of God as Father, Son, and Holy Spirit, and they worshiped, prayed, baptized new believers, and celebrated the Eucharist in the name of this same God. This became the liturgical and confessional language of the church from the very beginning, which in turn provided the language that Christian thinkers used in their more technical theological writing.

God is one; God is three persons, Father, Son, and Holy Spirit. How is that possible?

The second question concerned Jesus Christ. If Jesus Christ really was divine, again as Thomas confessed, then what does that say about Jesus Christ as human? The apostles came to know Jesus over three years as a real man. When telling his story, they described him as napping, eating, spitting, drawing in dirt, touching lepers, healing disease, holding children on his lap, teaching, arguing, and weeping. They witnessed this wide range of human actions and emotions *before* Jesus was crucified and raised from the dead. But they wrote his story *after* the pivotal events of Holy Week and Easter Sunday, the experience of Pentecost, and the emergence and growth of the early church. Their confession that Jesus was God did not change their conviction that he was truly human. There is nothing in the accounts—not even a hint—that Jesus only *pretended* to be human but was in the end only divine. It seems logical that divinity would swallow up humanity like sunlight a candle. But their memory of knowing Jesus as a real person told them otherwise. Jesus did not give the impression of being human. He was human.

How could both divine and human coexist in one person?

These questions might seem technical, abstract, and impossibly complex to us, like quantum physics. But early Christians started not with the questions but with experience. It was never a matter of speculation but of careful and deliberate reflection on their personal knowledge of the man Jesus. Suddenly they found themselves exploring a new and different landscape. Their starting point was what they had "seen and heard." Experience preceded theology, worship preceded doctrine, testimony preceded writing. They drew maps about him after they had come to know him.

This was no easy task. How can someone describe color to people who see only in black and white? How can someone describe three dimensions to people who live only in two? Early Christians faced an impossible set of circumstances.

They could have followed an easier pathway. There were alternatives available to them. Roman elites would have applauded them for it. But they rejected these as untrue to the experience of the first disciples, who encountered the resurrected Jesus and called him Lord and, in the years that followed, proclaimed the gospel in the power of the Holy Spirit.

The first and most obvious of these alternatives was bitheism. There are two gods, not one. The problem in this case is making a meaningful distinction between the two gods without subordinating one to the other. If one god is Father and the other god is Son, the Father would seem to be superior to the Son, which would make the Son a lesser god. Moreover, if there are two gods, why limit it to two? Why not three, or four, or fifty? Suddenly we are thrust back into the world of ancient polytheism.

A second was to make the triune language of God describe role and function, not identity. There is really only one God. But this God plays multiple roles, as if he were an actor onstage playing three parts in a Greek drama. He plays the role of Father at one moment, Son at another moment, and Spirit at still another moment, switching roles and costumes as the play unfolds. But this seems hard to reconcile with the stories of the Gospels—Jesus' baptism, for example.

A third was to assign to Jesus Christ an exalted status, more than human but still less than divine. Perhaps God adopted Jesus at his birth or baptism or after his resurrection because Jesus, as good and pious as he was, proved himself worthy of it. Or God created the Son first so that he could serve as God's agent to create everything else and then, at the proper time, become human as Jesus Christ. In short, the Son was a hybrid of sorts, a new kind of creature that was neither divine nor human but something between the two.

These three alternative explanations circulated as live options around the ancient world—and within Christian circles, too. They had their attraction and advocates. In each case they provided a theological vision of God that was more compatible with Roman religion. But they did not square with the experience of the first disciples. So the church rejected them as falling short of describing the landscape the apostles traveled. There is one God. This one God is Father, Son, and Holy Spirit. God is a unity with distinction; God is one in relationship. And Jesus is both divine and human.

Gregory of Nazianzus, once again, wrote with brilliance and beauty about this complex issue. He reflected on the process and then explained, clarified, and defended the outcome. Gregory was active and influential at the second great council of the church, known as the Council of Constantinople (381), where he helped refine and finalize the language of the Nicene Creed. There is good reason why he is called "the Theologian" of the Eastern Orthodox Church. He had the mind of a scientist and the sensibility of a poet, which made him an exceptionally good writer, both clear and cogent. He is at his best in the "Five Theological Orations." In these five short books—it is hard to believe he preached them as sermons—he explored the nature of God as Trinity and Christ as both divine and human.

Gregory argued at the outset that the goal of theology is not knowledge of theology itself but deep, personal, intimate knowledge of God. It is relationship. But that introduces us to the essential problem. How can we *know* God? God is by definition inaccessible, indescribable, and incomprehensible simply because God is God. There is an infinite chasm between God and creation, a chasm so wide that nothing can cross it. We long for God. Nothing in this world can satisfy us. Yet we cannot grasp the very God we long to know.

So we commit idolatry instead and find a substitute for God. This seems a natural solution because even when we push human capacity to its limit and use the best tools at our disposal—the tool of human reason, for example—we still cannot fathom God. Our powers are limited; so limited, in fact, that we can hardly understand the things of this world—birds, spiders, fish, sea, air—to say nothing of God. So theology is far more difficult than it might at first appear. "All truth, all philosophy, to be sure, is obscure, hard to trace out. It is like employing a small tool on big constructions, if we use human wisdom in the hunt for knowledge of reality."[22]

But what if God took the initiative to make God's very self known to humanity? That is the genius and gift of the incarnation. God came to humanity because humans could not get to God. We see God in the face of Jesus Christ. But if that is true, Gregory wondered, then what do we actually learn about God, about God *as God actually is*? We discover that there is both unity and distinction in God. There is one God, and this one God is known as Father, Son, and Holy Spirit not only because God reveals himself to be so but also because God *is* so. The Son is "begotten" of the Father from, through, and in all eternity. The Holy Spirit "proceeds" from the Father, again from, through, and in all eternity. God is not bound by time; there is no becoming in God, only *being*. God has always been and will always be one God—Father, Son, and Holy Spirit. They are distinct as persons, to be sure, but share and do all things in common (for example, creation and redemption) because they are perfectly, eternally united in the same substance.

Gregory looked for illustrations in human experience to explain the Trinity, but he found them inadequate and misleading. He mentioned source, spring, and river; he experimented with sun, beam, and light. In the end, he concluded, they fell short. Again, how can two dimensions grasp the essential nature and experience of three dimensions, or black, white, and gray grasp the essential nature of color? "For my part, though I have examined the question in private so busily and so often, searching from all points for an illustration of this profound matter, I have failed to find anything in this world with which I might compare the divine nature. If a faint resemblance comes my way, the more significant aspect escapes me, leaving me and my illustration here in this world."[23]

Gregory faced a different challenge when trying to explain the incarnation. He could use biblical stories about Jesus to make sense of it because the incarnation occurred in actual human history, though it, too, remained a mystery. God the Son became the man Jesus Christ to save and redeem a lost world. Thus the one who was completely divine was in fact completely human, too. "He remained what he was; what he was not, he assumed." The Son existed in perfect unity with Father and Spirit. But he chose to become a human being "because of something, namely, your salvation, yours, who insult him and despise his Godhead for that very reason, because he took on your thick [embodiment]." Thus "man and God blended," yet remained distinct, neither bleeding into the other. Jesus Christ was

> begotten—yet he was already begotten—of a woman. . . . That it was from a woman makes it human, that she was a virgin makes it divine. On earth he has no father, but in heaven no mother. All this is part of his Godhead. He was carried to the womb, but acknowledged by a prophet as yet unborn himself, who leaped for joy at the presence of the Word for whose sake he had been created. He was wrapped in swaddling bands, but at the Resurrection he unloosed the swaddling bands of the grave. He was laid in a manger, but was extolled by angels, disclosed by a star and adored by Magi.[24]

It might appear at this point that these early Christian leaders neglected to explain the identity and role of the Holy Spirit. The first version of the Nicene Creed, written in 325, mentions the Holy Spirit almost in passing. When it was revised in 381 at the Council of Constantinople, the bishops who convened there chose to say more. "We believe in the Holy Spirit, the Lord, the giver of life, who proceeds from the Father through the Son, who with the Father and the Son is worshiped and glorified." Gregory's good friend Basil, bishop of Caesarea (in Asia Minor), wrote an entire book on the Holy Spirit that shaped the church's understanding of both the Spirit's divine nature and the Spirit's distinct role in salvation history. He argued from both Scripture and reason that the Holy Spirit, as the Third Person of the Trinity, is rightly called Lord and worthy of worship. He draws people into the very being of the Triune God, where there is perfect beauty, goodness, truth, light, life, and love. He also empowers the church to bear witness to this same God as we know him through Christ and in the power of the Holy Spirit.[25]

Full Restoration

There was something more at stake here than drawing the most precise and accurate theological map possible. A map reveals something of the landscape; but the point is to explore the landscape itself. Theology tells us about God; but the point, as Gregory argued, is to know God.

This book is about the Third Way, which proved to be unique in the ancient world—so unique that Rome called it the Third Way. It was unique as belief; it was unique also as a way of life. It would not accommodate to Rome, nor isolate itself from Rome. Instead, it immersed itself in Rome, quietly challenging Rome's policy of absorption or elimination. At the heart of this movement was its view of God as epitomized in the incarnation. Celsus thought it impossible that God would become human, at least human in the way Jesus was, because God *could* not become human in that way. But early Christians proclaimed that God did become human because God loves humans and all of creation.

The incarnation revealed the two primary purposes of divine revelation, both of which became foundational to early Christian belief and the Third Way.

The first is restoration of relationship. God chose incarnation out of love. Origen asserted, "But consider whether the Holy Scripture shows more compassion for humankind when it presents the divine Word, who was in the beginning with God . . . as becoming flesh in order to reach everyone."[26] Clement of Alexandria (d. 215) argued similarly. "It was in his love that the Father pursued us, and the great proof of this is the Son whom he begot from himself and the love that was the fruit produced from his love. For this he came down, for this he assumed human nature, for this he willingly endured the sufferings of man, that by being reduced to the measure of our weakness he might raise us to the measure of his power."[27]

According to these early Christian writers, the incarnation demonstrates that God loves humanity and thus took the initiative to repair the broken relationship. But the incarnation does more. It reveals that God not only loves humanity but also that God is love within God's very being. God *loves* because God *is* love. God's love is eternal because God is an eternal relationship. As Clement argued, we are saved *into love*. Christians are invited into the eternal, perfect, glorious love that exists within the very being of God as Father, Son, and Holy Spirit.

The second is restoration of image. The incarnation not only reveals the face of God; it also reveals the face of humanity as God intends humans to be. Jesus Christ is truly God; he is also the true human. The death and resurrection of Jesus make us right with God and restore us to our true humanity as revealed in Christ. As Irenaeus argued, "The only true and steadfast Teacher, the Word of God, our Lord Jesus Christ, who did, through His transcendent love, become what we are, that he might bring us to be even what He is himself."[28]

Salvation therefore consists of full restoration of relationship and image. God is both initiator and final destination. There is restoration of relationship: "For our sake he [God] made him [Christ] to be sin who knew no sin, so that in him we might become the righteousness of God" (2 Cor. 5:21). There is restoration of image: "Now the Lord is the Spirit, and where the Spirit of the Lord is, there is freedom. And we all, with unveiled face, beholding the glory of the Lord, are being changed into his likeness from one degree of glory to another; for this comes from the Lord who is the Spirit" (2 Cor. 3:17–18). The apostle John adds, "Beloved, we are God's children now; it does not yet appear what we shall be, but we know that when he appears we shall be like him, for we shall see him as he is. And every one who thus hopes in him purifies himself as he is pure" (1 John 3:2–3). We are made children; we are also called to live that way, to become like Jesus Christ, the true human.

Jesus Christ is therefore the perfect and final mediator. He is both window and mirror. We see *through* him into the very being of God as Father, Son, and Holy Spirit, and we gaze *at* him to see what we are and what we will become in him. There was a reason why early Christians were adamant about the incarnation. Nothing less than restoration—of broken relationship and of broken image—was at stake.

The incarnation set the trajectory for everything that would follow in early Christianity. Again, Irenaeus grasped this as well as anyone. In the incarnation, the Son became flesh to become the "dispenser of grace" to humanity by revealing God to humans and presenting humans to God. In the incarnation the Son became flesh to reveal a God who loves because God *is* love. And in the incarnation the Son became flesh to repair and renew the broken image so that humans could become what God intended them to be. He willed full, final, and complete restoration of relationship and image. "For the glory of God is a living man; and the life of man consists in beholding God."[29]

5

Authority

If there is an early church leader who might seem especially strange to us, it is Ignatius of Antioch. He was bishop of Antioch in the late first and early second centuries, which separates him from the apostles by only one generation. Eusebius, the fourth-century historian, says that he was the second to serve as bishop in that important city.

A city with a population of over one hundred thousand, Antioch was located in Syria, which served as a major crossroad between the Roman Empire and the empires to the east, among them the Persian. Travelers passed through it regularly, and large numbers of immigrants settled there, much like border cities today, which often resulted in ethnic tensions and social unrest. The city was known for its disasters, too; it averaged a disaster such as a major flood, fire, or invasion every fifteen years or so for centuries.[1]

Antioch saw a Christian witness shortly after the birth of Christianity, and it quickly became the center of operations for the mission to the gentiles. The apostle Paul served as a teacher there for one year before the church commissioned Paul and Barnabas to embark on their first missionary journey in the late 40s. Paul returned to Antioch on at least two occasions to report on the progress of the mission.

Ignatius was taken prisoner in Antioch during the reign of the emperor Trajan (98–117) and transported to Rome for trial and execution.

Eusebius tells us that Ignatius was most likely fed to wild beasts in the Colosseum sometime in the early second century, though he was not entirely certain. The emperor Vespasian began construction on the Colosseum in AD 72, and his successor, Titus, completed it around AD 80, using Jewish money and slaves after Rome conquered Jerusalem. The Colosseum seated some fifty-five thousand people. Emperors used it to provide entertainment for the masses, which included an array of blood sports, such as gladiatorial combat, the hunting of exotic animals, and the gruesome execution of enemies and criminals. Still standing today, the Colosseum is an architectural masterpiece, both in design and size, very much like modern arenas.[2]

Eusebius recounts that Ignatius, on his way to Rome, crossed Asia Minor and then Macedonia under strict military guard, though not so strict to prohibit him from visiting churches and writing letters along the way. His seven letters to churches (and one letter to his young protégé, Polycarp, the bishop of Smyrna) provide a window through which to view the life of a fledgling church that remained after the apostles had passed from the scene, a church that must have seemed fragile, like a sapling fighting for survival on the banks of a flooding river. The young church faced an uncertain future. Eusebius says as much when commenting on the tone and content of Ignatius's letters. "In particular [Ignatius] warned them to guard most carefully against the heresies which were then first becoming prevalent, and exhorted them to hold fast to the apostolic tradition, which, as he was now on his way to martyrdom, he thought it necessary for safety's sake to set down clearly in writing."[3]

Ignatius seems a real person in these letters. He writes with emotion, and he often shifts randomly from one topic to the next as if he is writing under duress—which he was. His concerns involve a wide range of issues: martyrdom, leadership, heresies, the nature of Christ, the gospel message, church unity. It is entertaining and puzzling reading and sometimes, considering the charged, almost apocalyptic language he uses, foreign to modern tastes.

In this case we must set aside modern tastes. His writing challenges us—even demands us—to step out of our cultural setting and into his, which requires both imagination and sympathy, of the same kind we might use when exploring a new and—at least to us—exotic culture.

For example, Ignatius *wanted* to die as a martyr. He pled with Christians in Rome to refrain from intervening on his behalf to spare his life. He hoped that the beasts would consume his entire body so that he could become a pure loaf of bread and thus a real Christian. "I am the wheat of God, and am ground by the teeth of the wild beasts, that I may be found the pure bread of God." Hoping that the consumption of his entire body would make him less troublesome to the church, he also claimed that his martyrdom would make him a true disciple. "Then shall I be a true disciple of Jesus Christ, when the world shall not see so much as my body."[4]

Ignatius defended the office of bishop, going so far as to say that Christians should view the bishop as a direct representative of Jesus Christ. "It is manifest, therefore, that we should look upon the bishop even as we would look upon the Lord Himself, standing, as he does, before the Lord."[5] Or again: "It is therefore necessary, whatsoever things ye do, to do nothing without the bishop."[6]

He was hardly charitable when writing about opponents. Calling them "heretics," he demanded complete avoidance of them. They are as dangerous, he said, as poison slipped into a favorite drink. "For there are some vain talkers and deceivers, not Christians, but Christ-betrayers, bearing about the name of Christ in deceit, and 'corrupting the word' of the Gospel; while they intermix the poison of their deceit with their persuasive talk, as if they mingled aconite with sweet wine, that so he who drinks, being deceived in his taste by the very great sweetness of the draught, may incautiously meet with his death."[7]

What are we to make of this peculiar man? He seems frightening and fanatical, and thus offensive to modern sensibilities. But could his eccentricity really be more our problem than his?

The subject of this chapter is Third Way authority, as it was defined, defended, and exercised in the first few centuries of the Christian movement. Our perspective is affected—and probably skewed—by the centuries that separate us from them, most of which tell a story of Christian dominance. We still see vestiges of it today—big, sometimes ornate churches in downtowns across America; megachurches in many suburbs; bestselling Christian books; Christian universities; Christian media stars, athletes, and entertainers; Christian political influence; Christian news sources and websites and cable TV shows. The evidence of Christian presence and power—however used or abused—is too obvious to overlook or deny. When reading early Christian writers like Ignatius, we scrutinize them in light of our experience of Christendom. When writing about them, even academics have trouble shaking the sensibilities and suspicions of conducting their research in light of the church's abuse of power over the centuries. Ignatius in particular does not fare well under that kind of scrutiny.

His circumstances, however, were in fact very different from ours. In his day there were no church buildings, nor any of the other kinds of visible Christian influence and dominance that we see and experience every day in the Western world. He served as leader of a movement that faced enormous challenges. We know the outcome; he did not.

That he wrote letters *on his way to martyrdom* in the Roman Colosseum illustrates the point. The apostles were dead; Ignatius, a first-generation bishop, was about to die, too. Heretics were making inroads; Roman persecution appeared to be on the rise; controversy threatened church unity; gentiles were flooding into the church. The leadership seemed hardly up to the task, considering the problems the church faced. What would happen to the church under this kind of pressure? The prospects for the church's survival seemed dim, or so it might seem to us.

But not so to Ignatius. He wrote with passion and confidence because he viewed his circumstances in light of the gospel, which told a story of God's victory over sin, death, Satan, and hell. No amount of difficulty could convince Ignatius to believe otherwise.

Still, however confident, Ignatius and other Christian leaders confronted daunting challenges. How could they advance the church's mission, defend the unity of the faith, win converts, plant churches, and train leaders in the face of so much opposition and trouble? And it was not just a question of how. It was also a question of who and what. Who would bear the burden of responsibility, and what would they actually do to maintain gospel faithfulness?

These questions all focus on the issue of early Christian authority.

The English word for "authority" comes from the Latin *auctoritas*, as "author" comes from the Latin *auctor*. *Auctoritas* had to do with office, institution, and expertise. It implied legitimacy. Cicero contrasted *auctoritas* with *potesta,* or "authority" with "power." The former was more positive, requiring institution, position, preparation, and prudence; the latter more negative, usually leading to destructive outcomes, whether intended or random.

It is helpful to think about how we use the word today in everyday speech. It can refer to authority of office (say, a Supreme Court judge), to the authority of institution (the police department), or to the authority of expertise (a scholar or physician or musician). We assume the same when defining authority in the church. There is the authority of office (bishop, vicar, or pastor); there is the authority of institution (the general assembly or the papacy); and there is the authority of expertise (the founder of a megachurch, the author of a bestselling Christian book, or the pastor of a local congregation).

This definition is clear enough. Still, the lingering influence of Christendom affects its connotative meaning, especially as it applies to how we understand *religious* authority. Christian institutions, like the Roman Catholic Church and World Vision, to name only two, command respect and exercise considerable influence; papal pronouncements often appear on the front page of newspapers; famous Christian leaders attract huge followings and pack arenas when on tour; and bestselling Christian books make the *New York Times* bestseller list.

Ignatius lived in a very different world from ours. The church was just getting started in his day and thus had little time and opportunity to develop the beliefs, offices, and institutions that would later provide a clearly defined and widely respected structure of authority. Ignatius makes no sense if we do not take into account his very fragile world. What challenges did he face?

Troubles Ahead

The first challenge was the death of the apostles. Far from fading from the scene after Jesus' death and resurrection, the original eyewitnesses and followers of Jesus remained active, playing an important role in the first decades of the movement. Some remained in Jerusalem; others traveled, and testified as they did, which created a rich and dense culture of witness, story, and teaching. Even Paul claimed that he had "received" much of what he knew about the essential outline of the Jesus story from eyewitnesses (1 Cor. 15; Gal. 2). This repository of witness saturated the church and circulated as the church grew. It is highly probable, for example, that Peter provided much of the information that Mark used when writing his Gospel, most likely in Rome.

The apostles carried the additional authority of being commissioned by Jesus himself to "go," "make disciples," and "baptize." They became the official leaders of the church, which eventually included James, the Lord's brother, and Paul. The proceedings of the Jerusalem Council, as reported in Acts 15, offer evidence of the kind of authority that Peter, Paul, and James exercised. Apostolic writings only reinforced that authority. The apostles were the original witnesses, the first leaders, the founders and pillars. They knew Jesus; they heard his teaching; they received his commission; they called him Savior and Lord.

What would happen to the movement after the titans of that first generation passed from the scene?

The second challenge was the growth of the church. It is hard to estimate raw numbers—how many actual believers there were, in how many churches, in how many cities and towns—by, say, the year 150. The New Testament informs us that there were churches in Rome before Paul traveled there. In addition, there were churches in Syria, Asia Minor (coastal and inland), Greece, Macedonia, and Alexandria. We know this part of the story of the church's early expansion best because Luke tells it. But it is hard to imagine that an equal number of churches were not planted in North Africa and lands east of Jerusalem.[8]

The church was especially successful in reaching gentiles. But that success posed a problem. Gentiles required more from the church than Jewish converts because they understood less. They carried the beliefs and habits of their former way of life into their new faith, which would have made it easy to create a kind of hybrid religion of old and new,

82

the religious equivalent of white supremacy's use of Christian symbols and ideas.

How could the church welcome gentile converts without accommodating to the culture, on the one hand, or rejecting and condemning the culture, on the other? If Christian leaders had made inclusion of gentiles too easy, the faith itself would have eventually yielded to Rome's pluralism and suffered irreversible erosion. If Christian leaders had made inclusion too hard, converts would have given up in discouragement, finding the demands of church membership excessive, even punitive.

The third challenge was the threat of persecution. Christians encountered opposition from Jews right from the beginning of the movement, as Luke reports in Acts. Jewish leaders imprisoned Peter and John, hounded Paul out of synagogues and cities, applauded the execution of James (the apostle), and urged the stoning of Stephen, the first Christian martyr. But all things considered, Jewish opposition was limited in severity and in scope.

Roman opposition was far worse. The first Roman persecution occurred in AD 64. The historian Tacitus wrote a detailed account. He assigned responsibility to the emperor Nero, by then unpopular, crude, and corrupt. As Tacitus reported, a fire broke out in Rome, devastating a large portion of the city. Rumors began to spread that Nero had ordered it started so that he could rebuild Rome to his own glory. And Nero did in fact construct a large and lavish palace after the fire.

At first Nero tried to appease the masses with gifts and the gods with sacrifices, but neither succeeded in proving his innocence and diminishing the hostility. So he blamed the Christians, using them as a scapegoat. They proved to be a convenient target because of their "abominations" and "hatred of the human race"—the former referring to their peculiar practices, like the Eucharist and love feast, the latter their unwillingness to participate in popular forms of Roman entertainment, like the games, which Christians considered immoral.

A sadistic tyrant, Nero excelled in cruelty. Upon his order, Roman soldiers arrested and executed Christians. They clothed some in animal skins and then turned wild and hungry dogs loose on them, and they tied others to posts and set them on fire, using them as human torches to illuminate the night for palace parties. Nero used this brutal persecution to entertain the citizens of Rome. "Nero had thrown open his gardens for the spectacle, and was exhibiting a show in the circus, while he mingled with the people in the dress of a charioteer or drove about in a chariot." He was so severe that Romans began to pity Christians, even though they despised their religion. We have no idea how many Christians were executed, but the persecution was severe enough to move Tacitus to write about it.[9]

The persecution did not stop with Nero. In AD 96 the emperor Domitian initiated another one, mentioned by the historian Dio Cassius.[10] This persecution is most likely the one John described in highly symbolic language in the book of Revelation. Again, we have no idea how many died. But the numbers were high enough to inspire John to condemn Rome as the devil's instrument.

Imperial policy changed in the second century, becoming less random and capricious, though no less severe. The great emperors of that century—Trajan and Hadrian are two notable examples—followed a "don't ask, don't tell" policy. Appearing more measured, these emperors nevertheless continued to persecute Christians for no other reason than that they were Christians. Their use of the emperor cult, which was far more prominent in the second century than in the first, made the Christian worship of Jesus increasingly offensive and dangerous. As Tertullian put it, Christians were accused only of the "crime of a name" and not the "name of a crime." Roman officials targeted Christian leaders (especially bishops) in particular, which is why Ignatius died in Rome, Polycarp in Smyrna, and Pothinus in Lyons. Roman officials assumed that public executions would intimidate church members and break apart the movement. Obviously their strategy did not work.

Still, Ignatius and his fellow church leaders had good reason for concern. The movement was new, small, and fragile. It was like a team of mostly young athletes squaring off against a team of seasoned professionals. What would happen to the movement if Rome succeeded in killing off much of its leadership? And Rome had the power and organization to do just that.

The fourth reason for concern was the emergence of movements that presented a view of Jesus that departed from the teachings of the apostles. No movement was more threatening to the fledgling church than Gnosticism. The term itself poses problems because it applies to a wide range of movements that differed, sometimes sharply, from each other. If the canonical Gospels seem like four movements of a single symphony, Gnostic writings seem like separate pieces of music altogether. Still, the majority of Gnostic schemes shared certain features in common.[11]

All religions address a problem and then offer a solution. In the case of Gnosticism, the "problem" was the existence of the material world, including the human body, which seemed in the minds of Gnostic teachers to be destined for decay, destruction, and death. Where did the body come from? Why save it, as bad as it is? If it could not be saved, then what about the "spirit" in people? That exposed a second problem. Gnostic teachers believed that divine reality is totally "other," inaccessible and unknowable. Even the most spiritual people lack the capacity, as ignorant as they still are, to understand and know God. How then is knowledge of God even possible?

Gnostics were confident they had answers. Probably the most prominent Gnostic teacher of the second century was Valentinus. We learn about him from his critics—Tertullian, Irenaeus, and Hippolytus. But we also have several fragments of his writings and one book that he in all likelihood authored, *The Gospel of Truth*. We know enough to stitch together his story and basic ideas.[12]

Valentinus grew up in Alexandria and made his way to Rome around the year 140. He attracted followers who hoped to reach enlightenment through secret Gnostic wisdom. He was a prolific author (psalms, hymns, homilies, epistles), though most of his writings have been lost. He seems to have cut a powerful figure, too—educated, articulate, urbane, persuasive. He preached winsomely and widely, won disciples, started churches, and even aspired to the office of bishop. Church leaders in Rome rejected his candidacy and then excommunicated him. He eventually moved to Cyprus, where he continued his work. There the trail of his story runs cold.

But his influence continued. The churches he founded survived to the fourth century, and in a few cases even longer. He inspired a number of students to follow or adapt his system of religious ideas, to the extent that a kind of "Valentinian school" emerged, having two main branches, a western and an eastern.

What made his ideas so compelling? Valentinus developed a complex scheme to explain the origin of the material world and to lead people back to God, who is by definition pure spirit.

According to Valentinus, ultimate spiritual reality consists of an inconceivable and unknowable being, Bythos (depth). Emerging from this being are fifteen pairs of aeons, emanations, or eternities, like rays of light radiating from the sun. These aeons are called the "Pleroma" (fullness) or "Totality." Though occupying an exalted status, the Pleroma does not know and cannot understand its divine source.

The last of these aeons is Sophia (the Greek word for "wisdom"). It is through her that the material world came to be. As the Gnostic story of creation goes, Sophia longed with passion to know the Father, but the Father was incomprehensible to her. Sophia, therefore, lived in ignorance, agony, and misery. Her grief and tears produced three beings—Christ, who hastened back to his Father; the demiurge, who in ignorance created the material world; and the devil, who is the enemy of God.

The Gospel of Truth thus claims: "For this reason error became powerful; it worked on its own matter foolishly, not having known the truth. It set about with a creation, preparing with power and beauty the substitute for the truth."[13] Out of compassion Christ sent Jesus into the corrupt world as messenger and savior. Jesus suffered and died, as all creatures do, but then returned, as an immaterial and imperishable being, back to the Father. "For this reason Jesus appeared; he put on that book; he was nailed to a tree; he published the edict of the Father on the cross. O such great teaching! He draws himself down to death though life eternal clothes him. Having stripped himself of the perishable rags, he put on imperishability, which no one can possibly take away from him."[14] "Truth," one of the highest aeons, sent the Holy Spirit to guide the elect to salvation.

Not all, however, can be saved, but only the elect. Gnosticism is in fact for the few, not the many. Only some can be enlightened, not all. Only some carry a spark of divine light in them. Only some are capable of understanding the "secrets" of Gnostic teaching, which is why Gnostic teachers always traced the source of truth back to *one* apostle (Thomas in some accounts, Judas in others, Mary Magdalene in still others, and so forth), the only one who was sufficiently spiritual to understand. In fact, the word "Gnostic" refers to the special knowledge insiders received to attain salvation. Knowing, not believing and obeying, was primary.

As both preacher and writer, Valentinus was esoteric. His ideas were *supposed* to be esoteric because he had to use language to explain the infinite and ineffable, which is by definition incomprehensible. He told very few stories about Jesus. His Jesus was more mystic and sage than anything else. Valentinus taught that Jesus made an appearance on earth to show the way to "true interiority," which only some—those capable of enlightenment—could understand and achieve.

Valentinus attracted followers but also—and not surprisingly—critics. His most formidable critic was Irenaeus, who used every rhetorical weapon at his disposal to expose the deception of his scheme. "Error, indeed, is never set forth in its naked deformity, lest, being thus exposed, it should at once be detected. But it is craftily decked out in an attractive dress, so as, by its outward form, to make it appear to the inexperienced . . . more true than the truth itself."[15] Irenaeus argued that Valentinus, as well as other Gnostic teachers (and there were many), twisted the Bible to fit their peculiar view of Jesus. "They gather their views from other sources than the Scriptures; and, to use a common proverb, they strive to weave ropes of sand, while they endeavor to adapt with an air of probability to their own peculiar assertions the parables of the Lord, the sayings of the prophets, and the words of the apostles, in order that their scheme may not seem altogether without support."[16]

Irenaeus charged that Gnostics condemned the very world that God created, rejected the very Christ who came as a real man, dismissed the very crucifixion that won a complete salvation, denied the very resurrection that was the firstfruits of a restored humanity, and indulged or debased the very body that was destined to share in resurrection glory. He believed that Gnosticism was a mortal threat to the gospel and to the church.

But who is to say Irenaeus was right, Valentinus wrong?

This question leads us back to the issue of authority. By the time Ignatius wrote his letters, Peter, Paul, and James were already dead, as was John, the apostle who lived the longest. Nero and Domitian had turned the brutal power of Rome against Christianity. Gentiles were flooding the church; their numbers would only grow over time. Gnostics were providing alternative views of Jesus. How could the church survive, to say nothing of flourish, under these perilous circumstances? The church could not appeal to imperial Rome for help (the emperor Constantine would not emerge for another two hundred years), nor could it simply eliminate the opposition. Roman bishops did excommunicate Valentinus, to be sure. But Valentinus did not suddenly disappear. His movement in fact lasted for another two centuries.

The battle would be won or lost not in the arena but in the marketplace. Persuasion would have to prevail, not coercion. Authority would have to be more organic than organizational, more relational than institutional, more fluid than formal.

Authority in the early Christian period functioned like a circulatory system, a vast network of arteries that circulated gospel blood from one central organ, the heart.[17] That heart was Jesus Christ, who lived a public life and taught, trained, and commissioned a large and identifiable circle of disciples. After his death, resurrection, and ascension, those disciples continued the movement, bearing witness that Jesus Christ was the incarnate Son of God, Savior and Lord. The momentum did not diminish after the death of the first generation either. A second generation took over, and then a third generation, the main arteries circulating life through relationship, witness, teaching, and leadership. And the heart of the movement continued to be Jesus Christ.

The church developed and used three sources of authority to keep this circulatory system strong, secure, stable, and vital.

Belief

The first source of authority was a basic confession of faith, which emerged almost immediately, traveling with Christians as they spread the gospel and planted churches. In the second century it came to be known as the "rule of faith," "canon of truth," or "symbol of faith." These various rules of faith stated, in clear, pithy, concrete language, what Christians believed about the essential gospel, which focused on the person and work of Jesus Christ.[18]

We find evidence of this in the New Testament. As dominant and independent as he seemed to be, Paul cited a basic set of beliefs that he claims to have inherited, not invented. He was responsible, he said, to hand on this tradition, which was central to his calling as an apostle. "For I delivered to you as of first importance what I also received," he wrote to Christians in Corinth, "that Christ died for our sins in accordance with the scriptures, that he was buried, that he was raised on the third day in accordance with the scriptures, and that he appeared to Cephas, then to the twelve. Then he appeared to more than five hundred brethren at one time, most of whom are still alive, though some have fallen asleep. Then he appeared to James, then to all the apostles" (1 Cor. 15:3–7). Likewise, he summed up essential Christian belief in his first letter to Timothy, as if quoting an early rule of faith. "Great indeed, we confess, is the mystery of our religion: He was manifested in the flesh, vindicated in the Spirit, seen by angels, preached among the nations, believed on in the world, taken up in glory" (1 Tim. 3:16).

Christian leaders continued to use these brief summaries of Christian belief, which always focused on Jesus Christ as God's Son incarnate, as crucified and resurrected. Living one generation after the apostles, Ignatius cited what seems a formulaic confession:

> But our Physician is the only true God, the unbegotten and unapproachable, the Lord of all, the Father and Begetter of the only begotten Son. We have also as a Physician the Lord our God, Jesus the Christ, the only-begotten Son and Word, before time began, but who afterwards became also man, of Mary the virgin. . . . He was in a mortal body; being life, He became subject to corruption, that He might free our souls from death

89

and corruption, and heal them, and might restore them to health, when they were diseased with ungodliness and wicked lusts.[19]

Justin Martyr appealed to that same basic formula, which was foretold in the Old Testament. "In the books of the prophets we found proclaimed beforehand that Jesus our Christ would come, would be born through the virgin, become man and heal every sickness and disease, raise the dead, be hated and unrecognized, be crucified, die, and be raised again, and ascend into heaven, who is and is called the Son of God, and that certain men would be sent by him to every race of men to preach these same things."[20]

After explaining the Gnostic scheme, Irenaeus cited the rule of faith as his first and primary argument against the heresy. He stated that, however dispersed throughout the world, the church confessed faith in the same truths about God the creator, Jesus the redeemer, and the Holy Spirit, source of power for the church's ministry and witness. Thus the church believes "in one God, the Father almighty, Maker of heaven and earth, and the sea, and all things that are in them; and in one Christ Jesus, the Son of God, who became incarnate for our salvation; and in the Holy Spirit, who proclaimed through the prophets the dispensations of God, and the advents, and the birth from a virgin, and the passion, and the resurrection from the dead, and the ascension into heaven in the flesh of the beloved Christ Jesus, our Lord, and His [future] manifestation from heaven in the glory of the Father."[21]

A contemporary of Irenaeus living in North Africa, Tertullian stated a rule that sounded much the same. "There is only one rule of faith, unchangeable and unalterable: that of believing in one only God, omnipotent, the creator of the world; and his Son Jesus Christ, born of the Virgin Mary, crucified under Pontius Pilate; on the third day raised again from the dead; received into heaven; now sitting at the Father's right hand; who will come to judge living and dead, through the resurrection also of the flesh."[22]

Hippolytus of Rome, another contemporary, compiled a manual of instruction for the churches, which included a rule of faith used in the church's rites of initiation. The presiding bishop was instructed to ask baptismal candidates three questions. The second asked: "Do you believe in Christ Jesus, the son of God, who was born of the Holy Spirit and Mary the virgin and was crucified under Pontius Pilate and was dead [and buried] and rose on the third day alive from the dead and ascended in the heavens and sits at the right hand of the Father and will come to judge the living and the dead?"[23]

No official church council wrote these rules of faith, imposing them on the church, nor a dominant leader, like Augustine. These summaries of belief surfaced organically and independently, stating, as Irenaeus argued, what the whole church, however separated by distance, language, and culture, believed. The origin was more grassroots than hierarchical. The process was more bottom-up than top-down. Scattered across the Mediterranean world, the church nevertheless functioned as if it were one, holding all essential beliefs in common. "She also believes these points [of doctrine] just as if she had but one soul, and one and the same heart, as if she had but one heart and one soul, and she proclaims them, and teaches them, and hands them down, with perfect harmony, as if she possessed but one mouth. For, although the languages of the world are dissimilar, yet the import of the tradition is one and the same."[24]

This came to be known as "orthodoxy." Far from being novel or speculative or creative, it was rooted in the original teachings of the apostles, who bore witness to the person and work of Jesus Christ.

Book

The second source of authority was a book—*the* book. Most of the texts now included in the New Testament had functional authority long before they were officially canonized as Holy Scripture, as we learned in chapter 3. The church quoted from them, preached on them, memorized them, copied and circulated them, and used them in worship.

It was not simply as sacred Scripture, however, that these texts functioned authoritatively. It was *as a book*, too. This book played a pivotal role as a material object in early Christianity, as important to the movement as an MRI machine to an orthopedic surgeon or a computer to a physicist. Christianity was a "bookish" religion from the very beginning, a value and practice Christians inherited, at least in part, from the Jews.[25]

Most, though by no means all, converts in the early Christian period were illiterate. The more-literate leaders of the church read the book of Christians aloud, especially in worship, and then expounded on it. Paul commanded his young protégé, Timothy, to read from the Old Testament in carrying out his pastoral duties in worship (1 Tim. 4:13). Peter mentioned that Paul's writings were being used as authoritative texts in worship (2 Pet. 3:14–18). By the early second century, pastors read from the writings of the apostles. In this way they could keep the words of the apostles alive as if the apostles were still present, telling stories about Jesus and explaining his victory over sin, death, and hell. In a sense, the original orality of Christianity was thus carried on. Justin stated that the churches studied the "memoirs of the apostles" on Sundays, though churches had only one copy, which means that they read the memoirs of the apostles *aloud*.[26] Irenaeus argued that the four canonical Gospels—and *only* those four—were widely acknowledged as providing multiple perspectives on the same story, the story of Jesus, his ministry, death, and resurrection.[27]

But it was not simply the *use* of the book that set the Christian movement apart. It was also *the book itself*. Early Christians were committed enough to these texts to translate, copy, and circulate them. Scholars have noted the abundance of extant manuscripts, which bears witness to the importance of the book based on sheer quantity. Written in Greek, the language of the people Christians were trying to reach, the book of Christians was translated into Latin, Coptic, and Syriac by the end of the third century. Such translating, copying, and circulating was no small task, considering the magnitude of the work involved. Many of the apostolic writings were long (e.g., Luke and Acts), demanding a great deal from the church to produce multiple copies.

Christians made use of the codex, a fairly new technology in the ancient world, which resembles the modern book. The ancient world was much more familiar with and dependent on the scroll. Christians quickly adopted the codex for certain texts—those now included in the New Testament. There was a simple reason for this. Readers could turn to any part of it quickly and conveniently, unlike the scroll. The weekly—and even daily—use of it in worship (Hippolytus urged Christians to gather *every morning* for worship) required a text that would allow for easy access to all parts, which favored the codex over the scroll. It fit the church's commitment to the book.

Bishop

The third source of authority was the office and function of bishop. The earliest post-apostolic writers we know of mentioned and outlined the duties of the office of bishop. Both Clement of Rome, for example, and Ignatius of Antioch (as we have already observed) argued that the apostles themselves appointed bishops to carry on their ministry after they were gone. The chief duty of bishops was to be faithful to the apostolic witness. The office itself was far less important than the function. There was little these early bishops would—and could—gain from the office. They presided over small and marginal churches. They were more likely to die as martyrs than anyone else, and they carried virtually no cultural status in the larger Roman world. It seems unlikely, therefore, that bishops would have sought such a leadership position largely to serve their own interest. There was simply too much risk and cost and too little reward, as defined by conventional Roman standards of status and power.

Besides, most of the pastoral work happened at the local level, carried out by ordinary believers. We know that on the eve of Constantine's conversion, there were some 1,400 bishops in the empire, exercising spiritual oversight over some 5,000,000 believers who were worshiping in some 65,000 churches, which means that on average one bishop was responsible for 46 churches and 3,500 believers. Those numbers imply that bishops carried a heavy burden of responsibility. But they also imply that local leaders—presbyters, deacons, deaconesses, lectors, exorcists—provided the daily pastoral care. In short, the main arteries of bishops circulated blood through the thousands of capillaries of lower—and local—offices, which had the effect of flattening hierarchy and democratizing authority.

Early Christian leaders defended the importance of "apostolic succession" to preserve the ministry of and message about Jesus. The apostles appointed leaders who could be trusted; those leaders did the same, which was intended to create and sustain an unbroken succession from the apostles to the generations that followed, forming a circulatory system that moved from the heart outward, bringing life to the world.

Still living in the first century, Clement, the bishop of Rome, traced his office through the apostles back to Jesus Christ himself. God sent his Son, Jesus. Jesus in turn commissioned the apostles, who proclaimed the gospel around the Mediterranean world. Finally, the apostles appointed bishops, who not only continued to preach the gospel but also pastored churches. "Christ therefore was sent forth by God, and the apostles by Christ. . . . Having therefore received their orders, and being fully assured by the resurrection of our Lord Jesus Christ, and established in the word of God, with full assurance of the Holy Ghost, [the Apostles] went forth proclaiming that the kingdom of God was at hand." Having established churches, these same apostles "appointed the first-fruits . . . to be bishops and deacons of those who should afterwards believe."[28]

Irenaeus charged bishops to be faithful to the work of the apostles, who passed on their ministry to the second generation—and beyond—by the succession of bishops, "by which they have handed down that Church which exists in every place, and has come even unto us, being guarded and preserved without any forging of Scriptures, by a very complete system of doctrine." This culminated, Irenaeus noted, in the "pre-eminent gift of love, which is more precious than knowledge, more glorious than prophecy, and which excels all the other gifts [of God]."[29]

He cited the life of Polycarp as an example of how succession worked. On the one hand, Polycarp learned from the apostle John; on the other hand, he mentored Irenaeus when he was still a young man, before Irenaeus left for Lyons, where he eventually was appointed bishop. This succession of episcopal leadership comprised three generations that spanned 170 years. "But Polycarp also was not only instructed by apostles, and conversed with many who had seen Christ, but was also, by apostles in Asia, appointed bishop of the Church in Smyrna, whom I also saw in my early youth, for he tarried [on earth] a very long time, and, when a very old man, gloriously and most nobly suffering martyrdom, departed this life, having always taught the things which he had learned from the apostles, and which the Church has handed down, and which alone are true."[30]

Bishops did their best to shepherd the flock, though of course in actual practice they sometimes failed, as the historical record indicates. We know of noble bishops, to be sure; we also know of scoundrels and rogues. The best of them visited churches, preached regularly and prayed faithfully, taught catechumens, administered sacraments, led delegations, convened local and regional councils, and wrote letters of encouragement, council, and rebuke, all of which kept the apostolic circulatory system reasonably functional and healthy.[31]

Back once more to Ignatius, with whom we started this chapter. He had good reason for worry, considering the dire circumstances he faced as a second-generation leader of the church. But he also had confidence—in the power of the gospel, which was summed up in the rule of faith, preserved in the book, and passed down through the ministry of bishops, of which he was one.

Still, there is something peculiar about these three sources of authority. They all point to Jesus Christ, which should be obvious by now. But Jesus himself seemed to have no authority at all, at least as it was—and still is—conventionally understood. He did not attend a school, or study under a master, or found an institution, or hold an office, or lead an army, or write a book. At the end of his life even his closest companions deserted him. He died a lonely death on the cross, utterly abandoned and forsaken by all but a few.

Yet this man, his disciples believed, wielded an authority that no one had ever witnessed before. Authority is by definition derivative; his was inherent. Authority is official; his was personal and original. Authority is often coercive, won and wielded through the exercise of power; his was humble and sacrificial, surrendered rather than seized. People responded to him with utter amazement. They said he taught with authority—and not as the scribes and Pharisees—stilled raging storms, healed the sick, restored sight to the blind, cast out demons, even resuscitated the dead, all by saying just a word. His authority seemed to come from God. The apostles believed he *was*—and is—God.[32]

This authority carried over into the life of the early church. Not that early Christians claimed to have the same authority. Their authority *was* derivative, founded on Jesus Christ. They bore witness to him, as did the next generation and then the one after that until, as Irenaeus noted, the church had reached the known world, like a massive circulatory system of life. And everywhere, he said, there was the same belief, the same book, the same office of bishop, all pointing to the same person, Jesus Christ.

Rome did not know quite what to make of it or what to do about it. This Third Way authority surprised and threatened Rome because it was a different kind of authority. Christians refused to contend with Rome on Rome's terms. They quoted Jesus: "My kingdom is not of this world" (John 18:36 NIV), which seemed innocent enough. But Rome discovered that it was far from innocent. Though not *of* this world, Jesus and his followers had everything to do *with* this world, as we shall see.

6

Identity and Community

Early Christianity began largely as a rural movement. Jesus himself commenced his ministry in Galilee, not Jerusalem, and many of the first leaders of the church grew up in a rural setting. Peter was a small-town fisherman, not a big-city businessman. The Christian movement continued to thrive in rural areas, too. Pliny the Younger complained to Trajan, for example, that Christianity was spreading into the countryside as well as the cities, which Justin confirmed in his *First Apology*, mentioning that Christians gathered for worship every Sunday in rural settings (as well as in cities), and Tertullian claimed that Christians could be found everywhere in the empire, except of course in the temples. None of this should surprise us, considering the rural origins of Jesus and his first followers.

What is surprising, however, is how rapidly the Christian movement expanded into Greco-Roman cities. The church was born in the city of Jerusalem on the day of Pentecost, and Jerusalem became home base for the apostles. But the Christian movement established a witness in Antioch, too, even before Paul's conversion on the Damascus road, which occurred within the first decade of the birth of Christianity. We know that by the end of the apostolic period there were churches in Antioch, Ephesus, Corinth, Philippi, and Rome, all large Greco-Roman cities, and we know the names of at least some of the people who evangelized in those cities (Paul, Silas, Timothy, Apollos, Priscilla and Aquila, and others). Ministry in urban centers continued, too, mostly through the work of ordinary Christians whose names have long been forgotten but whose influence remains.[1]

These were a different kind of city than ours. We tend to value privacy and property in modern Western cities. Homeownership is the ideal, though apartment living has become increasingly popular—and often necessary, especially in cities with a high cost of living, like San Francisco, London, Paris, and New York. Modern houses have eliminated the front porch in favor of decks and patios in the backyard, where gardens grow, families barbecue, and children play. Fences keep out all intruders—and neighbors, too, for that matter. Apartments do not allow for the same kind of spacious living, but they still protect privacy.[2]

We treat our homes as if they were a refuge. When leaving them, we travel mostly by car from one destination to the next, as if cars functioned as a kind of wormhole between the worlds of home and stores, markets, gyms, schools, work—and churches, too, which, as if they were fortresses surrounded by a concrete moat, are no more open to the neighborhood than most modern houses are. Modern city planners view churches as "dead space" because they rarely welcome passersby, unlike coffee shops, markets, bakeries, pubs, restaurants, and galleries.

It is impossible to understand the success of the early Christian movement unless we recognize the difference between ancient cities and modern ones and the impact of ancient cities on how the church grew. So we must begin with a brief exploration of cities in the Roman Empire. What were they like?

Roman Cities

Many Roman cities were surprisingly large, though it is hard to determine exact population figures. Rome's population numbered between 750,000 and 1,000,000, Alexandria's 400,000, Ephesus's 200,000, Antioch's 150,000, and cities like Pergamum, Sardis, Corinth, and Carthage's around 100,000, and many more between 30,000 and 80,000.[3]

These cities were impressively sophisticated, even according to modern standards. Many had neighborhood water fountains (still present, e.g., in Rome), underground sewage systems, public latrines, wide boulevards with water features, and parks. They were dense, too—as dense as modern cities like Singapore and Calcutta.

Rome's Regionary Catalogue, published in the early fourth century, indicated that there were 1,782 private houses and 43,580 apartment buildings in the city, which means that most people lived in very close quarters. Main city streets were wide, paved with stone (which made them washable), and lined with shops, but most streets were narrow and crowded with people, covered in dirt, and filthy. One could easily walk across the entire city of Rome in less than a day, which indicates how small the area was for the million or so people who lived there.[4]

Roman society was divided along class lines. There were the few who were wealthy and powerful (less than 5 percent) and the many who were relatively poor and powerless. The rich lived in large, private houses and often owned country estates, too, where they could withdraw to escape the summer heat and the threat of natural disasters, such as plagues, fires, and floods, which were especially prevalent and dangerous in cities.

The houses of the upper class were spacious and beautiful. Upon entrance guests would pass through a front door into a vestibule, which would then lead to a meeting hall and dining room. Behind these public rooms were the kitchen, bedrooms, workshop, quarters for servants and associates, places for storage, and more. Houses had one or more inner courtyard that allowed natural light to flood interior rooms, and they provided indoor plumbing and fresh drinking water, piped in from an aqueduct. They were decorated with thin slabs of marble, which were often inlaid with mosaics and then affixed to interior walls, much like wallpaper in modern houses. They bustled with activity, too, because they functioned as the center of both family life and commerce, with space set aside for both. In addition to parents and children, the houses of the wealthy included slaves and household servants, cooks, managers, business associates, messengers, and clients. An excavation of a large home in Ephesus reveals a footprint of more than seven thousand square feet.

The poor (either working or destitute), comprising over 95 percent of the population, lived very differently. There was a "middling" class (similar to our lower-middle class), which included artisans, merchants, shop owners, freemen, skilled laborers, and the like. But many teetered close to poverty or fell into it. There were no government services to depend on, though Rome, as well as other large cities, did dole out free bread and provide free entertainment for the masses. Still, most people had to depend on kinship networks or the patronage system for survival.[5] Class distinctions were clear and decisive.[6]

The vast majority of urban dwellers lived in apartment buildings, which ranged in height from three to eight stories. They were poorly constructed, and thus vulnerable to destruction by fire, flood, and earthquake. The best—and most expensive—apartments were located on the first and second floors. They often housed one extended family and contained multiple rooms, which might include servant quarters, a business, and a shop. Poorer families lived on the upper floors, which were far less roomy and expensive, clean and convenient, safe and secure. There was very little natural lighting, no plumbing, no running water, and no adequate ventilation. They were cold in winter and hot in summer. People cooked on charcoal braziers, used chamber pots at night, and discarded all waste in open sewers during the day when, safer from rampant crime, they dared to venture out in public.

Considering the cramped conditions, odor and noise from the street, and general lack of comfort, urban dwellers tried to spend as much time as they could in public places, thus avoiding the confinement of such bleak quarters. They enjoyed public "baths" (much like modern spas or health clubs), which were open to all, including women, and offered an opportunity to bathe, converse with friends, exercise, and relax. They also frequented temple and shrine, forum and marketplace, circus and stadium, where they loitered, shopped, met friends, caught up on the latest gossip, and watched all forms of entertainment, from street jugglers to races at the circus. Petty crime was a constant problem, as was prostitution.

There was virtually no privacy in these cities. Consequently, the life of ordinary people was always on display, a spectacle for the world to see. What people believed, how they behaved at work and home and marketplace, where they shopped and worshiped and traveled, who they counted as friends (and enemies)—this was all a matter of public knowledge. Such a public life was bound to lead to conflict, and the constant influx of immigrants, traders, and travelers created tensions of all kinds. The city of Antioch, for example, had eighteen identifiable ethnic groups, most of which lived in ethnic enclaves but clashed in public places.[7]

The Christian movement took root and flourished in this urban world. The purpose of this chapter is to understand why and how.

At just this point, however, we face a temptation. That the movement succeeded is beyond question. Rome's response to Christianity provides evidence enough—as we see, for example, in the criticism of Celsus, Galen, and Porphyry, all Roman intellectual elites. Romans took notice of the movement and responded with curiosity, interest, enthusiasm, suspicion, or hostility.

But the movement's success can easily lead to an error in judgment on our part, which is to idealize and romanticize it, as if the movement embodied a kind of pure Christianity. Such a judgment is not true to the facts and not helpful to us. It might have been successful; that does not mean it was without weakness. There was clearly a gap between aspiration and outcome, conviction and behavior. The historical record is clear about this. Ignatius of Antioch, for example, leveled harsh criticism against the Jews, as did the Epistle of Barnabas, forgetting the Jewish origins of Christianity and violating the law of love Jesus taught. Polycarp became the ideal Christian martyr, to be sure; but not all Christians followed his example. Pliny informed the emperor Trajan that threat and torture often worked, pressuring Christians to forsake Christ and to return to the temples. Christian leaders feuded, too, as we observe in the controversy over how the church dealt with believers who had committed apostasy during the Decian persecution (249–51) but then wanted to return to the Christian fold. Some church leaders urged tolerance; others advocated severity. We know that the controversy turned nasty and caused deep division.

Still, the fact remains that Christians did stand out; they did leave an impression; they did flourish. The movement did grow over a period of some 250 years, often under trying circumstances.

Early Christianity functioned as a new and peculiar kind of resistance movement that Rome had never seen before. The connotation of a resistance movement in our day implies protest against a political party, ideology, or policy, which the resistance movement seeks to overthrow and replace. But early Christians did not directly challenge Roman hegemony or complain about a political regime or policy (except unjust persecution). Christians related to Rome with a certain degree of ambivalence. They testified that they prayed for Caesar but refused to worship him. They aspired to serve the needy of the empire but not under the Roman terms of reciprocity. They viewed Jesus as the rightful king but never revolted against Rome or set up an alternative government in exile, as if their movement was exclusively political.

They claimed that they followed a different king (and a different *kind* of king) and lived for a different kingdom (and a different *kind* of kingdom)—"not *of* this world," as Jesus said, but certainly *for* it. This king and kingdom struck the Romans as strange, menacing, even dangerous, though in a way that was hard to define. Jesus claimed absolute lordship but refused earthly throne, weapon, army, and image. He demanded complete allegiance from his followers but sacrificed his life for them. He invited all to become citizens of his kingdom but had no territory over which he ruled. He announced the creation of a new humanity and the formation of a new community, regardless of background, ethnicity, and social status. Christians believed that the world, which included the Roman Empire, was a part of God's kingdom, not outside it. It was God's to rule and theirs to serve and care for. Thus they prayed, "Thy kingdom come, thy will be done, on earth as it is in heaven."

Rome, therefore, had to contend with a movement it could not defeat in the traditional way. It discovered over time that, short of complete annihilation, it could not defeat it at all.

How did this movement prove to be so effective?

I want to return now to the ancient document I mentioned in the first chapter, *The So-Called Letter to Diognetus*. We have to read such documents with a careful and critical eye, as if we were detectives in

102

search of clues, because it is hard to determine how reliable they are in telling us the truth about the early Christian movement. Does this letter actually describe with accuracy what in fact was true about the early church? Does it prescribe what the author wished the church to be? Or does it distort the truth? How can we know for sure which alternative is the right one?

We do know that the Christian movement grew and became a formidable force in the Roman world long before Constantine, the first Christian emperor, came to power in the early fourth century. If anything, some scholars argue that the gradual emergence of a Christian empire undermined true—and original—Christianity rather than strengthened it; or, short of that, it changed it into something very different from what it had been before Constantine.[8] There are reasons why the church grew in numbers and influence. The challenge is in discovering what those reasons were.

This letter gives us three clues that might explain why Christianity succeeded as a movement in the Roman world.

New Identity

First, the letter states that Christians took on a new and peculiar identity as followers of Jesus, an identity that crossed traditional barriers. Christians did not introduce a new culture, at least according to Rome's definition of "culture," symbolized by the obvious markers of language, clothing, diet, custom, rite, ritual, art, and architecture. "For Christians cannot be distinguished from the rest of the human race by country or language or custom."[9] Christians did not wear "Christian" clothes or shop in "Christian" stores or speak a "Christian" language or build "Christian" houses of worship. Archaeologists can find scant evidence of a Christian material presence in the ancient world, with the exception of religious texts (the New Testament) and a few works of art (mostly found in catacombs).

But Christianity had an impact all the same. Erecting no church buildings, Christians aimed to be "living stones," as Peter put it (1 Pet. 2:5). Refusing to visit pagan temples and burn incense in worship, they

hoped to emit the "aroma of Christ" (2 Cor. 2:15). Never once portray-
ing images of their God (at least in this early period), as the Romans
did, Christians strived to reflect the image of God by how they lived
(1 Pet. 2:21). Christians formed an identity that transcended Roman
categories. They shared much in common with everyone else, yet they
were still different. "They live in their own countries, but only as aliens.
They have a share in everything as citizens, and endure everything as
foreigners. Every foreign land is their fatherland, and yet for them every
fatherland is a foreign land."[10]

The author was echoing the language and life of Paul. As a radical
Pharisee, Paul considered himself "blameless" under the Jewish law.
In his mind Judaism was the superior religion and his religious accomplishments proof of it. "If anyone else has reason to be confident in
the flesh, I have more: circumcised on the eighth day, a member of the
people of Israel, of the tribe of Benjamin, a Hebrew born of Hebrews;
as to the law, a Pharisee; as to zeal, a persecutor of the church; as to
righteousness under the law, blameless" (Phil. 3:4–6 NRSV).

Then Paul had an encounter with Jesus Christ on the Damascus
road, which set in motion a series of events that changed him and the
entire Christian movement. Surprising everyone, Paul became a radical Christian and the primary apostle to the gentiles, the very group of
people he had once despised.

Paul described this dramatic change in one of his letters. As a Phari-
saic Jew, Paul divided the world into two groups: observant Jews and
everyone else. Such was the "human point of view" that informed his
perspective on the world. He viewed Christ from that same perspective,
believing him to be a messianic pretender and Jewish rebel. And he also
despised Christ's disciples, then known as "Christians," because they
posed a threat to his Jewish beliefs and way of life. Christians claimed
that Christ had come to "fulfill" ancient Judaism. But Paul believed
that Christ was really threatening to destroy it.

His encounter with Jesus changed his entire perspective—and life.
Paul discovered that Jesus Christ, the one crucified, had been raised
from the dead. This Jesus, he came to believe, was truly the Messiah
and Son of God.

Paul's conversion transformed how he understood himself and everyone else. In Christ, people become completely new. "From now on, therefore, we regard no one from a human point of view; even though we once knew Christ from a human point of view, we know him no longer in that way. So if anyone is in Christ, there is a new creation: everything old has passed away; see, everything has become new!" (2 Cor. 5:16–17 NRSV).

Paul was quick to acknowledge, however, that much of the "old" remained, which his letters addressed time and again. He exhorted believers to grow into their new identity and to live in a manner worthy of the gospel—in short, to become who they already were in Christ. But Paul acknowledged that their behavior continued to be appallingly "old," falling far short of their new identity in Christ. Christians might have been adopted children, but they still lived as if they were homeless orphans.

His conversion transformed how he viewed the human community, too. Christ, Paul asserted, broke down the "dividing wall of hostility" (Eph. 2:14) between Jew and gentile, exposing and condemning any and all claims that made one group feel superior to the other. Christ died for all because they were sinners; Christ rose for all to redeem them. No group had an advantage over another group; no group could assert superiority over another. Christ had made one new person out of two, or ten, and a million (Eph. 2:11–22). Christ's death and resurrection introduced a new way of understanding how being an individual and belonging to a community are no more mutually exclusive than being an athlete and belonging to a team. "There is no longer Jew or Greek, there is no longer slave or free, there is no longer male and female; for all of you are one in Christ Jesus" (Gal. 3:28 NRSV).

Of course that was not entirely true either, as the church in Corinth sadly illustrated, divided, as it was, into various factions. It was obvious that the "old" persisted there, too. Paul reasoned, however, that the *primary* identity of Christians—adopted children of God through Christ—transformed all *secondary* identities, subjecting them to the rule of Christ. Occupying the same position in the social order as before, true disciples learned to be a different kind of person in the social order—a different kind of Jew or Greek, ruler or citizen, elite or barbarian, master or servant, male or female, husband or wife, parent or child (1 Cor. 7; Eph. 5:21–6:9).[11]

The book of Acts tells the story of how identity in Christ—the "new creation"—began to shape and change social identity, however slowly and incompletely. The church became a community that welcomed outsiders—gentiles, women, slaves—because Christ came to make all people new. The church was not only for Jews, God's chosen people; it was also for gentiles. The very group that had at one time been "far off" had been brought "near" through Christ. The story of Cornelius's conversion in Acts 10 epitomizes this dramatic shift. Peter, of all people, was the one who welcomed him into the Christian fold. As Peter discovered in a dream, God declared all foods clean; likewise, God welcomed all peoples, regardless of background and ethnicity, into the church.

All of this explains why the author of *The So-Called Letter to Diognetus* argued as he did. This radical message confronted an ancient world deeply divided by gender, ethnicity, education, and socioeconomic inequality. The Christian movement challenged these inequalities, however subtly, and achieved at least modest success in crossing demographic, racial, ethnic, and economic boundaries. Primary identity in Christ began to transform secondary identities. Clement of Alexandria, a Christian teacher in Alexandria in the late second century, argued that Jesus Christ loves, and thus makes people loveable, which in turn inspires Christians, no matter their social location, to love others, too, with Christ's love.[12] Living under the law of love, the Christian movement tended to flatten the social order without destroying it.[13]

The author of *The So-Called Letter to Diognetus* argued that it was Jesus Christ who changed everything. He was the way *to* new life. He made the unrighteous righteous; he turned sinners into saints; he transformed the ungodly into his followers. "In his mercy, he took up the burden of our sins. He himself gave up his own Son as a ransom for us—the holy one for the unjust, the innocent for the guilty, the righteous one for the unrighteous, the incorruptible for the corruptible, the immortal for the mortal. For what else could cover our sins except his righteousness?" The sole duty of Christians was to look to Jesus and trust him as "Nurse, Father, Teacher, Counselor, Healer, Mind, Light, Honor, Glory, Might, Life."[14]

But Jesus Christ modeled a new way *of* life, too. Once finding life in him, Christians were called to live *like* him, and thus to imitate him. "And when you have acquired this knowledge, think with what joy you will be filled! Think how you will love him, who first loved you so! And when you love him, you will be an imitator of his goodness." The author explained what such imitation would accomplish, too. Masters would turn into servants, the strong would care for the weak, the wealthy would honor the poor. Those in power would no longer behave as they had previously, for "it is not in this way that any man can imitate God, for such things are alien to his majesty."[15]

To the early Christians, Jesus himself set the standard. Jesus numbered women among his disciples; no traditional rabbi followed this practice. He healed lepers, then considered unclean and cursed; embraced children, then treated as marginal and unimportant; and cared for the poor, then considered unworthy of mercy. He loved wayward sinners, as the story of the prodigal son illustrates so well. Christians tried to do the same. Another apologist writing in the second century, Athenagoras, an Athenian, put it this way: "But among us you will find uneducated persons, and artisans, and old women, who, if they are unable in words to prove the benefit of our doctrine, yet by their deeds exhibit the benefit arising from their persuasion of its truth: they do not rehearse speeches, but exhibit good works; when struck, they do not strike again; when robbed, they do not go to law; they give to those that ask of them, and love their neighbors as themselves."[16]

Christian martyrs had a similar impact. Martyrs became a new kind of hero. To be sure, their death did not accomplish what Christ's did; it had no salvific power to it, as the story of the martyrdom of Polycarp makes clear.[17] Still, martyrdom demonstrated that Christian identity took precedence over all other identities, thus testifying that faith was far more important than wealth, fame, and position. Writing about martyrdom, Origen exhorted the faithful to yield the first place to those who had suffered and died for Christ. Christians "should get out of the first seats" for the people who, because of their love for God in Christ, "trample upon the deceitful fame most people seek."[18]

Their example challenged how Rome defined social status. Tertullian noted the complete reversal of values that martyrdom symbolized. Martyrs seemed to be the victims; far from it, they were the victors. They languished in prison; but they were really enjoying freedom. "Wherefore, O blessed, you may regard yourselves as having been transferred from prison to what we may call a place of safety. It is full of darkness, but you yourselves are light; it has bonds, but God has made you free. . . . The Christian outside the prison has renounced the world, but in the prison he has renounced a prison, too. It is of no consequence where you are in the world—you who are not of it."[19]

The story of the martyrdom of Perpetua, a new Christian, mother of a newborn, and member of the upper class, illustrates the point. As a wealthy Roman woman, she was raised knowing that identity came primarily through empire and family. But as a Christian, she chose instead to identify with Christ and the Christian community, however great her loss of earthly status. Her father pled that she return to the family. "Do not abandon me to be the reproach of men. Think of your brothers, think of your mother and your aunt, think of your child, who will not be able to live once you are gone. Give up your pride! You will destroy us all!" But Perpetua refused. Simply being Christian created a new identity for her and conferred a new status upon her, in her mind one far loftier than her old one.[20]

This movement—of ordinary people from diverse backgrounds— challenged the elites of the Roman world. The lower classes in particular had little to lose but much to gain in following Jesus, which made the conversion of Perpetua, a member of the upper class, so unusual and unnerving. The Christian movement had a transformative impact, though without ever trying to achieve such an impact directly (as if the primary goal of Christians was to reform Rome). Justin Martyr summed up the idealistic vision that animated the movement, especially as it was embodied in the Christian way of life. The impact was simply Christians living as Christians. "We who formerly delighted in fornication, but now embrace chastity alone; we who formerly used magical arts, dedicate ourselves to the good and unbegotten God; we who valued above all things the acquisition of wealth and possessions, now bring what we have into a common stock, and communicate to everyone in need; we who hated and destroyed one another . . . now, since the coming of Christ, live familiarly with them, and pray for our enemies."[21]

New Commonwealth

There was a second reason why Christianity became such an influential—and threatening—presence in the Roman world. Once again we return to *The So-Called Letter to Diognetus*, where the author states that the Christian movement formed a new *oikoumene*—"commonwealth"—a term Rome used exclusively of itself.[22]

The Roman Empire had united the entire Mediterranean world under the rule of Caesar. Comprising many cultures, tongues, and ethnicities, the empire secured the Pax Romana, the "peace of Rome." A network of roads allowed for relatively safe travel; a vast army kept borders secure and cities reasonably stable; a common coinage allowed for convenient financial transaction from one part of the empire to another; a political system established a sense of order across a huge expanse of territory within which diverse peoples lived. By the second century, the emperor, elevated to the status of a god (especially in the east), became the symbol and embodiment of the Roman *oikoumene*.

It would seem that the Roman commonwealth and Christian commonwealth would clash, as if they were two opposing armies fighting over the same territory. But the Christian movement did not challenge Rome directly. Early Christianity was never intentionally subversive and revolutionary. The movement operated under a completely different set of principles, so unfamiliar to Rome that Rome did not know quite how to respond. It bears repeating: Christians did not angle for power, march on Rome, tell the emperor how to rule, or work for his demise. Following Paul's counsel to Timothy, they only wished—and asked—to be left alone (1 Tim. 2). Christians functioned much like a young, idealist teacher who lands a job in a failing school. It is her first job, a chance to get started in her career. Her only aspiration is to help the students in her classroom learn and grow into mature adults. She works hard, introduces fresh ideas, cares deeply for her students, and over time wins them over, which only rattles the administration and threatens some of the veteran teachers. Much to her surprise—and perhaps naivete—she faces severe opposition. Over time her methods of teaching and love for the students transform the school, a consequence she never aimed for. All she wanted was to do her best as a teacher.

Early Christians believed that the church embodied a new *oikoumene*, only of a very different kind from Rome's. Irenaeus, as we have already observed, affirmed that churches, though scattered around the Mediterranean world, were united in Christ. They confessed the same faith, followed the same order of worship, received the same sacrament of Eucharist, read the same Bible, and obeyed the same ethic of love. Everywhere, he argued, that church believed and practiced the same thing, as if it had but one heart, one mind, one will, one voice.[23]

Tertullian, a contemporary of Irenaeus, noted that Christians did not pursue the kind of position and power Romans did because they followed a different God and belonged to a different body. This body had universal jurisdiction, as if it were an empire within the empire, but it was a strange kind of empire because it showed no interest in Rome's way of doing empire. He noted that there was nothing more alien to Christians than political activity. Still, he wrote, as Christians "we acknowledge only one universal commonwealth, the whole world." The church, he continued, was united "by a common religious profession, by a godly discipline, by a bond of hope. We meet together as an assembly and congregation that as an organized force we may assail God with our prayers."[24]

Clement of Alexandria, still another contemporary of Irenaeus, noted the same kind of unity. These three leaders—Irenaeus, Tertullian, and Clement—did not live near each other, know each other, or read each other's works, yet they asserted the same universal *oikoumene*. "In essence, in idea, in origin, in pre-eminence we say that the ancient Catholic Church is the only church. . . . The pre-eminence of the church, just as the origin of its constitution, depends on its absolute unity: it excels all other things, and has no equal or rival."[25]

Living a generation later, Cyprian, bishop of Carthage, repeated the same argument. He served as bishop when the emperor Decius initiated an empire-wide persecution in 251. He fled from Carthage to safety so that he could continue to exercise his duties as leader of the church, and he received severe criticism for it. Ironically, Cyprian suffered martyrdom during the Valerian persecution in 258. His most famous work is on the unity of the church. He believed that the church is one, however widespread and diverse. Using the metaphors of the sun and its rays, trunk and its branches, fountain and its streams, he argued that singularity and multiplicity are not mutually exclusive. There is one source, Jesus Christ; there are many manifestations—one source of light, but many rays; one trunk, but many branches; one fount, but many streams. "Thus also the Church, when the light of the Lord is poured forth, though she sheds her rays of light throughout the whole world, nevertheless the light is one that I spread everywhere, but the unity is not cut off from the body." Changing metaphors, he confessed the church was like a mother of many children. "From her womb we are born, by her milk we are nurtured, by her spirit we are given life."[26]

There was something profoundly audacious about this claim. The Christian movement was at this time small and marginal, considering the size and sophistication of the empire. Yet the leaders of the church claimed that the church constituted a new *oikoumene*, though it had little to show for it.

What did Rome make of this peculiar *oikoumene*? What could it do about it? Rome considered it a cancer within the empire, spreading the disease through Rome's entire body, challenging its authority and way of life. But Christians believed the opposite. Christianity was the source of life and health, like white blood cells, combating the cancer— brutality, social stratification, abuse of power, greed and materialism, and immorality—that was Rome. The two could not coexist forever. One would have to give way to the other.

New Household

There was a third reason why Christians launched such an influential movement in the empire. The *oikoumene*—the universal body of the church—also existed as an *oikos*, a "household." Universal was also

111

particular; global, local; big, small—especially in the most basic form in which the church existed: the house church. It was in cities in particular that house churches spread, multiplied, and flourished.[27] In such a setting Christians could not hide. They lived and worshiped in the same apartment buildings as their pagan neighbors; they shopped in the same markets; they visited the same public places. But they did not live in the same way. The author of the letter to Diognetus explained what set Christians apart. Christians, he wrote, "marry, like everyone else, and they beget children, but they do not cast out their offspring. They share their board with each other, but not their marriage bed. . . . They obey the established laws, but in their own lives they go far beyond what the laws require."[28] Christians also refused to visit temples, participate in public festivals, and honor the emperor as a god.[29]

The *oikos*—the local house church—created a new kind of family. God ruled—and loved—as Father, which implied that all members, regardless of social status, were brothers and sisters. Paul's appeal to Philemon set the trajectory, for he exhorted Philemon to welcome his slave, Onesimus, back as a brother in Christ. Christianity did not abolish ancient social roles and hierarchy but subjected them to a different standard. Husband and wife, parent and child, slave and free, citizen and barbarian, Jew and gentile were members of the same family, and subject to the rule of Christ.[30]

The new *oikos* thus began very gradually to transform the old order, though never completely and perfectly. Unlike the Roman father, who ruled the household, even exercising the power to determine whether a newborn would live or die, the Christian father was expected to serve. Unlike Roman women, whose primary responsibility was to marry and produce male heirs, Christian women were encouraged to use their gifts in the church and were even allowed to remain single with no loss of social status.[31] Unlike Roman children, who were assigned a subordinate status until becoming adults, Christian children were treated as disciples and welcomed in worship as full participants.[32]

House churches functioned as mission outposts. Christians attracted attention, not because they were loud and obnoxious but because they were different. That difference repulsed some, especially Roman officials, but impressed and attracted many others—relatives, friends, neighbors, and associates. Observing Christian behavior, they would show interest and ask questions. Christians in turn would invite them into their homes for a meal and then to worship, which would sometimes lead to enrollment in a formal process of training that led to membership in the church (a subject to which we will return in chap. 9). In short, public contact was inherently evangelistic, as natural as neighborliness when walking a dog or companionship when joining a climbing or a quilting club is today. Evangelism was a process that gradually resulted in a change of belief (rule of faith), belonging (the house church), and behavior (the ethic of the kingdom), culminating in the rites of initiation—baptism, confirmation, and Eucharist—and thus full inclusion into the community of faith.[33]

The Christian feast—known as the agape feast—symbolized the difference between the Christian way of life and the pagan way of life. Refusing to participate in pagan feasts, Christians hosted their own. The purpose was not to appease the gods or indulge the appetites, both of which typified Roman feasts. Instead, it was to express gratitude to God and love for one another. Clement of Alexandria declared, "The meal occurs because of love, not love because of the meal, which is a proof of a generous and shared good will." It served as a foretaste of the feast of the heavenly kingdom. It was the holy assembly of love. "Love then is a pure thing and worthy of God, and its work is generosity. . . . Love is not a meal, but let the banquet depend on love."[34] Such love was not confined to the Christian community alone; it also included outsiders and outcasts. Tertullian claimed, "Our feast shows its motive by its name. It is called by the Greek word for love. Whatever is reckoned the cost, money spent in the name of piety is gain, since with that refreshment we benefit the needy. . . . As is so with God, there is a great consideration for the lowly."[35]

How could Rome suppress such a movement? Christianity infiltrated cities, one relationship at a time, one apartment building at a time, one marketplace at a time, as if releasing white blood cells into the bloodstream of the Roman Empire. It was slow, laborious work. But over time it began to challenge and purge the cancer and corruption of Rome, at least as Christians viewed it. Christians were aware of the impact, and spoke of it. Writing in hyperbole, as he often did, Tertullian announced, "Men cry out that the state is beset by Christians; that there are Christians in the countryside, in the villages, in the islands. That people of both sexes, of every age and condition, even of high position, are passing over to the Christian society: this they lament as though it were a calamity. And yet for all that they are not stimulated to consider whether there may not be some good in it that they have failed to notice."[36]

The early church thus launched a different kind of movement in the ancient world. Christians did not clamor for relevance or try to assert power. Their king was so different from Caesar, their kingdom so different from the empire, that to overthrow Caesar and his empire would have actually violated the central principles of the movement. Such a movement, unique as it was, confused and rattled Rome. It proved highly adaptable, resourceful, and successful in functioning within the empire. Not that it was entirely successful. No renewal movement ever is, as history shows, even in the case of the movements we most admire and wish to emulate.

I want to conclude this chapter with two brief anecdotes, both from experiences in international travel. An anecdote has little power to prove a point, but it can illustrate one. In 2000 I spent the summer in Africa. My three children, then quite young, accompanied me, and they spent a great deal of time serving at an orphanage while I taught at a Christian university. On Sundays we attended a vibrant evangelical church in Nairobi. I had the privilege of getting to know the pastor, if just a little. Over lunch one day he asked me to think about the many times Christians in America refer to themselves as "American Christians." He wondered what that phrase actually meant. He would allow, he said, for "Christians who happen to live in America," just as he saw himself as a Christian who happens to live in Kenya. But the strong identification of Christianity and America seemed heretical to him because it tempted Americans to confuse the two identities, and thus to import American culture (e.g., wealth) to other parts of the world, always "in the name of Christ." "As a Christian," he said, "you are my brother.

As an American," he continued, "you want to be my master." He challenged me to choose between the two.

A few years later I flew to Costa Rica with my two sons to visit my daughter, who was traveling and serving in Central America. During our eight-day visit we spent two nights in a hostel in a small town. I rose early one Sunday morning to take a walk around the neighborhood. I just happened to be strolling past a small Protestant church when the pastor and his wife emerged to tidy the grounds before members arrived for worship. I stopped briefly to watch them. They eyed me with suspicion, as if thinking to themselves, "What is this gringo doing in our town, staring at us?" I pointed to the cross affixed to the steeple and then, looking at them, put my hand over my heart. Observing this gesture, their countenance immediately changed. They approached me, smiling brightly, and embraced me. We tried our best to communicate a little of our stories, with very modest success. It was clear that what mattered most—in fact, the only thing that mattered at all—was our common faith in Christ. I was no longer a white American tourist wandering the neighborhood; I was a Christian brother.

This is what began to happen, in fits and starts, with the emergence of Christianity in the ancient world. Converts took on a new identity; they joined a new *oikos*; they became members of a new *oikoumene*. "I am a Christian," they confessed. That was all they said; that was all they needed to say.

7

Worship

A number of years ago I attended a concert featuring one of the great classical improvisation artists of this generation, Gabriela Montero. This was no ordinary concert, because Montero was there to introduce the art of classical improvisation to the large and curious audience that was as unfamiliar with it as I was. She explained in her opening comments that classical improvisation was all the rage in the late nineteenth century, when such luminaries as Chopin and Liszt squared off against each other in friendly competition to demonstrate who was the better musician. She wanted to revive the magic of that lost art.

She asked the audience for a volunteer to hum a tune to her—any tune, including ones she might not know. A number of hands immediately shot up. She called on one young man who stood and hummed the first few measures of the "Imperial March" from *Star Wars*. She listened attentively, all the while smiling (she admitted later that she had never heard of it!), and then sat at the piano for perhaps a minute in total silence, her hands resting on the keyboard. Finally she started to play, composing a new piece of music on the spot, all the while weaving the tune through the entire composition, shifting fluidly from one style of music (say, baroque) to another (Romantic). She even composed a fugue. At the end of the concert the audience erupted in applause, almost levitating with a standing ovation, as if they had never heard such a thing before. Which was true enough—no one in the audience had ever witnessed such artistic genius.

That experience set my mind in motion. I started to think about other examples of improvisation—theatrical, for example. Like its musical counterpart, this form requires a high degree of skill. A group of actors gathers on stage. A member of the audience randomly describes a setting, suggests a few imaginary props, assigns roles, and outlines a plot. Then the actors must act something out as if they were in a real play, writing an impromptu script. As you can imagine, the best improvisational actors have had a great deal of experience onstage. They have played different characters, learned to work with props and a cast, studied blocking and movement, and read scripts written by a variety of playwrights from William Shakespeare to August Wilson. They have mastered these roles so thoroughly that they can draw on them as resource and inspiration.

I thought about sports, too, especially basketball and soccer, two highly improvisational team sports. Athletes must constantly adjust to the random flow of the game. The offense tries to move the ball down the court or field to score; the defense tries to block the advance and steal the ball, which puts them immediately on the offensive. The action moves back and forth fluidly and unpredictably. The game is constantly changing, which requires athletes to adapt quickly to new conditions. This is possible only if they have attained mastery, which frees them to make the necessary adjustments and thus gain an advantage over their opponents. In short, these sports are improvisational.

The best improvisational musicians, actors, and athletes surrender their freedom in order to attain mastery, which actually—and paradoxically—gives them a different kind of freedom, the freedom to excel at improvisation. They submit to the training of a master, practice scales and lines and drills, and learn multiple skills until, steeped in discipline, they can perform without making a cacophony of sound or creating little more than chaos. They learn that such discipline leads to the kind of freedom that only the most accomplished artists and athletes experience.

Early Christians, living as cultural outsiders, learned how to be *impro-visational* disciples among a Greco-Roman people who did not under-stand, nor always welcome, the new religion of Christianity.[1] Christians never knew from one day to the next what circumstances they would face, what challenges awaited them. The cultural landscape in which they lived made little room for Christianity, largely because Christianity departed so dramatically from how religion functioned in antiquity. This setting required Christians to learn the art and skill of improvisation. It prepared them for the unexpected; it made them creative and resourceful; it equipped them to be effective witnesses in the Roman world.

The church developed resources to assist them. For the most part they tried to internalize these resources, which inculcated the knowledge, beliefs, skills, disciplines, and virtues they needed to live as disciples. Not that every Christian pursued this course of action. But enough did to create and sustain a movement over many generations, like a championship college basketball team that keeps "reloading" year after year, making the team perennially competitive even when star players graduate or turn pro.

The primary setting for this kind of preparation was worship.[2] Con-sidering the Christian view of God as triune, worship served not only as the primary setting but also as the ideal setting. Christians practiced discipline—say, reciting the Lord's Prayer, memorizing Scripture, and offering their resources to God—*before* God, who is truth, goodness, and beauty, which enabled them to live *for* God in the Roman world. Worship of the Triune God drew them into the very being of God as love, which empowered them to love as God does.

To understand the uniqueness and success of early Christianity in the ancient world, therefore, we must explore how early Christians worshiped and how worship helped form disciples.

At first glance it would seem that little has changed. Christians have been worshiping in much the same way for some two thousand years, with very little variation. Worship might be less liturgical now than it was in the first few centuries, but it nevertheless follows the same basic script: prayers, songs, Bible reading, message, Eucharist (also known as communion or the Lord's Supper), offering, dismissal.

Two texts illustrate this. The first was written by an outsider to the Christian movement, a prominent Greco-Roman official, who described early Christian worship to the emperor, Trajan, after hearing complaints about Christians. We have met this man—Pliny the Younger—before. Writing at the beginning of the second century, he observed that Christians "were in the habit of meeting on a certain fixed day before it was light, when they sang in alternative verses a hymn to Christ, as to a god, and bound themselves by a solemn oath, not to any wicked deeds, but never to commit any fraud, theft or adultery, never to falsify their word, nor deny a trust when they should be called upon to deliver it up; after which it was their custom to separate, and then reassemble to partake of food—but food of an ordinary and innocent kind."[3]

The second comes from the pen of an insider, Justin Martyr. An adult convert and Christian philosopher, Justin wrote a defense of Christianity around AD 150, arguing that its way of life posed no threat to Rome. He devoted several chapters to explaining how Christians worshiped.

And on the day called Sunday, all who live in cities or in the country gather together to one place, and the memoirs of the apostles or the writings of the prophets are read, as long as time permits; then, when the reader has ceased, the president verbally instructs, and exhorts to the imitation of these good things. Then we all rise together and pray, and, as we before said, when our prayer is ended, bread and wine and water are brought, and the president in like manner offers prayers and thanksgivings, according to his ability, and the people assent, saying Amen; and there is a distribution to each, and a participation of that over which thanks have been given, and to those who are absent a portion is sent by the deacons. And they who are well to do, and willing, give what each thinks fit; and what is collected is deposited with the president, who succours the orphans and widows, and those who, through sickness or any other cause, are in want, and those who are in bonds, and the strangers sojourning among us, and in a word takes care of all who are in need.[4]

What is striking about these two ancient texts—and I could cite others, too—is how familiar their descriptions of worship seem to us, though we are separated from them by two millennia.

Does that mean there is little to learn about worship from these early Christians? That is hardly the case. The elements and order of worship might be similar, then as now; but the environment in which Christians lived was so different that it radically altered how they understood and experienced worship. What might appear to be similar is simply not the case. It is as different as painting by the numbers and painting as an artist.

We tend to view worship as one activity among many, taking its place alongside job, home, school, sport, and hobby. We "go to church" in the same way we go to work or to the gym. Moreover, for many of us, religious devotion favors the personal and private—studying the Bible and praying, reading Christian books, listening to Christian music and podcasts, decorating our homes with Christian art—over the public and communal, probably because it is more convenient. Worship is an event that occurs for one hour on Sunday; it plays a fairly limited role in the lives of most Christians, including serious Christians. Our spotty attendance in worship is proof enough of that. When we do attend worship, we tend to approach it as consumers, expecting good music (according to our own tastes), an inspiring sermon, and friendly people.

Early Christians viewed worship as a communal discipline around which their lives were ordered and organized. It played a central role in the movement because it prepared them for the challenges of discipleship in the larger Roman world.[5] At least that was the intent, though of course outcome fell short of aspiration, as it usually does. Christians depended on worship; their world revolved around it; they committed themselves to the regular discipline of it. It was at the heart of their faith, not simply one small expression of it, because worship ordered their lives around the center of life, the Triune God. They viewed worship as they did food and sleep and air. It was a spiritual necessity to them. Without it they put their spiritual lives at risk.

How did it function so differently for them?

Time and Place

Romans participated in countless festivals and feasts, always to honor the gods and goddesses and to give thanks for their provision. They

121

visited temples and shrines to offer them sacrifices and to seek their favor, and they kept household deities to ask for blessing in matters pertaining to domestic life. They practiced such devotion to secure Rome's prosperity, and their own as well. We have no reason to doubt their sincerity. Still, their approach was different from Christianity, more transactional than relational, more appeasement than praise.

Christian worship provided an alternative. It began with the Christian view of time and place. The first Christians were all Jews. As observant Jews they honored the Sabbath and attended the synagogue. But they also began to worship on the first day of the week, which they called "the Lord's Day."[6] Ignatius of Antioch identified the Lord's Day as the proper day for worship; he argued that it rightly replaced the Jewish observance of the Sabbath. Those who once lived according to the ancient practice arrived at a new hope when they began to follow Jesus. "And after the observance of the Sabbath, let every friend of Christ keep the Lord's Day as a festival, the resurrection-day, the queen and chief of all days . . . on which our life both sprang up again, and the victory over death was obtained in Christ."[7] Tertullian believed that Christians should view the Sabbath as they viewed circumcision—obsolete in light of Christ's work of redemption. "It follows, accordingly, that, inasmuch as the abolition of carnal circumcision and of the old law is demonstrated as having been consummated in its own times, so also the observance of the Sabbath is demonstrated to have been temporary."[8]

Justin Martyr explained the reason why the Lord's Day emerged as *the* day for worship. Christians, he reported, gathered on the first day of the week, whether they lived in city or countryside, because God created light on the first day of the week, and he brought his Son back from the dead on the first day of the week, too, which was also called "The Eighth Day" or the day of re-creation. "But Sunday is the day on which we all hold our common assembly, because it is the first day on which God, having wrought a change in the darkness and matter, made the world; and Jesus Christ our Savior on the same day rose from the dead."[9]

In addition to the weekly rhythm of the Lord's Day, Christians followed a daily rhythm, too. They turned to God multiple times each day, both privately and communally, like young children who keep circling back to their parents to express a need or a joy. This rhythm of daily worship began early in the church's history.[10] The Didache, which could be dated to as early as AD 100, if not earlier, urged Christians to pray the Lord's Prayer three times a day.[11] Another manual of church practice, the *Apostolic Tradition*, compiled in the early third century, probably by Hippolytus, instructed that Christians pray at the third, sixth, and ninth hours (9:00 a.m., 12:00 noon, 3:00 p.m.), and it cited the events surrounding the death of Christ to explain why. In the third hour "Christ was displayed nailed to the tree." In the sixth "as Christ was fixed on the wood of the cross that day was divided, and a great darkness descended." Finally, in the ninth hour, for "at that hour Christ, pierced in the side, poured forth water and blood and lit up the rest of that day and brought it so to the evening."[12] In what he called the "3+2" principle, Tertullian urged that followers of Jesus pray privately (or with family) in the early morning and late evening, and communally during the third, sixth, and ninth hours, thus ordering the day around worship. He also advised reciting the Lord's Prayer and the Psalms. Clement and Origen urged Christians to follow the same pattern, believing that such a practice would lead to "ceaseless prayer."[13] Hippolytus said that the discipline of daily prayer would keep Christ "always in mind."[14]

Place mattered, too, but not as we understand religious place in modern religion, which is oriented almost exclusively toward a building. Here the historical record is more complex. Christians associated holiness with a person—Jesus Christ, the incarnation of God in human flesh, who had come to earth and, after his ascension, had sent the Holy Spirit so that Jesus would continue to be present in the life and ministry of the church. The apostles reported that Jesus had predicted the destruction of the temple and then claimed it would be rebuilt in three days, an oblique reference to his resurrection. Christians believed that Jesus Christ replaced the Jewish temple. They could therefore worship God anywhere, for they believed God was everywhere. Any setting for worship would do as "the place where the Holy Spirit abounds."[15]

Early Christians found the setting of the house church to be as suitable for worship as any place because they worshiped God "in spirit and

123

in truth," which made Roman temple, shrine, and altar unnecessary—
and idolatrous. But they also worshiped at sites where martyrs were
buried, venerated objects of spiritual value (like the bones of saints),
and used baptismal fonts and other ritual objects in worship. The building as such was not as important in early Christian worship as holy
heroes and sacramental practices, which allowed early Christians, at
least in part, to maintain the connection between holiness and person,
especially *the* person, Jesus Christ, whom they called Lord.[16] All holiness derived from him.

Early Christians also worshiped with their bodies. They stood to
pray, raising their hands toward God. They turned to the east in anticipation of Christ's coming, which they associated with the dawn
of a new day—or more accurately, a new age. Clement of Alexandria
explained, "And since the dawn . . . is the image of the day of birth . . . ,
in correspondence with the manner of the sun's rising, prayers are made
toward the sunrise in the east."[17] Origen added, "There are four cardinal
points—north, south, east, and west. It should be immediately clear
that the direction of the rising sun obviously indicates that we ought
to pray inclining in that direction, an act which symbolizes the soul
looking towards where the true light rises."[18]

They signed the cross to claim Christ's power and protection over
them. Though the cross did not appear in Christian art until many centuries later, Christians signed with the cross almost from the beginning.
They viewed the cross not as an art object to display or wear but as a
spiritual practice to seek protection from the devil. Hippolytus believed
the sign of the cross functioned as a spiritual shield to ward off temptation and the devil. "If you are tempted, reverently sign yourself on the
forehead. For this sign of the passion is shown and is proven against
the Devil if you make it in faith, and not so that you might show it to
people, but present it through knowledge like a shield."[19]

These various practices had a focus—Jesus Christ. Early Christians
believed that it was because of him—his life, death, and resurrection—
that they should worship on the first day of the week. It was because
of him that they were free to worship everywhere, and not simply in
certain places deemed holy. It was because of him that they turned east

when praying, expecting that Christ would return as surely as the sun rises every morning. It was because of him that they made the sign of the cross, which protected them from evil. Early Christians oriented and organized their lives around God as they knew him in the face of Jesus Christ. They believed that they did not have to appease the gods; instead, they were free to worship the one true God—Father, Son, and Holy Spirit.

Word and Words: The Liturgical Script

The centrality of Jesus Christ shaped their use of language in worship, too. Words—written, read, recited, memorized, proclaimed, sung, and prayed—all pointed to the Word made flesh. When Christians worshiped, they worshiped the Word by using words that bore witness to him.

Early on the church developed a kind of "liturgical script" that the faithful learned, internalized, and mastered as a resource for the improvisational work of discipleship. We find evidence of this early on in the history of the church: the "Two Ways" of the Didache, the many rules of faith that appeared in early Christian literature, the liturgy of worship outlined in the *Apostolic Tradition*, hymns and key biblical texts (psalms, for instance), the words of institution in the administration of the sacraments, and of course the Bible, which played the dominant role. These sources provided words for the community of the Word.

The church functioned primarily as an oral culture. Many Christians could read, of course, and churches had copies of sacred texts such as the letters of Paul, John, and Peter, as well as the four Gospels and the Acts of the Apostles, that they used in worship.[20] But in most cases churches had only one copy of these texts, not many. Thus, however literate, the church functioned—and by necessity *had* to function—as an oral community of the Word. Such a community required relationship since all information—liturgy, prayers, hymns, rules of faith, practices, authoritative texts—was passed down primarily from reader to congregation, teacher to student, pastor to people. Relationship implies accountability. New Christians might have learned less information in this early period, but they would have certainly learned it better. The scarcity of books also meant that Christians were prone to memorize texts, because that was the only convenient and consistent means of access they had to them. Wealthy households might have had a small collection of books; most households had no books at all. If they wanted to retain knowledge of texts, they had to memorize them.[21]

Lectors, as they were called, read Scripture in worship. And it appears they read it often and at length. Even during Paul's lifetime, his letters were read aloud in worship and then circulated to other churches to do the same (Col. 4:16). In his description of worship, Justin referred to this same practice. He explained that when Christians gather, lectors read "the memoirs of the apostles or the writings of the prophets" for "*as long as time permits.*"[22] Tertullian explained that Christians met together regularly to listen to the Word. "We assemble to read our sacred writings, if any peculiarity of the times makes either forewarning or reminiscence needful. However it be in that respect, with the sacred words we nourish our faith, we animate our hope, we make our confidence more steadfast; and no less by inculcations by God's precepts we confirm good habits."[23]

Exposition and explanation followed the reading. Justin related that the "president" of the congregation—no doubt a bishop or an elder—would exposit the Word after someone had read the Word. Such proclamation was less like the formal sermon we hear today and more like an informal exploration, or a "gloss," which usually involved the congregation in some way. The setting itself—the house church—made excessive formality inappropriate. Even the great preachers of the fourth century—John Chrysostom comes to mind here—expected, and even encouraged, at least some degree of response to their preaching.[24]

Early Christians prayed Scripture, too. They prayed the Lord's Prayer, the very words of Jesus. So important did that prayer become in the early church that by the fourth century, bishops and pastors would not even teach it to catechumens until just before or after their baptism. It functioned as one of the *disciplina arcani*—"secret rites"—of the church. Tertullian believed that the Lord's Prayer summarized the writings of the entire Bible. Scholar Roy Hammerling reflects on the place of the Lord's Prayer in early Christian worship. "The Lord's Prayer," he writes, "was like a holy of holies for early Christians, the heart of the temple of scripture and the central courtyard of Christian living. . . . And so it was treasured, loved, and cherished as a jewel of unsurpassed worth, a pearl of great price."[25]

In his book on prayer, Tertullian drew a sharp line between what he called "old-world prayer" and Christian prayer, the former practiced by Jews (and, by inference, others) who expected immediate earthly benefit, the latter by Christians who looked for a different kind of outcome. The former asked God for "the good life," the latter for "the blessed life." The former claimed deliverance from "fires" and "beasts" and "famine," the latter cried out for the power to believe and endure. Old-world prayer was incomplete because it did not pray in the name of Christ. Christian prayer "does not station the angel of dew in mid-fires, nor muzzle lions, nor transfer to the hungry the rustic's bread; it has no delegated grace to avert any sins of suffering; but it supplies the suffering, and the feeling, and the grieving, with endurance: it amplifies grace by virtue, that faith may know what she obtains from the Lord, understanding what—for God's name sake—she suffers."[26]

Christians sang Scripture or hymns based on Scripture. Paul sometimes cited short statements of faith in his letters that have a poetic ring to them, which implies they were probably recited—and even sung—in worship (1 Tim. 3:16). The same is true in the case of the beautiful "Christ Hymn" of Philippians 2:5–11. We find clear evidence of the production and recitation of poetry and hymns in the second century. Clement of Alexandria concluded his famous *The Instructor*, a primer on Christian belief and behavior, with a poem. The first stanza reads:

> Bridle of colts untamed,
>> Over our wills presiding;
> Wing of unwandering birds,
>> Our flight securely guiding.
> Rudder of youth unbending,
>> Firm against adverse shock;
> Shepherd, with wisdom tending
>> Lambs of the royal flock:

> Thy simple children bring
> In one, that they may sing
> In solemn lays
> Their hymns of praise
> With guileless lips to Christ their King.[27]

By the fourth century the Christian movement could boast several great poets, among them Prudentius, who wrote in Latin, and Ephrem, who wrote in Syriac.[28] Some of these poetic texts were turned into hymns; so, too, were liturgical texts, like the Liturgy of St. James, the source of the hauntingly beautiful Advent hymn, "Let All Mortal Flesh Keep Silence." The great Ambrose (340–97), bishop of Milan, wrote many hymns for worship, among them this well-known hymn, which many congregations still sing today.

> O splendor of God's glory bright,
> From light eternal bringing light;
> Thou light of light, light's living spring,
> True day, all days illumining:
>
> Come, Holy Sun of heavenly love,
> Shower down Thy radiance from above,
> And to our inward hearts convey
> The Holy Spirit's cloudless ray.
>
> O joyful be the passing day
> With thoughts as clear as morning's ray.
> With faith like noontide shining bright,
> Our souls unshadowed by the night.
>
> O Lord, with each returning morn
> Thine image to our hearts is born;
> O may we ever clearly see
> Our Savior and our God in Thee![29]

Christians had reason to strive for mastery of this liturgical script because they never knew what awaited them once leaving worship and reentering ordinary life. We can only imagine the challenges that Christians faced in home, marketplace, and neighborhood, to say nothing of the experience of Christians in dungeon and arena. Many of the stories of early martyrdom provide evidence of the internalization of the Word. Before dying, the martyrs sang hymns, recited Scripture, prayed, recalled the drama of Christ's death, and saw visions of heaven. They demonstrated that they had internalized the liturgical script of the church so deeply that they were able to draw on it even under the extreme conditions of martyrdom. The account of the martyrdom of Perpetua reports that Perpetua and her companions actually sang a hymn together in the arena before they were put to death.[30] In short, they put to use the resources they had mastered in worship, which enabled them to remain faithful under pressure. It was the key to their resiliency; they learned to live as improvisational disciples.

Word and Sacrament

Christians feasted together as a weekly, if not daily, discipline. Meals, as Andrew McGowan suggests, "were not merely one sacramental part of a community or worship life but the central act around or within which others—reading and preaching, prayer and prophecy—were arranged."[31] Meeting in domestic settings, as if they were a family, churches were small enough to make the communal meal possible.

The administration of the sacraments played a dominant and formative role in worship, too. The ordinary meal set the stage for the sacramental meal, which pointed to the Word made flesh. The incarnation showed how it was possible for something to be "this, and the other," as Robert Wilken puts it. Human and divine, body and spirit, material and spiritual were united in Christ, the latter not nullifying the former. The same was true in the case of baptism and Eucharist.[32]

Early Christians believed that water remained water in baptism but became something else, too. Justin Martyr believed that washing in water led to rebirth in the name of the Triune God.[33] Irenaeus referred to the power of "moisture" to bring dry things to life. The Spirit used baptism in the same way. "And as dry earth does not produce fruit unless it receives moisture; we so, who are at the first 'a dry tree,' would never have yielded the fruit of life without the 'voluntary rain' from above."[34]

Clement of Alexandria outlined the spiritual benefits of baptism, again giving the impression that water, once consecrated, had power to accomplish everything believers needed. "This work is variously called grace, and illumination, and perfection, and washing: washing, by which we cleanse away our sins; grace, by which the penalties accruing to transgressions are remitted; and illumination, by which the holy light of salvation is beheld, that is, by which we see God clearly. Now we call that perfect which wants nothing. For what is yet wanting to him who knows God?"[35]

These early writers and pastors set baptism in a larger landscape of ritual observance.[36] The Didache, for example, instructed the faithful to fast before being baptized.[37] Justin warned that candidates for baptism should not only learn the faith but also "live accordingly."[38] Tertullian reported that the church should baptize during the Pasch (our Holy Week, most likely on the Saturday) or on the day of Pentecost, though he was quick to add that "every day is the Lord's: every hour, every time, is suitable for baptism; if there is a difference in the *solemnity*, there is no distinction in the *grace*."[39] And any kind of water or place would do.[40]

The Eucharist followed the same pattern. Common, earthly elements— bread and wine—had supernatural, transformative power. Ignatius called it the "medicine of immortality" and "an antidote to ward off death."[41] Justin noted the parallel between incarnation and Eucharist. He argued that Christians did not receive bread and cup as if they were common food and drink, just as Jesus was not merely a man, though he was that, too. Thus as Jesus Christ, "having been made flesh by the Word of God, had both flesh and blood for our salvation, so likewise have we been taught that the food which is blessed by the prayer of His word, and from which our blood and flesh by transmutation are nourished, is the flesh and blood of that Jesus who was made flesh."[42] Irenaeus believed that God created the human body; Christ became a body in the incarnation for the sake of humanity's salvation; through Christ God would redeem the human body, thus claiming the whole person—body and soul—for "incorruption." He argued that the same logic applies to the Eucharist. God uses the material substances of bread and cup as surely as he used the material incarnation, death, and resurrection of Jesus to bring fallen sinners back to life.[43]

Early Christian writers believed that Christ was truly present in bread and cup; the Eucharist re-presented Christ's saving work on the cross and mediated grace to the faithful. Wilken concludes, "Here was a truth so tangible, so enduring, so compelling, that it trumped every religious idea. Understanding was achieved not by stepping back and viewing things from a distance but by entering into the revealed object itself."[44]

Word and the World

Early Christians believed that worship prepared them for the demands of discipleship once they left places of worship (mostly house churches, but also halls, courtyards, and even caves) and reentered daily life in the Greco-Roman world. Worship trained them for witness and service; worship cultivated virtue; worship showed them how to live in the world as followers of Jesus.

The Sermon on the Mount provided the template. The Didache, for example, borrowed extensively from the Sermon on the Mount in outlining the "Two Ways" of life that people could follow. One was the way of life, the other the way of death; the difference between the two was infinite.[45] First, there was the way of life: "Now, this is the way of life: 'First, you must love God who made you, and second your neighbor as yourself.' And whatever you want people to refrain from doing to you, you must not do to them." And then there was the way of death: "But the way of death is this: First of all, it is wicked and thoroughly blasphemous: murders, adulteries, lusts, fornications, thefts, idolatries, magic arts, sorceries, robberies, false witness, hypocrisies, duplicity, deceit, arrogance, malice, stubbornness, greediness, filthy talk, jealousy, audacity, haughtiness, boastfulness."[46]

The Didache linked seemingly lesser sins with greater consequences, just as Jesus did in the Sermon on the Mount. It thereby emphasized the importance of motive, not simply behavior. One could attempt to limit sin to smaller things, as if to keep it hidden; but in the end it would lead to greater sin, and to spiritual ruin. "My child, flee from all wickedness and from everything of that sort. . . . Do not be jealous or contentious or impetuous, for all this breeds murder. My child, do not be lustful, for lust leads to fornication. . . . My child, do not be a liar, for lying leads to theft. Do not be avaricious or vain, for all this breeds thievery. My child, do not be a grumbler, for grumbling leads to blasphemy."[47]

Christian teachers used the pedagogical device of the Two Ways to shape Christian behavior according to kingdom principles, and thus to train believers to resist the temptations of the world and to live as citizens of the true kingdom. Clement applied the Two Ways to food and all forms of luxurious living, and Tertullian to the enjoyment of entertainment.[48] Tertullian underscored the significant difference between the Greco-Roman way of life and the Christian way of life. The former indulged the appetite as if the world were all there is; the latter resisted the temptations of the world because of the greater reality of the kingdom, which would redeem and reclaim the world. Christians, he concluded, rejected worldliness, but not the world as such. "Would that we did not even inhabit the same world with these wicked men! But though that wish cannot be realized, yet even now we are separate from them in what is of the world; for the world is God's, but the worldly is the devil's."[49]

Early Christians practiced virtuous behavior in worship first, which prepared them for the more difficult task of living virtuously in the Roman world. The exercise of generosity is a good case in point. We can find no references in early Christianity to tithing, the standard we tend to use today. Early Christians emphasized freedom and stewardship, which kept them from imposing a measurable—and often legalistic—standard on the faithful. Worship provided an opportunity for people to give; but leaders never *required* people to give. They could therefore give in faith and out of freedom. Thus Tertullian explained, "Though we have a kind of money-chest, it is not for the collection of official fees, as if ours were a religion of fixed prices. Each of us puts in a small donation on the appointed day in each month, or when he chooses, and only if he chooses, and only if he can; for no one is compelled and the offering is voluntary."[50] Clement underscored the importance of motive. "So that it is not he who has and keeps, but he who gives away, that is rich; and it is giving away, not possessing, which renders a man happy; and the fruit of the Spirit is generosity. It is in the soul, then, that riches are."[51] Whatever the amount, the collection went to the aid of orphans, widows, sick and diseased, and prisoners.[52]

These, then, were the primary—and early Christians would say necessary—elements of worship: observing the Lord's Day, following daily rhythms of prayer, signing the cross, reciting the Lord's Prayer, memorizing the liturgical script, learning the Two Ways, practicing discipline, cultivating virtue, receiving the sacraments, and the like. They worshiped to orient their lives around the Triune God. Worship in turn prepared them to be improvisational disciples in the Roman world. How they were able to do this mystified the Romans as much as Gabriella Montero mystifies her audiences.

Early Christians viewed worship as creating an environment akin to heaven—a foretaste of the kingdom, reality as God defines it, truth instead of falsehood. Of course worship offered only a brief glimpse and experience. Early Christians understood that they would have to return to ordinary life and, in the setting of home and neighborhood and marketplace, live out their commitment to gospel and kingdom. And so they prayed, "Thy kingdom come, thy will be done, on earth as it is in heaven," believing that God would answer that prayer, at least in part, through the kind of people they were becoming in worship.

8

Life in the World

The stories of two towering fourth-century figures illustrate the theme of this chapter—the difference between how Christians and Romans lived in the world. And there was a difference, too, according to both Roman and Christian observers, who noted that Christians, unlike many (or most) Romans, upheld high moral standards in their daily behavior and responded to the "least of these" with uncommon compassion and care. Not that every Christian lived such an exemplary life, of course. Still, there is enough evidence to prove that Christians set an example that Romans noticed, sometimes criticizing it and sometimes applauding it. It was one reason why the Christian movement had impact on Roman society.

The first figure admired it; the other lived it. The first resided in Rome and spoke Latin; the other in Asia Minor and spoke Greek. The first ruled the empire as emperor; the other served the church as bishop. The first lived in splendor; the other lived in poverty. The first championed traditional Greco-Roman religion; the other worshiped the Triune God. The first wrote a book to expose Christianity as false; the other wrote books to defend Christianity as true. They never met, though they certainly knew of each other. There is some evidence—not confirmable—that they exchanged letters.

Julian the Apostate

The first figure is the emperor Julian, known as "the Apostate" because he attempted to turn the empire, which in his day was rapidly becoming Christian, once again into a pagan one.[1] Born in 331, he was a nephew of Constantine, the first Christian emperor who, only eighteen years earlier, had reversed imperial policy, granted legal status to Christianity, and allowed Christians to practice their religion in freedom. After Constantine's death, his son Constantius assumed the throne. He ordered Julian's father, along with eight other relatives, murdered. Julian was spared from the brutal purge. But he never forgot it.

Following the typical pathway of the elite, he studied under the best of teachers, both Roman and Christian. He dabbled in traditional religion and joined the cults of Cybele and Mithras, both mystery religions. Eventually he converted to the traditional religion of Rome, though keeping it secret from the imperial family to preserve his life.

Julian openly declared himself a follower of traditional religion in 361, the year he became emperor. That Julian returned to it is not entirely surprising. The old religion still held sway among the educated elite; dominated cityscapes with its thousands of temples, shrines, monuments, inscriptions, and sculptures; and shaped the cultural narratives and practices of the empire through the popularity of its many myths, festivals, and rituals.

Julian devoted himself to restoring the old religion. He studied and cherished its literature, embraced its beliefs, such as they were, and dutifully observed its rituals. He ordered that traditional religious practices be renewed throughout the empire. Further, he allowed only the adherents of traditional religion to teach philosophy, literature, and rhetoric, arguing that the only people qualified to teach these subjects had to demonstrate sympathy for them, if not outright belief in them.

Not that Julian was a purist. Like many Roman intellectuals, he practiced traditional religion even as he believed in the existence of one transcendent, mysterious, inaccessible, incomprehensible God, as Plato affirmed. He saw no contradiction between the two. They addressed different needs—one the needs of the empire, the other the needs of the soul.

Julian's policy in effect limited Christians from filling educational posts, and it undermined their efforts to integrate Christianity and classical culture into a larger intellectual whole. Julian argued that it had to be either Christianity or classical culture; it could not be both. "But now that the gods have granted us freedom it seems to me absurd for men to teach what they disapprove. If they are real interpreters of the ancient classics, let them first imitate the ancients' piety toward the gods. If they think the classics wrong in this respect, then let them go and teach Matthew and Luke in the church."[2]

Julian faced opposition from Christians, as his popular title—"the Apostate"—implies; the sheer growth and power of the church made such opposition inevitable. But he also received support. Many Romans, especially members of the elite, wondered about the viability of an empire that had benefited from the benevolence of the gods since its founding but had rejected the Roman gods in favor of the Christian God. Could there be a Roman Empire without traditional religion? Some thought it was impossible.

But Julian was smart and strategic, too. He never coerced Christians to return to the old religion, and even granted them the freedom to practice their own, though he considered them misguided. As he mandated in his edict to the people of Bostra, "They may hold their meetings, if they wish, and offer prayers according to their established use . . . and for the future, let all people live in harmony. . . . Men should be taught and won over by reason, not by blows, insults, and corporal punishments. I therefore most earnestly admonish the adherents of the true religion not to injure or insult the Galileans in any way. . . . Those who are in the wrong in matters of supreme importance are objects of pity rather than hate."[3]

Julian grew up in a Christian home and thus knew Christianity as an insider. After becoming emperor he wrote a book against Christianity, entitled *Against the Galileans*. Julian charged that Christians worshiped a man and imposter, not God, for the true God is transcendent, unable and unwilling to become a human being. Besides, if God did become human, why would he limit himself to becoming only one, and then, of all people, *this* one—Jesus of Nazareth, an uncultured Jew? And what made the Jews more special than any other people on earth anyway?

He asserted that Christianity was an apostasy of Judaism, a ruinous departure from it rather than a fulfillment of it. Where it remained faithful to Judaism, he argued, it reinforced the worst in it: the domination of a tribal deity. "If he is the God of all alike, and the creator of all, why did he neglect us [Romans]?" God is a spiritual being who is Lord of all and known by all. The true and high God is not the property of any one group of people. The best way to know God, Julian argued, was through nature, however imprecise and unclear. "All humanity, without being taught, have come to believe in some sort of divinity." It was arrogant of Christians to think otherwise, which clearly made them inferior to the more generous and sophisticated Romans.[4]

We will never know how successful his efforts to restore traditional Roman religion might have been. His premature death in 363, a mere eighteen months after he became emperor, cut short his ambitious plans. In 382 the emperor Theodosius pronounced Christianity the official religion of the empire, making it highly unlikely that Julian's vision would ever be realized. Still, the world looked very different during Julian's brief reign. It seemed possible to reinvigorate the traditional religion and push Christianity aside. He was confident that he would succeed because in his mind traditional religion was the superior religion.

With one exception.

He admitted with frustration that Christians had clearly surpassed traditional religion in their moral way of life and care for the poor. In a letter to Arsacius, high priest of Galatia, he reasoned that restoration of pagan rites and rituals, temple worship, and pagan education was not enough. Christians clearly held the advantage in service and godliness of life. "Why, then, do we think that this is enough, why do we not observe that it is their benevolence to strangers, their care for the graves of the dead and the pretended holiness of their lives that have done most to increase atheism [Christians were often accused

138

of atheism because they did not worship images of the gods]? I believe that we ought really and truly to practice every one of these virtues."[5]

Julian charged Arsacius to promote similar values and behavior among the priests in his district. He promised that he would use the wealth and power of the empire to assist them. He would open hostels and dole out grain and wine, assuring that at least one-fifth would go to the truly destitute, with the remainder going to strangers and beggars. "For it is disgraceful that, when no Jew ever has to beg, and the impious Galileans support not only their own poor but ours as well, all men see that our people lack aid from us."[6]

It was obviously not a problem of resources. Traditional religion, after all, had at its disposal the wealth of the empire, in addition to the patronage of wealthy local officials who often served as priests as well as politicians. It was a problem of moral vision or, better put, the absence of one. Julian admitted that traditional religion did not teach a virtuous and benevolent way of life, mandate care for the poor, or establish institutions to serve the most vulnerable, like widows and orphans. Julian's religion could not compete with Christianity, at least on this one point.

Basil of Caesarea

The second figure is Basil of Caesarea, also known as Basil the Great, a contemporary of Julian's (Julian died in 363, Basil in 379).[7] Born into a prominent Christian family, he was one of ten children, several of whom would eventually be elevated to sainthood in the Eastern Orthodox Church. Basil enjoyed the privileges of growing up in an upper-class home, which meant he received the best education, first in Caesarea, then in Constantinople, and finally in Athens. He was a brilliant student, but also inclined toward conceit, as his younger brother, Gregory of Nyssa, charged. The influence of his older sister, the godly Macrina, inspired him to repent, to seek God, and to dedicate his life to the church as a preacher and leader. He traveled to Egypt to learn from the desert fathers and mothers. Upon his return to Cappadocia (central modern Turkey), he founded a monastery and committed himself to a life of study, simplicity, poverty, and service.

But Basil's abilities and ambitions were too great to be confined to a monastery. He was recruited as a lector in Caesarea, then ordained a priest, and finally elevated to the office of bishop in 370. In these various roles, he involved himself in many of the important controversies of the day. His influence spread throughout the eastern half of the empire, as is evidenced by his vast correspondence (some 366 letters are extant). He used his position to organize, reform, and guide the church during a period of calamity and conflict. However gentle and calm, he did not hesitate to make decisions that aroused suspicion, if not open opposition, from friends and enemies alike. A high-ranking Roman official once wrote to Valens, the emperor, "We have been worsted, Sire, by the prelate of this church. He is superior to threats, invincible in argument, uninfluenced by persuasion."[8] Even members of his closest circle sometimes complained about his dominant personality and political maneuvering.[9]

Basil was especially known for his commitment to uphold justice and show mercy, especially on behalf of the poor. As his biographer and friend, Gregory of Nazianzus, noted, he committed himself to "the support of the poor, the entertainment of strangers, the care of maidens, legislation written and unwritten for the monastic life." After assuming the office of bishop, he founded a community to care for the destitute, which took on the honorific title "the Basileiad," a place of refuge that grew so large that it became its own city. It welcomed and housed immigrants, provided medical care for the sick (e.g., lepers), and trained the unskilled for jobs. It met social, physical, and spiritual needs. Nazianzus described it in lofty terms: "Go forth a little way from the city [Caesarea], and behold the new city, the storehouse of piety, the common treasury of the wealthy, in which the superfluities of their wealth, aye, and even their necessities, are stored, in consequence of his exhortations, freed from the power of the moth, no longer gladdening the eyes of the thief, and escaping both the emulation of envy, and the corruption of time: where disease is regarded in a religious light, and disaster is thought a blessing, and sympathy is put to the test." The first of its kind, it was replicated in other dioceses, too, though on a smaller scale. Nazianzus lauded it as superior to the pyramids of Egypt and the other Wonders of the Ancient World.[10]

Basil appealed to the rich to fund the Basileiad. By the fourth century the church was attracting an increasing number of Roman elites, which changed the entire composition of the church. The days of persecution had ended; an imperial church was on the horizon. This change of circumstances tempted church leaders to seek the approval of the rich, to view wealth as a sign of God's favor, and to court their support and influence, all at the expense of the church's historic suspicion and criticism of wealth, as we see, for example, in the ministry of Jesus. No doubt some—perhaps many—yielded to this temptation.

But not Basil. He called the rich to repent of greed and materialism, to avoid luxury, and to steward their resources to assist those who were less fortunate. His preaching sounds as harsh today as I am sure it did in his day. In one of many sermons on the topic, Basil charged that if the rich truly loved their neighbors, they would have divested themselves of their wealth long ago. "But now your possessions are more a part of you than the members of your own body, and separation from them is as painful as the amputation of one of your limbs. Had you clothed the naked, had you given your bread to the hungry, had your door been open to every stranger, had you been a parent to the orphan, had you made the suffering of every helpful person your own, what money would you have left, the loss of which to grieve?"[11]

The Basileiad was the first hospital founded in the Western world. Romans had their physicians and healing centers, to be sure, but only for the elite. But they had nothing like the Basileiad, which served all who had need, especially the sickest and the poorest. It set a trajectory of health care in the Western world that has continued to this day.[12]

The Essential Difference

Julian complained about exactly this kind of Christian service. In spite of the loftiness of his position and the vast resources of the empire, he could not motivate priests to follow the same way of life, nor replicate the church's ministry to the needy. But the difference went deeper than ethics. Christians worshiped a God who loved humanity in and through his Son, Jesus Christ. This Jesus, Son of God, Lord of lords, King of kings, had "given his life as a ransom for many" and, "though rich, had become poor." How could Christians, the "poor" whom Jesus had made "rich," not act with generosity toward "the least of these"? It would be like a lottery winner, once utterly destitute, refusing to give a penny of his unearned fortune to the very group of people—the poor—to whom he once belonged.

Basil did not speak alone. His younger brother, Gregory, bishop of Nyssa, and his close friend, Gregory, bishop of Nazianzus, made similar arguments. These three exercised such far-reaching influence that they have become known as the Cappadocian fathers. On this matter, at least, they spoke with one voice. Basil argued that God became a lowly human being in Christ, weak and powerless, so that "we might be rich in divinity." He inquired whether or not his parishioners were willing to follow the same example of tenderness and compassion. What about the most needy? Are they to be overlooked and dismissed? "Surely not, my brothers and sisters! This is not the way for us, nursed as we are by Christ, who brings back the one gone astray, seeks out the lost, strengthens the weak. This is not the way of human nature, which lays compassion on us as a law, even as we learn reverence and humanity from our common weakness."[13]

Gregory of Nyssa pointed to the example of Jesus Christ, who lowered himself and took on fragile human flesh in order to cure all human ills. How then could wealthy Christians ignore and avoid the very people for whom Christ came, lived, and died? If Christ came for *all*—the sickest as well as the healthiest, the least as well as the greatest—then his followers should serve *all*. "The Lord of the angels, the king of celestial bliss, became man for you and put on this stinking and unclean flesh, with the soul thus enclosed, in order to effect a total cure of your ills by his touch. But to you, you who share the nature of this brokenness, you flee your own race."[14]

And Gregory of Nazianzus reminded the rich and healthy that the poor and sick "have been made in the image of God in the same way you and I have, and perhaps preserve that image better than we, even if their bodies are corrupted." They were heirs of the kingdom, too.[15]

The Cappadocians inherited a tradition of theology and practice, going back three hundred years, which informed and inspired them. They could not have accomplished what they did—the founding of the Basileiad, for example—out of thin air, no more than Thomas Edison could have invented the electric light bulb out of thin air or Beethoven composed his five piano concertos out of thin air. Edison built on the inventions and discoveries of others, like Benjamin Franklin, just as Beethoven was indebted to Bach and Mozart. Basil, Nazianzus, and Gregory drew on rich history of the church's thought, witness, and ministry, which included the sacrifices of thousands of countless and nameless Christians.[16]

There is a clear pattern of thought in early Christian writing. How Christians lived, the argument went, grew out of who Jesus was and what Jesus accomplished. Tertullian cited Jesus' example as the primary reason why Christians should forsake pride and practice humble service. If Jesus never claimed power for himself and refused to be crowned king, how could his followers do otherwise? If he turned "coldly from all pride," as well as all "dignity and power," how could his followers depart from this same course? If they hoped to be useful to the kingdom, they would have to imitate its king.[17] Clement of Alexandria argued similarly. Jesus impoverished himself because he loved the unworthy. And who could ever claim to be anything other than unworthy? If such is the case, then how could the followers of Jesus judge others as unworthy? "Do not you judge who is worthy or who is unworthy. For it is possible you may be mistaken in your opinion."[18] The author of *The So-Called Letter to Diognetus* contrasted the way Romans conceived of God with the Christian view of God. The difference between the two explained why Christians *lived* differently, too. "But any man who takes upon his neighbor's load, who is willing to use his superiority to benefit one who is worse off, who supplies to the needy the possessions he has as a gift from God and thus becomes a god to his beneficiaries—such a man is an imitator of God."[19]

Way of Life

We know, therefore, what early Christians believed. We know why they believed it. And we know that they put Jesus Christ at the center of it all.

But did Christians back then actually *live* this way? Did they really demonstrate that kind of devotion and sacrifice? Was the Christian way of life *that* different from that of the Romans?[20]

How can we find out?

Pagan Criticism

First, we can investigate the writings of Greco-Roman elites. They were certainly aware of the growth and impact of Christianity. They commented on it, often in a spirit that communicated both scorn and jealousy.

Julian admitted as much, as I have already pointed out. His own efforts to restore traditional religion faced the challenge of having to compete with the Christian way of life. He discovered that traditional religion was simply not up to the task.

He was not alone. Other Roman critics noted, often disparagingly, how Christians lived. Take, for example, two second-century writers. The first we have met before. Celsus, a philosopher and friend of the emperor, Marcus Aurelius, observed with dismay that Christians viewed all people as having equal dignity before God, which made Christians successful in reaching the lower classes. "In private houses also we see wool-workers, cobblers, laundry-workers, and the most illiterate and bucolic yokels, who would not dare to say anything at all in front of their elders and more intelligent masters."[21] The second, Galen, a physician, wrote about the exemplary conduct of Christians. His comments sounded a note of grudging respect, as Julian's did. Christianity, he observed, produced people whose moral life rivaled the teaching and conduct of the philosophers. "For their contempt of death is patent to us every day, and likewise their restraint in cohabitation. For they include not only men but also women who refrain from cohabiting all through their lives; and they also number individuals who, in self-discipline and self-control in matters of food and drink, and in their keen pursuit of justice, have attained a pitch not inferior to that of the genuine philosopher."[22]

Apologists

Such were the observations—and complaints—of outsiders. Insiders made the same point. A number of pastors and apologists ("defenders" of the faith) cited concrete examples of Christian behavior to show how unique and exemplary the Christian way of life was. It would have made no sense to cite such evidence in their arguments if it was palpably untrue.

Christians, they said, were humble, gentle, generous, compassionate, kind, and patient. They refused luxury and avoided popular forms of entertainment, choosing instead to live chastely and modestly. They opposed violence, arguing that it would be far better to be a victim than a perpetrator. They condemned idolatry and prohibited church members from practicing it or working jobs that somehow promoted it. They protected the sanctity of marriage and the marriage bed, opposed divorce, held husbands accountable to the same moral standard as wives, and honored women—virgins and widows—who chose not to marry or marry again. They condemned abortion and infanticide, and they rescued infants who had been abandoned and left to die. They supported orphans, widows, and prisoners, cared for the sick and buried the dead, not just their own but their neighbors', too. They welcomed people into their homes and gave sacrificially to those in need. Christian leaders identified these and other examples—observable to all—to illustrate how Christians lived, and how they lived better than the Romans.

Clement, bishop of Rome, writing only one generation after the apostles, commended believers living in Corinth for their obedience, acknowledging that he had heard reports of their heroic way of life from travelers who crossed his path. "For who ever dwelt even for a short time among you, and did not find your faith to be as fruitful of virtue as it was firmly established? Who did not admire the sobriety and moderation of your godliness in Christ? Who did not proclaim the magnificence of your habitual hospitality?"[23] After exposing the corruption of the

Roman way of life—abortion, adultery, violence, infant exposure—
Athenagoras testified that Christians not only rejected these bankrupt
patterns of life but blessed Romans when they were being persecuted,
for "it is not enough to be just (and justice is to return like for like),
but it is incumbent on us to be good and patient of evil."[24] Tertullian
explained how Christians dispersed their money. Their contributions,
he wrote, are "the trust funds of piety." Christians, he continued, perhaps exaggerating to make the point, did not spend their money on
parties, games, and other forms of Roman entertainment, but instead
gave their money for "feeding and burying the poor, for boys and girls
destitute of property and parents; and further for old people confined
to the house, and victims of shipwreck; and any who are in the mines,
who are exiled to an island, or who are in prison merely on account of
God's church—these become the wards of their confession."[25]

Exemplary Stories

Early Christian authors told stories to illustrate how Christians lived
so sacrificially for the welfare of society. All religions tell stories to
establish an ideal standard and thus to promote good behavior. What
set these Christian stories apart in the ancient world was the way of
life they described—the way of Jesus, which modeled sacrifice not as
an end unto itself, as if sacrifice itself was an ultimate good, but as a
means to the end of redemption and resurrection.

Some of these stories focused on famous Christians, like Cyprian,
bishop of Carthage, and Origen, a brilliant Christian teacher and
writer, both of whom lived in the third century. It was not unusual in
the Greco-Roman world to write the biographies of such beloved and
admired people.[26]

But others focused on the heroic behavior of ordinary Christians.

One notable example concerns a plague that swept through the ancient world in AD 250.[27] It is hard to determine the exact number of
deaths, but scholars estimate that up to a fifth of the population of the
empire died. At the height of the epidemic, thousands perished daily in
the city of Rome alone. The fatality rate was so high that some cities

fell into ruin and military campaigns had to be stopped. It tested the mettle of the empire, and it tested the faith of Christians.

Dionysius, bishop of Alexandria, wrote in an Easter message, "Out of the blue came this disease, a thing more terrifying . . . than any terror, more frightful than any disaster whatever."[28] Pontius, Cyprian's biographer, described it as incomprehensibly dreadful. It invaded every home, killing too many people to count. The impact was catastrophic. "All were shuddering, fleeing, shunning the contagion, impiously exposing their own friends, as if with the exclusion of the person who was sure to die of the plague, one could exclude death itself also. Meanwhile, there lay about the whole city, no longer bodies, but the carcasses of many, and, by the contemplation of a lot which in their turn would be theirs, demanded the pity of passers-by for themselves. No one regarded anything besides his cruel gains."[29]

Many bishops used the pulpit to address the hard questions that inevitably surface on such occasions and to provide comfort and hope. They preached on such themes as God's sovereignty, the suffering of Jesus, the last judgment, and the resurrection of the dead. They also interpreted the catastrophe as a kind of divine test. Cyprian asked his congregation whether they would show the same kind of generosity to victims that God extends to the least deserving. Jesus taught that God causes the sun to rise and set for everyone's benefit, and sends forth rain to nourish everyone's crops, showing kindness to friends and enemies alike. "Should not one who professes to be a son of God imitate the example of his Father? It is proper for us to correspond to our birth, and it does not become those who are clearly reborn in God to be degenerate, but, as a son, the descendent of a good father, should rather prove the imitation of his goodness."[30]

The Christian faith made a practical difference in the lives of people, offering hope in the face of acute suffering and calling people to serve the afflicted. In general, Christians faced the plagues with courage, nursed the sick, and buried the dead. They believed that because God loved them, as undeserving as they were, they were duty bound to love others. Again, the contrast between Christians and Romans was noticeable, at least according to Christian observers. Cyprian, for example,

147

charged Christians to care for everyone, and not simply Christians. He proclaimed "that there was nothing wonderful in our cherishing only our own people with the needed attentions of love, but that one would only become perfect by doing something more than the publican or the heathen, overcoming evil with good, and practicing clemency which was like the divine clemency, loving even his enemies."[31]

Dionysius wrote movingly of the sacrifices that Christians had made on behalf of the sick and dying. Christians, he said, "showed unbounded love and loyalty, never sparing themselves and thinking only of one another. Heedless of danger, they took charge of the sick, attending to their every need and ministering to them in Christ, and with them departed this life serenely happy." They discovered soon enough that, however Christlike their behavior, they would not be spared from the same fate that had already taken the lives of others.

Dionysius interpreted their sacrificial deaths in light of the sacrifice of Christ. A number of the sick had recovered, while their caretakers had died. So Dionysius reasoned that perhaps the caretakers had suffered vicariously, dying in the place of those who had survived. It might have been faulty science, but it was persuasive theology. "For they were infected by others with the disease, drawing on themselves the sickness of their neighbors and cheerfully accepting their pains. Many, in nursing and curing others, transferred their death to themselves and died in their stead, turning the common formula that is normally an empty courtesy into a reality."[32]

Dionysius also mentioned that Christians buried the dead, and they showed great tenderness by first washing their bodies and wrapping them in graveclothes. Again, these actions set Christians apart from their Roman neighbors, who would have nothing to do with the dead. "The heathens behaved in the very opposite way. At the first onset of the disease, they pushed the sufferers away and fled from their dearest, throwing them into the roads before they were dead and treating unburied corpses as dirt."[33]

Ironically, Christians survived the plagues at higher rates than Romans, even though Christians were more willing to be exposed to the deadly contagion. Why? First, they cared for the sick. Such care ensured that a higher percentage of the afflicted would survive, even if there were no actual cure available. Basic nursing care—sips of broth, cold rags on the forehead, tender backrubs, a change of bedding, visits from loving friends—strengthened the sick and helped at least some of them to outlive the contagion. Second, Christians who survived became immune and thus provided a workforce of healthy people who were no longer susceptible to the disease. These survivors made themselves available to the sick, which in turn increased survival rates even more. Finally, Christians believed in, prayed for, and experienced miracles, which resulted from the powerful work of the Holy Spirit. Miraculous cures and demon exorcisms occurred with enough frequency to leave an impression on pagans, who interpreted these manifestations of power as evidence that the Christian God was real, thus making "physically and dramatically visible the superiority of the Christian's patron power over all things."[34]

Organized for Action

Finally, Christians organized for action by creating institutions to support and expand their ministry to the needy. As we know, institutions are necessary once service moves beyond the immediate, spontaneous, and personal. It is one thing to give twenty dollars to a homeless person standing on a street corner with sign in hand that reads, "Homeless. Anything helps. God bless." It is another thing altogether to get that person off the street and into a bed and job.

There is good evidence that the church quickly and effectively organized for action and, through the institutions they founded, accomplished concrete good. Take, for example, widows. In his first letter to Timothy, Paul outlined a set of standards to guide churches in the care of widows. Young widows were to marry; older widows were to receive support from families or, if destitute, from the church. If the latter, they could join an order of widows, but only under certain conditions: they had to be at least sixty years old, pledge to remain single, and devote themselves to prayer and service. This policy became the standard for the early church over the next few centuries.[35] In time, widows took on other duties, too, such as sewing clothes, mentoring younger women, and visiting the sick.[36]

Deacons collected and distributed food and funds, cared for the sick (as widows did), visited prisoners, and provided for the needy. So critical was their work, and so dependent were the vulnerable on their work, that Hippolytus issued a stern warning if deacons delayed in fulfilling their duties. If a deacon "receives a gift which is to be given to a widow or to a poor woman or to a person busily occupied with the affairs of the church, he should hand it over on that same day. If not, on the following day he should add to it from what is his and so give it, since the bread of the poor was delayed a while with him."[37] Deacons answered to the bishop and assisted him in the execution of charitable duties. As churches grew in size and influence, the work of deacons became more complex and demanding, like a farm that keeps adding more crops, more acres, more laborers, and more machinery to its expanding operation. By the early third century, churches had established the office of subdeacon to assist deacons. The church also formed an order of deaconesses to provide similar pastoral services for women.[38]

Exorcists contributed to the church's ministry, too, though the office itself was never an ordained one. This office in particular might seem especially strange to us living in the West, because many today reject the existence of demons, reasoning that such belief manifests ignorance and superstition. Obviously, early Christians did not reject their existence; if anything, they took the influence of demons very seriously. But their belief in demons might not have been as superstitious as it appears. They believed that physical and emotional problems often resulted from the influence of demonic powers; but they also acknowledged human responsibility and allowed for natural causes.

Exorcists functioned in two ways: they exorcized the demons of catechumens who were preparing for the rites of initiation (baptism, confirmation, and Eucharist), and they exorcized demons that were tormenting the faithful. Minucius Felix described the type of problems that exorcists confronted: "the evil spirits disturb their life; they disquiet their slumbers; creeping also into their bodies, they secretly terrify their minds, distort their limbs, break their health, and feign diseases."[39]

Christian exorcists appeared to get results, too. Justin boasted of "how many persons possessed by demons, everywhere in the world and in our own city, have been exorcized by many of our Christian men." Irenaeus claimed that "some people incontestably and truly drive out demons, so that those very persons often become believers."[40] Exorcists read psalms to the afflicted, prayed for them, visited and fed them, and blessed them with the sign of the cross, as well as cast out their demons.[41]

One office in particular presided over this entire ministry of benevolence and service: the office of bishop, though presbyters played a similar role under the supervision of bishops. As I have already noted, the office of bishop emerged early in the history of the church. Both Clement of Rome and Ignatius of Antioch lifted up the office as central to the health and governance of the church. In early Christianity their primary responsibility was pastoral: they preached the Bible, disciplined the faithful, prepared catechumens for church membership, led in worship, baptized, administered the Eucharist, and shepherded the flock. Not until well into the fourth century did bishops wear distinctive clothing, occupy the pulpits of cathedrals, and begin—at least in some cases—to live like the religious counterpart to the Roman senator.[42]

We learn the most about their work from fourth-century documents. Three bishops (Gregory of Nazianzus, John Chrysostom, and Ambrose of Milan) wrote books on pastoral care, and the church compiled a manual that outlined their pastoral responsibilities. These documents show that bishops managed the affairs of the church and supervised large staffs, not as bureaucrats but as leaders and servants. Thus the *Constitutions of Holy Apostles* mandated that bishops pay the most attention to the most vulnerable, "exhibiting to the orphans the care of parents; to the widows the care of husbands; to those of suitable age, marriage; to the artificer, work; to the unable, commiseration; to the strangers, a house; to the hungry, food; to the thirsty, drink; to the naked, clothing; to the sick, visitation; to the prisoners, assistance."[43]

In his book on pastoral care, John Chrysostom used the metaphor of the physician to describe the kind of care bishops were supposed to provide. "It is impossible to treat all his people in one way, any more than it would be right for the doctors to deal with all their patients alike." Thus "the shepherd needs great wisdom and a thousand eyes to examine the soul's condition from every angle."[44]

Not surprisingly, these leaders outlined the necessary qualifications for the office, too. They held bishops accountable to lofty standards—so lofty, in fact, that some candidates tried to avoid office altogether, even fleeing when they heard reports that the church planned to ordain them. The demands were just too great, the standards too high. Nazianzus wrote, "A man must himself be cleansed before cleansing others, himself become wise, that he may make others wise; become light, and then give light; draw near to God, and so bring others near."[45] Ambrose of Milan charged, "He who endeavors to amend the faults of human weakness ought to bear this very weakness on his own shoulders."[46]

Conclusion

By the third century the church was fully engaged in ministries of all kinds and thus developed a structure to do it effectively and efficiently. As demand grew, so did complexity and reach of organization. In AD 251 Cornelius of Rome wrote a letter to Fabius, bishop of Antioch, enumerating the offices serving the church there: "There are one bishop [for a region in the city], forty-six presbyters, seven deacons, seven subdeacons, forty-two acolytes, fifty-two exorcists, readers, and door-keepers."[47] By then some "1,500 widows and distressed persons" were receiving the church's services in some official way.[48]

This kind of ministry had flourished for nearly three centuries before Basil arrived on the scene, which explains why—and how—Basil could found the Basileiad, the first Christian hospital. The fruitfulness of Basil's ministry was the harvest of three hundred years of Christian service that inspired him—and confounded Rome.

Galen commented on it in the second century, as Julian did in the fourth century. They grudgingly conceded that the Christian way of life was exemplary, and they wished that their own religious tradition could produce similar results. It certainly had the resources; but it lacked the kind of belief system and moral vision that would motivate Romans to pursue it and sustain them in it.

152

However attracted to the Christian way of life, Julian nevertheless rejected Christianity. It seems that he could not—or would not—acknowledge and accept the inextricable connection between the Christian way of life and its source—Jesus Christ, whom Christians called Savior and Lord. Julian wanted to divide what Christians united. He wanted the fruit but spurned the faith that gave rise to it.

But could the two be separated? Julian tried but failed. Basil argued that Christian service was dependent on the source of faith that inspired it. The two could therefore not be severed. The Christian way of life and its influence in the world could not stand on its own. Jesus Christ was—and had to be—at the heart of it.

9

Crossing to Safety

Consider this curious turn of events: In his account of the early expansion of Christianity, Luke tells the story of several conversions—among them the Ethiopian eunuch, the Pharisee Saul (later known as Paul), Cornelius the centurion, and the Philippian jailer—relating how these conversions occurred and what followed in their wake. In each case, conversion resulted in immediate baptism.[1]

Now fast-forward to the middle of the second century. It is clear that conversion no longer leads to immediate baptism. There is a delay between an initial interest in or conversion to Christianity and the administration of baptism—a long delay, too, sometimes up to three years. It is a puzzle. Why the change?

This may seem an obscure question. But it is actually far from irrelevant, for it introduces us to one of the central practices of the early Christian period that not only allowed for the survival of the Christian movement but also contributed to its growth—under very difficult circumstances. This central practice was embodied in the structure of the early Christian "catechumenate."

I came to this discovery quite by accident. I took a standard church history course in seminary, and I continued to read extensively during my early years of pastoral ministry. I returned to formal education in my midthirties to earn a PhD in the history of Christianity at the

University of Chicago. Then I settled into a teaching career at Whitworth University. Years later while doing research for another project, I happened upon a word that I had not heard before or, if I had, did not remember. The word was "catechumenate." I was familiar with the word "catechism," of course, and understandably so, being an heir and disciple of the Reformation. But "catechumenate" was alien to me. Why, I wondered, was this idea and practice, as central as it was in early Christianity, not included in my seminary education?

My discovery of this word awakened my curiosity. And so I began to explore, and was introduced to one of the most effective training programs in the history of the church.

There was good reason for its development in the early Christian period. The Christian movement began as a small sect within Judaism and spread quite rapidly and steadily, though unevenly, throughout the Roman world, eventually becoming a formidable rival to other ancient religions long before Constantine came to power in the early fourth century. The church demonstrated an unusual capacity to establish meaningful contact with unbelievers and yet maintain high standards of membership, to welcome outsiders into the church and turn them into committed disciples.

Over time the Christian movement began to reach a growing number of gentiles who knew little or nothing about Christianity. The difference between Greco-Roman religion and Christianity was great enough to require the church to create some kind of bridge between the two. Engineers build bridges, of course, to span a physical barrier—a river or canyon—that prohibits convenient and easy crossing. The barrier in this case was the chasm between the old world of traditional Roman religion and the new world of Christianity. The church had to build some kind of bridge that would allow gentiles to transition from one world to the other and thus become established believers.

The basic contours of the early Christian catechumenate appear in rough outline in the Didache and Justin's *First Apology*. Tertullian, Clement, and Origen assumed its existence, and Hippolytus outlined its basic structure. It is clear from these and other sources that the church, facing problems and challenges as it spread and grew, developed a rigorous training program to form people in the faith, to prepare them for church membership, and to equip them to be effective witnesses in the empire. This training program communicated very clearly that discipleship is not for a few special Christians but for all Christians, not an option but an expectation, not an addition to conversion but an essential feature of conversion.[2]

How did it work? Ordinary church members established the first point of contact with unbelievers, reaching out to their friends and neighbors in the name of Christ. They lived in the same world. They spoke the same language, lived in the same apartment buildings, shopped in the same markets, and worked in many of the same jobs and trades. They witnessed to their faith and drew friends and neighbors into the church. The church in turn created the catechumenate as an institutional bridge to help outsiders move from traditional religion to Christian faith. The church thus erected and maintained what sociologists call "permeable boundaries."[3] Avoiding both excessive accommodation to and isolation from Roman culture, the church began very slowly to engage, reach, and win the culture, from the bottom up rather than from the top down.

The catechumenate enabled converts to become functional disciples and thus helped to form a community of Christians whose example of faith and obedience provided a clear and winsome alternative to Christianity's major competitors—traditional religion, mystery religions, philosophical schools, and Judaism. Steady growth made the movement increasingly visible, which perpetuated the cycle of success. The relatively high level of commitment among its members, which the catechumenate itself helped to solidify, only strengthened momentum, as if it were a successful farm system feeding a major league club with a steady stream of great players. Not that other religions failed to make demands of adherents. Still, the Christian movement excelled at setting and maintaining high standards of membership.

Considering the cultural climate, nothing short of a rigorous training program would have sufficed. The catechumenate functioned much like a total immersion program in language study. Such a program becomes almost necessary with languages that are furthest removed from one's native language. It is one thing to learn a familiar dialect, which requires little more than casual exposure and practice because the difference is too slight to require much more. It is another thing to learn an alien language. A student must cross the bridge, leaving behind one linguistic world to enter another—and alien—one. The difference between the two is so great that nothing short of complete immersion will do.

It is hard for us to imagine today what it would have been like to face, day after day, the difficulty of reaching and winning converts in the ancient world. Paul usually launched his evangelistic enterprise in synagogues, which afforded him the luxury of assuming his audience had at least some level of knowledge about salvation history. The history of Israel itself served as the matrix for introducing the good news about Jesus Christ, who, according to Christian proclamation, fulfilled it. But Paul faced a different kind of challenge when speaking to a Greco-Roman audience, as we observe in Acts 17. They did not know the story; in fact, they lacked the categories that would make sense of the story. They did not think in terms of creation, fall, and redemption, of the death and resurrection of Jesus and his atoning sacrifice, of faith and obedience, and of Christ's kingdom rule. Moving beyond a Jewish milieu, the early Christians had to start from scratch.

These circumstances forced church leaders to consider carefully and to plan strategically how to move converts into the fold of Christianity. A simple conversion was not enough, for Romans had to be converted to an entirely different belief system and way of life that was as alien to them as a language like Chinese is to English speakers. This huge gap required time, patience, and purposefulness. Anything short of that would have undermined the very faith that Christian leaders proclaimed, Roman critics opposed, and martyrs died for, a faith rooted in the incarnation, death, and resurrection of Jesus Christ. To add Jesus to the pantheon of Roman gods and goddesses, as Porphyry advocated, and to present Christianity as just another option in the already crowded field of religion was one thing. A conversion to that kind of religion could have happened quickly and conveniently. Conversion to apostolic Christianity was another thing altogether.

Meaning and Metaphor

The word "catechumenate" is derived from the Greek term *katecheo*.[4] The word surfaces rather late in secular Greek, and it is not found in the Septuagint (the Greek translation of the Hebrew Bible) at all. Its basic meaning was to share an oral communication to an audience, to report and inform, and also "to sound from above," as poets and orators did in the ancient world when addressing an audience from a stage. In this sense it referred to a kind of public performance, a "sounding down- ward" of important ideas. Over time it was used in two ways: first, to recount something important; and second, to instruct someone, espe- cially in the rudiments of a subject or a skill.

It appears only a handful of times in the New Testament. The au- thors adopted and adapted a rare Greek word to convey something that no other word could do. Paul used it to refer to Jewish instruction in the law (Rom. 2:18) and to his commitment to speak five intelligible words in a known language rather than ten thousand words in an un- known language (1 Cor. 14:19), which implied these five words were especially fundamental and important. He contrasted the person who taught (again, in what appears to be a formal sense) with those who were being taught, which hints at some kind of formal teaching ministry in the church (Gal. 6:6).

Early Christian leaders also borrowed and adapted the language of Roman athletic competition to reinforce the importance of readiness, training, and rigor. They had a clear purpose in mind—preparation for actual competition, which in their case meant witness to the Roman Empire. A sense of urgency and seriousness prevailed. Prac- tice would be put to the test in real life; discipline would be put on the line. There could be no spectators in the church, only athletes, for spectators were sure to fail and fold under the pressure of living in a cultural setting in which suspicion was normal and persecution possible. Paul implied as much when he exhorted Timothy, "Train yourself in godliness, for, while physical training is of some value, godliness is valuable in every way, holding promise for both the present life and the life to come" (1 Tim. 4:7–8 NRSV). Paul had endurance in mind, especially because Timothy—most Christians, in fact—faced opposition.

The references to athletic training and competition appear often in early Christian literature, and the intent was nearly always the same—to encourage and charge Christians to submit themselves to a regimen of discipline. Christians needed fortitude to endure as disciples; as time went on they also needed courage to face death as martyrs. For example, in the famous story of the Gallic martyrs (AD 177), the writer explained the difference between those who were able to endure suffering and those who, facing the same test, had failed; that difference had to do with their willingness to live as spiritual athletes. "It was clear that some were ready to be the first Gallic martyrs: they made a full confession of their testimony with the greatest eagerness. It was equally clear that others were not ready, that they had not trained and were still flabby, in no fit condition to face the strain of a struggle to the death."[5]

The use of athletic metaphors underscored a view of discipleship that dominated the period—commitment to genuine faith in Christ, discipline of the appetites, cultivation of virtue, love for others, service to the needy, and faithfulness in persecution. Unlike athletic competition in the Greco-Roman world, however, spiritual training in the church was intended to include everyone—not simply men but also women, not simply the young but also the old and infirm, not simply elites but also ordinary people. The only qualification was a willingness to follow Jesus as Lord. Discipleship was not for the faint of heart but for those who were ready to be trained in the faith as an athlete is trained in a sport. Age, gender, physique, background, and social status were superseded by commitment to Christ and perseverance in the faith.[6]

Early Christian writers cited athletic metaphors often. It would have made perfect sense to their audience, too, because athletic competition was so popular and pervasive in the ancient world. Christians, however, turned the metaphor upside down, for in the competition Christians entered, they would win only by losing. Writing around the year 200, Tertullian challenged Christians to view themselves as athletes for Christ. He drew a parallel between Greco-Roman training and Christian training. Greco-Roman athletes submitted to a regimen of strict discipline and avoided luxury and rich food. Christians were equally committed to discipline, though under very different terms. "We, with the crown eternal in our eye, look upon the prison as our training-ground, that at the goal of final judgment we may be brought forth well disciplined by many a trial; since virtue is built up by hardships, as by voluptuous indulgence it is overthrown."[7]

Likewise, Clement of Alexandria identified spiritual training in Christ as one kind of training that stands alongside many others, such as the training of a scholar or orator or athlete. The goals were different, as we would expect, but the rigor was the same. Christians followed a program suitable for discipleship, which resulted in "moral loveliness." "And in the case of those who have been trained according to this influence: their gait in walking, their sitting at table, their food, their sleep, their going to bed, their regimen, and the rest of their mode of life, acquire a superior dignity. For such a training as is pursued by the Word is not overstrained, but is of the right tension."[8]

Christian writers continued to use the metaphor even after official persecution ended. To be sure, Christians no longer expected to die for Christ; but they could still live for him and, through rigorous training, become "bloodless martyrs." Thus the need to endure in faith remained. The cost would be different, of course. But there would still be a cost. Thus in one of his catechetical sermons Ambrose proclaimed to catechumens that they had been prepared for the contest; they were ready to wrestle to win a trophy. For Christians the contest was on earth; but the reward—the trophy—would be heavenly. "You wrestle in the world, but it is Christ's trophy you receive—the prize for your struggles in the world. And even though this prize is awarded in heaven, the right to the prize is achieved here below."[9] And John Chrysostom exhorted new Christians to imagine competing as spiritual athletes in a stadium filled with thousands of spectators. "Young athletes, the stadium is open, there are the spectators on the tiers of the amphitheater, in front of them is the leader of the games. Then, there is no middle ground, either you fall like a coward and leave covered with shame, or you act bravely and win the crown and the prize."[10]

161

Early Glimpses

Early Christian documents offer brief glimpses of the catechumenate, though an outline of the actual structure did not surface until after the year 200. For example, the Didache, which functioned as a training manual for the church, begins with a description of the "Two Ways," the one referring to the Christian way of life, the other referring to the pagan way of death. Echoes of the New Testament, especially the Sermon on the Mount, reverberate throughout the document. "There are two ways, one of life and one of death; and between the two ways there is a great difference. Now, this is the way of life: 'First, you must love God who made you, and second, your neighbor as yourself.' And whatever you want people to refrain from doing to you, you must not do to them."[11]

After outlining the Two Ways, the manual details several liturgical practices, including how the church should baptize new believers. The manual assumes candidates had already been instructed in the Two Ways before baptism, implying that baptism followed—rather than preceded—spiritual training. "Now about baptism: this is how to baptize. *Give public instruction* on all these points, and *then* 'baptize' in running water, 'in the name of the Father and of the Son and of the Holy Spirit.' . . . Before the baptism, moreover, the one who baptizes and the one being baptized must fast, and any others who can. And you must tell the one being baptized to fast for one or two days beforehand."[12]

In his *First Apology* Justin explained how the church in the middle of the second century baptized new believers. It is clear that an elaborate choreography was emerging, as if the rite was used as a way of inviting candidates to participate in the story of salvation, the rite serving as a segue into that story. It is also clear that baptism required more than belief; it also demanded a change of behavior, once again demonstrating that belief and behavior were seamlessly woven together. He explained what preceded baptism, as well as what happened when it was administered.

As many are persuaded and believe that what we teach and say is true, and *undertake to be able to live accordingly*, are instructed to pray and to entreat God with fasting, for the remission of their sins that are past, we praying and fasting with them. Then they are brought by us where there is water, and are regenerated in the same manner in which we were ourselves regenerated. For, in the name of God, the Father and Lord of the universe, and of our Savior Jesus Christ, and of the Holy Spirit, they then receive the washing with water.[13]

Origen, the most learned and prolific Christian writer of the third century, used Israel's journey from Egypt to the promised land as a metaphor for the catechetical process. He did not equate baptism with crossing the Red Sea, as we might assume, which happens early in the story, but with crossing the Jordan River, which means that the crossing of the Red Sea and passing through the wilderness belonged to the catechetical process. Once again, Origen underscored the importance of training. "When you abandon the darkness of idolatry and when you desire to arrive at the knowledge of the divine law, then begin your departure from Egypt. When you have been accepted into the crowd of the catechumens and when you have begun to obey the commandments of the Church, you have crossed the Red Sea. In the halts of the desert, each day, you apply yourself to listening to the law of God and to contemplate the visage of Moses, which discloses the glory of the Lord."[14] Catechumens would finally arrive at the shores of the Jordan River. Crossing that river was equated to the sacrament of baptism, which occurred at the end of the catechetical process.

Apostolic Tradition

By the early third century some kind of formal training program was in place. The most comprehensive description we have comes from the *Apostolic Tradition*. Written as a church manual in the early third century, it reached its final form in the fourth century.[15] The *Apostolic Tradition* outlined the basic structure of the ancient catechumenate, highlighting three features in particular: enrollment, instruction, and rites of initiation. What is immediately obvious upon reading it is the importance of relationships (or what sociologists call "social networks") and rigorous training, which culminated in a final induction ceremony that had a pageantry similar to a West Point graduation.

First, the document explained the process of enrollment. The Christian movement grew at the grassroots level, at least in the second and third centuries, with Christians reaching their relatives, friends, and neighbors through daily interaction in public places. Such a web of relationships modeled Christian community to outsiders, which meant that the church itself became a primary means of evangelization, a relational womb of rebirth.[16] Evangelism occurred in the setting of natural social relationships. Ordinary Christians took the lead.[17]

Once contact was made and interest awakened, believers invited their friends to meet with a church leader, who would examine them to see if they were ready to be enrolled in the catechumenate and thus become "catechumens." In most cases the believers who brought their friends served as the "sponsor," also known as the godparent, moving through the entire process with them as a companion and mentor. Mentorship, therefore, functioned as a necessary part of the training program.

At this first meeting church leaders would ask questions about background and discern level of interest. Were they really sincere about becoming a Christian? Sponsors would speak on their behalf, too, testifying that they were indeed ready. Here is how the *Apostolic Tradition* put it: "And those who brought them shall bear witness whether they have the ability to hear the word. They might be questioned about their state of life, whether he has a wife, or whether he has a slave."[18]

Among other things, the examination involved investigating the candidate's work history. "They shall enquire about the crafts and occupations of those who are brought for instruction."[19] Professions too closely associated with traditional religion were at the least questioned, and sometimes disallowed. This included professions that in any day or cultural setting would be considered unacceptable to Christians, such as prostitution or gladiatorial combat. But it also included occupations that would seem on the surface to be normal and legitimate, even from a Christian point of view. Still, these "normal" occupations supported traditional religion, however indirectly, which is why the church demanded that catechumens either quit them or, short of that, avoid excessive entanglement.

Thus sculptors could not make idols, actors could not play roles in dramas that taught traditional religion, teachers could not instruct children in ancient myths, and civil magistrates and military officers could not preside over ceremonies that buttressed the state's power, especially religious power. Church leaders did not view any profession as neutral, because at least some buttressed the dominance of traditional religion. In these and other cases, if the catechumen refused to desist, they were "to be rejected."[20] The prohibition of these professions demonstrated, yet again, the significant difference between Christianity and Greco-Roman religion, which the catechumenate both exposed and reinforced. Sometimes the church demanded a clean break from the past.

Second, the document mandated that church leaders provide instruction to catechumens and urged sponsors to sit through the instruction with them. Sponsors were thus exposed to basic instruction in the faith more than once. Moreover, sponsors served as a kind of relational bridge between the catechumens and the church, which put them in a position to clarify the instruction and apply it to the daily life of catechumens, as if participating in a kind of spiritual apprenticeship program.

No outline of instruction is evident or obvious in the early sources, though it is possible to postulate what it might have included and probably did include. Early apologetic works demonstrate how important the Old Testament story was, with Jesus serving as its fulfillment. The Didache, *The So-Called Epistle to Diognetus*, and Athenagoras's *Plea* indicate that catechumens received instruction in Bible, doctrine, and ethics. Early documents also spelled out spiritual and liturgical practices, such as daily recitation of the Lord's Prayer, baptism, and Eucharist.

The *Apostolic Tradition* stated the intended outcome of catechetical instruction, even if it did not outline the actual curriculum. The goal was not simply greater knowledge but also change of behavior. Information was to lead to formation, instruction to discipleship. Moreover, the manual required that instructors do more than teach; it mandated that they pray for catechumens, too. Finally, it made clear that catechumens

165

were welcomed into the fellowship of the church but could not become full and final members until after they were baptized. It reserved certain religious practices *for baptized members only*. After instruction and prayer, therefore, the catechumens were dismissed before members gave the kiss of peace, recited the Lord's Prayer, and received the Eucharist. Such exclusion from certain rites only buttressed their sacred quality. "Each time the teacher finishes his instruction let the catechumens pray for themselves apart from the men, both the baptized women and the women catechumens. . . . But after the prayer is finished the catechumens shall not give the kiss of peace, for their kiss is not yet pure. . . . After the prayer of the catechumens let the teacher lay hands upon them and pray and dismiss them. Whether the teacher be an ecclesiastic or a layman let him do the same."[21]

We learn more about the curriculum from fourth-century documents, including the catechetical sermons of several prominent bishops, among them Ambrose of Milan, Cyril of Jerusalem, Theodore of Mopsuestia, John Chrysostom, Basil of Caesarea, Gregory of Nazianzus, Gregory of Nyssa, and Augustine of Hippo. Some bishops wrote guidelines for catechetical teaching, too.[22] Thus a formal body of instructional material was widely available. Bishops told the biblical story (Cyril devoted some eighty hours to this), explained basic Christian beliefs (following an outline based on early rules of faith and similar to the later creeds—the Nicene, which was written in 325 and revised in 381, and the Apostles', which surfaced even later) and the Lord's Prayer, and outlined Christian ethical behavior, mostly by using the Ten Commandments and the Sermon on the Mount. Sometimes they explored the mysteries of the sacraments, called the Mystagogy, during the eight days after Easter (known as the Octave).

Third, at the end of the formal training period catechumens participated in the "rites of initiation," which usually occurred during Holy Week and culminated on Easter Sunday morning when the bishop administered baptism, confirmation, and Eucharist. These rites of initiation were intended to reflect a spirit of mystery, and they enabled the catechumens to pass from outsider to insider, from candidate to member, from seeker to believer. The rites invited candidates into the

story of salvation because the various rituals in which they participated embodied the story. These rituals included exorcisms, anointings,
fasting, vigils, scrutiny, renunciation of the devil, affirmation of faith,
trinitarian baptism, symbolic use of clothing, congregational welcome,
kiss of peace, recitation of the creed, administration of the Eucharist,
exhortation, and final instructions during Easter week.

Again we turn to the *Apostolic Tradition*. The final rites of initiation
began with another examination, with the sponsor bearing witness to
the catechumen's readiness. What catechumens believed mattered, of
course; but *how they lived* mattered, too. "And when they have chosen
who are set apart to receive baptism let their life be examined, whether
they lived piously while catechumens, whether 'they honored the widows,' whether they visited the sick, whether they have fulfilled every
good work. If those who bring them witness to them that they have
done thus, then let them hear the gospel."[23] In this case the "gospel"
most likely referred to some kind of creed, which candidates memorized
and then recited during the baptismal service.

During Holy Week, candidates were busy with last-minute spiritual
preparation. The atmosphere became heavy with anticipation, dense
with solemnity. Daily exorcisms implied that the devil himself would
be especially active in disrupting and undermining the process at the
very end. "Moreover, from the day they are chosen, let a hand be laid
on them and let them be exorcised daily. . . . But if there is one who
is not purified let him be put on one side because he did not hear the
word of instruction with faith. For it is impossible that the alien spirit
should remain with him."[24]

On the day before their baptism, catechumens fasted, kept vigil, and
prayed, all in preparation for the great event. Bishops in turn prayed over
them, breathed on them, and "sealed" forehead, ears, mouth, and nose
with the sign of the cross, as if to erect a spiritual wall of protection
around them. Finally, bishops read Scripture and instructed them.[25]

This rich choreography culminated in the administration of baptism,
confirmation, and Eucharist. The bishop prayed over the baptismal
waters. Then the candidates submitted to one last exorcism, renounced
the devil, confessed faith using a threefold formula that sounds much

like the Apostles' Creed, and were plunged into the baptismal waters three times. After baptism, candidates were anointed with the oil of thanksgiving and the oil of confirmation and then ushered into the church or hall to meet church members, who welcomed them with the kiss of peace. There they received their first Eucharist, which consisted not only of bread and wine but also of milk and honey, symbols of the food of the promised land and hope of the coming kingdom.[26]

Hippolytus concluded by exhorting new members to live out their faith through works of obedience. "And when these things have been accomplished, let each one be zealous to perform good works and to please God, living righteously, devoting himself to the Church, performing the things which he has learnt, advancing in the service of God."[27]

Thus by the early third century the catechumenate involved three discrete stages. It began with informal contact with nonbelievers, which led to formal enrollment, initial examination, and assignment of a sponsor or mentor. It then provided instruction in the biblical story, the creed, and the Christian way of life, assuming that such knowledge would lead to genuine change of life. Finally, it culminated in Holy Week, when church leaders scrutinized candidates one more time and led them through a highly choreographed process of initiation that involved fasting, prayer, vigils, exorcisms, anointings, baptism, confirmation, and Eucharist. Thus belief, belonging, and behavior were woven together into a seamless whole, no one element predominating over the others.

By the time we reach the fourth century the evidence is plentiful and cogent. We have Egeria's detailed description of the catechumenate in Jerusalem (as we shall see shortly), as well as her stirring account of the Great Week (Holy Week).[28] We have Cyril of Jerusalem's catechetical sermons, which corroborate Egeria's account; we also have the catechetical sermons of Theodore of Mopsuestia, Chrysostom, Ambrose, Nyssa, Nazianzus, Basil, and Augustine.[29]

The Catechumenate and Christendom

Christendom emerged during the Middle Ages as a result of the long and complex process of the Christianization of Europe. Christendom, as I defined in the first chapter, refers to the symbiotic relationship between church and state, Christianity and culture. It began to emerge in the fourth century, when Christianity became the official religion of the empire and the church one of the dominant institutions in the empire. Over time Christianity prevailed to such a degree that the vast majority of people living in the empire simply assumed that they were Christian, as if by default. Thus it was less likely that people *became* Christian by decision, commitment, and training; they simply *were* Christian by association with Christian culture.

Christendom changed the catechumenate. Evidence of this change surfaced as early as the fourth century. One sign of change concerned timing. The catechumenate was simultaneously lengthened and shortened. Christian families sometimes enrolled their children as catechumens when still young, though many of those children did not become functional catechumens—or *competentes*—until they reached adulthood. For example, Augustine's mother, Monica, enrolled him as a catechumen when he was a boy. But he did not submit to catechetical training (under Ambrose) until he was thirty years old.

Bishops adapted the catechumenate to this change of circumstances, though not without significant reservations. They shortened the actual period of formal training to a matter of weeks, which was a significant decrease from what it had been only a century earlier. They recruited catechumens to enroll as *competentes* during the season of Epiphany. The training program would then commence during the first week of Lent and end on Palm Sunday, just in time for the *competentes* to undergo the rites of initiation. Bishops had to teach a great deal of content in a short period of time. Cyril, bishop of Jerusalem, instructed catechumens three hours a day during the entire season of Lent. It seems unlikely that catechumens could have absorbed and applied so much information. It was a matter of too little time and too much information. Like runoff after a fierce thunderstorm, much must have been lost in the process.

Another sign of change involved the rites of initiation, which became increasingly grandiose and elaborate. We know the most about what happened in Jerusalem because we have access to Egeria's journal. Most likely a Spanish nun, Egeria went on pilgrimage to the Holy Land in the 380s. She recorded her experiences and observations for the nuns who were not able to travel with her. In her journal she devoted many pages to a description of the "Great Week" (our Holy Week) as it unfolded in Jerusalem. Constantine's mother, Helena, had persuaded her son to turn Jerusalem into a pilgrimage site, which set in motion the massive construction of churches and shrines. Holy Week became a major event and tourist attraction. Huge crowds of pilgrims flocked to the Holy City. But the event, as well as its popularity, changed the catechumenate, in effect separating the final initiation process from the training program that prepared people for it. It became a spectacle, like a showy commencement ceremony following a mediocre education.

Bishops were not pleased about the decline of the catechumenate. We can sense frustration and disappointment in their preaching. They did their best to recruit catechumens to become *competentes*, but they often met with little success. Ambrose of Milan labored long and hard to enroll catechumens but repeatedly failed. He felt like a fisherman who had labored all night long, catching nothing. "I, too, Lord, I know that for me it is dark, when you do not command. No one has yet inscribed, it is still night for me. I put out the net of the word at Epiphany, and I have not yet taken anything."[30] Basil of Caesarea wondered how it was possible for people who had attended worship for years to refuse to take the final step. "Catechized since you were young, do you still not give your accord to the truth? You who do not cease studying, have you not yet arrived at knowledge? You who are tasting life, explorer until old age, will you finish by becoming Christian?"[31]

Why, bishops asked, were catechumens attending worship at all? Was there some ulterior—and ungodly—motive? Ambrose thought so. "And here is one who comes to the Church because he is looking for honors under the Christian emperors; he pretends to request baptism with a simulated respect; he bows, he prostrates; but he does not bend his knees in spirit."[32] Gregory of Nazianzus thought postponement of baptism betrayed a dangerous presumption. He charged that some were thinking they could continue to sin that "grace may abound," as Paul wrote in Romans 6:1. "This would be to involve Christ in any unworthy commercial speculation: to burden ourselves with more than we can carry, to run the risk of seeing his ship totally perish and to lose in a shipwreck all the fruit of grace we did not know how to consume."[33] John Chrysostom reasoned that delay of baptism exposed a deeper problem: the assumption that catechumens could put off baptism to the very end, as Constantine had done. "Is it not the utmost stupidity to postpone the gift? Listen you catechumens and you who put off your own salvation until the last gasp."[34]

Still, these bishops would not compromise. They insisted that the rites of initiation had to mean something. They did not want to settle for superficial membership; they wanted to produce disciples. Cyril of Jerusalem cried, "Strip off, I beg, fornication and uncleanness and put on that brilliant robe, self-discipline."[35] Augustine warned against false confidence, as if baptism could work some kind of spiritual magic. "With the help of our Lord God, let us diligently beware henceforth of giving men a false confidence by telling them that if only they will have been baptized in Christ, no matter how they will live in their faith, they will arrive at eternal salvation."[36] Gregory of Nyssa even claimed that baptism would have no spiritual benefit without repentance and change of life. If life *after* baptism, he reasoned, was no different from life *before* baptism, then "the water is water, and the gift of the Holy Spirit nowhere appears in what takes place: the turpitude of the soul dishonors the image of God."[37]

The catechumenate eventually faded until it was almost forgotten as an important discipline of the early Christian movement. During the medieval period, almost everyone was baptized as an infant or baptized as an adult in a mass ceremony of tribal conversion. Renewal movements emerged to "Christianize" Christians and to disciple the baptized. The rite (later, the sacrament) of confirmation became the preferred method of confirming and thus completing the baptism of infants, usually years later. In some cases candidates for confirmation received instruction before they were confirmed, but not always. Monasteries preserved some features of the catechumenate in the novitiate, a three-year process that prepared novices to take final vows and become permanent members of a monastic community.

The long reign of Western Christendom is coming to an end. Nominal church membership is becoming less attractive than it used to be, and unbelief more compelling. The fading of Christendom is forcing the church to consider once again what it means to function as an outsider institution.[38] Such a change of status is also challenging the church to reconsider the role of the ancient catechumenate. What might recovery of this ancient institution mean? I will explore that question in the conclusion.

Conclusion

Now and Then

I did not set out to write the book you have before you. My original intent was to explore how the early Christian movement formed people in the faith, which I was going to title *The New Way*, meaning the new way of life Christians followed as a community and formed in converts. I assumed the topic was practical, a kind of historical "how-to" book on discipleship for the church today. My research on the catechumenate persuaded me that the early church's commitment to form people in the faith was the secret to its success in the Roman world. I thought it would be a "usable" history.

I eventually abandoned the project, not because it was wrong but because it was misleading and incomplete. Early Christians did not set out to establish a new way of life, grow the church into a formidable institution, and launch a reform movement that, to the surprise of Roman critics, exercised so much influence in the ancient world. The impact of this new faith was an unintended consequence of something else, something far more important.

What was the "something else" that made the Christian movement so unique and influential in the Greco-Roman world? It was not how Christians lived or how they formed people in the faith, at least not primarily. Rather, it was more fundamental than that. It concerned what Christians believed about the very nature of reality or, better put, *who*

173

they believed was at the center of reality—namely, Jesus Christ. The Third Way was a consequence of him.[1]

Early Christian sources are unrelentingly clear on this point. Jesus Christ shaped everything that followed in his wake. No one in the ancient world had ever encountered the likes of Jesus before. Rome had no categories for him, and neither did Jews. Not even his disciples could make sense of him until after the resurrection. Jesus Christ summoned his followers to a new way *of* life because he was first and foremost the way *to* new life. Without Jesus Christ there would have been no Third Way. The Third Way was the result of the apostolic experience of and testimony to the man Jesus who was the *Lord* Jesus. It was his uniqueness that made the early Christian movement unique.

Jesus said that his kingdom was "not of this world." That would seem to relieve Rome of worries about him, for Rome's kingdom was very much *of* this world. Yet Jesus' kingdom had everything to do *with* this world, too, as his own ministry demonstrated. His kingdom embodied a larger vision of reality, the reality of God's just and merciful rule over all of life. It transcended this world, to be sure; but it also promised to transform this world. His kingdom did not threaten Rome in an outwardly subversive way. Yet it was far more subversive at the same time. Rome had no idea how to suppress it, short of annihilation. But the very nature of the movement made such annihilation almost impossible. Christians did not accommodate to Rome. Neither did they isolate from Rome. Instead, they immersed themselves in the culture as followers of Jesus and agents of the kingdom, influencing it from within both as individuals and as a community. They announced that there was a truer way to believe and a better way to live than the first way (Roman) and second way (Jewish). They believed the Third Way was, in fact, the only way.

As we have seen, Rome *labeled* the Christian movement as subversive, too, though Rome could cite no evidence to level concrete charges against Christians. Rome witnessed Christianity's power to transform people, but such transformation did not set Christians apart as culturally isolated and peculiar. Rome resented its impact on the economy, popular forms of entertainment, and traditional religious practices, but Rome also benefited from the movement's benevolence and service.

For some 250 years the Christian movement grew steadily, if unevenly, exercising considerable influence as it did so. Rome simply did not know what to make of the Christian movement or what to do about it.

What can we learn today from the church's witness to Rome some two thousand years ago?

At the center, of course, was Jesus Christ himself—human and divine, crucified and resurrected, suffering servant and triumphant King, Son of Man and Son of God.

Early Christians believed that God had revealed himself in Jesus Christ. They claimed that this revelation showed the world who God is, as well as what kind of people humans were created to be. They believed Jesus was both window and mirror: a window through which they could see the very being of God and a mirror in which they could see the true human. Jesus Christ became the perfect and final mediator between God and humanity.

Early Christians claimed that the coming of Jesus Christ radically changed their understanding of the nature of God, too. God, they said, is one God in relationship, a triunity of love. This God of love, they believed, loves the people he created by inviting them to be participants and recipients of the love that exists within the very being of God as Father, Son, and Holy Spirit.

They viewed worship as a bridge between divine and human worlds, as if in worship Christians stepped into a liminal space between heaven and earth. They saw themselves not primarily as consumers who attended worship to hear a good sermon and sing a few familiar songs but as beholders of the unspeakable glory of God. How they viewed and practiced worship not only ushered them into the very presence of God but also prepared them to return to the ordinary life of market, home, and neighborhood as disciples of Jesus.

Christians embraced a new story, too. Their knowledge of Jesus changed their view of history. The story of Jesus opened their eyes to see history not as a narrative of the empire's achievements—and atrocities—but as a narrative of God's redemptive work in the world, which often occurs in quiet and mysterious ways. For them Bethlehem and Golgotha, not the Roman court, occupied center stage.

All authority, they confessed, comes from Jesus Christ, which completely redefined how they understood worldly authority. The incarnate Son of God emptied himself, taking the form of a servant. He came not to be served but to serve. He girded himself with a towel and washed the feet of the disciples. He prayed to his Father, "Not my will but yours be done" (Luke 22:42 NRSV). How Jesus exercised authority set the pattern for how Christians should exercise it. They believed that all true authority points to him; leaders are called to bear witness to Jesus and to imitate his example.

Jesus Christ reshaped identity. He promised to make people new creatures; he broke down dividing walls of hostility; he transformed how his followers saw themselves and treated "the other." Primary identity in Christ changed all earthly—and secondary—identities. There was still marriage, to be sure, but it would be a different kind of marriage. There were still Jew and gentile, but the gospel made them one.

Christians became a nation within a nation, a new *oikoumene* that spanned the known world, crossing traditional cultural barriers. Their primary loyalty was to fellow believers, not to nation or race or tribe or party or class. Christians met mostly in house churches, too, which created a new kind of family. God was true Father; they were all brothers and sisters. The Christian movement was therefore both radically global and local at the same time. Rome pitted rich against poor, citizen against barbarian, male against female, master against slave. Not so in the Christian movement. Both *oikoumene* and *oikos* had the effect of undermining and transforming the traditional social order.

They lived differently in the world, too. Christians were known as the people who cared for the "least of these," challenging Rome's patronage system and culture of honor and shame. Jesus, the one who was rich, became poor to make the poor rich. How could his followers do otherwise, considering what their master had done for them? They organized for action to meet practical need; they served the most vulnerable and despised in society.

Of course early Christians did not do any of these things perfectly. Even the best teams still lose, the greatest musicians still flub, the sharpest entrepreneurs still fail. Early Christians lost, flubbed, and failed, too. But they aspired to follow Jesus all the same. And they did so with enough consistency and success to attract Rome's attention, which is why Rome identified the Christian movement as a new way or a "Third Way."

Rome's various responses—fascination, confusion, suspicion, opposition, persecution—only underscored how unique the movement was. It was not easy to understand and to follow then, considering that pre-Christendom setting, nor is it today, considering our increasingly post-Christendom setting. And this is why the early Christian movement established the catechumenate as a strategy of formation.

The catechumenate was both inherent to the faith and necessary for its survival and growth. It was *inherent* because discipleship was the only possible response to the lordship of Jesus Christ. Conversion to Christ implied conformity to Christ. The church did not function like a club with various levels of membership—some associate members and others full members. Not every Christian became a serious disciple. Still, standards were high because the identity of Christ was clear. Christians believed he was Lord.

And it was *necessary* because the church faced stiff opposition and competition in the ancient world. The difference between Roman religion and Christianity was so great that the church had to develop a process to move people from the old world of traditional religion to the new world of Christianity. Anything short of that would have resulted in accommodation or isolation, and thus to the decline and eventual death of Christianity, at least as the apostles defined it.

Christendom—the symbiotic relationship between church and society, Christianity and culture—made the Third Way unnecessary. Why follow the Third Way if it was the only way? Not that Christendom lacked serious Christians. The history of the church tells the story of countless renewal movements—monastic, mendicant, and Wesleyan, for example. But these were *renewal* movements, intended to awaken a moribund Christendom. The unstated assumption behind these movements was that the Western world was Christian, however nominal most Christians appeared to be.

We are no longer living in that world, which is why the early Christian movement has so much to teach us.

177

There is competition now, sometimes fierce. As long as Christians assume we are still living under the old arrangement of Christendom, the church will continue to decline in the West, no matter how ferociously Christians fight to maintain power and privilege. If anything, the harder Christians fight, the more precipitous the decline will be, for cultural power and privilege will come at an increasingly high price. Christians will either accommodate until the faith becomes almost unrecognizable, or they will isolate until their faith becomes virtually invisible.

Now, as then, the church needs disciples who trust in and confess that Jesus is Lord and try to live accordingly, who orient their lives around the worship of the Triune God and understand the Christian story as their story, who view themselves as new creatures in Christ and as members of a global community of faith, and who strive to imitate Jesus in all areas of life, serve the "least of these," and steward their resources as if everything they have belongs to God, which of course it does. Nothing short of a change of church culture will suffice—from a culture of entertainment, politics, personality, and program to a culture of discipleship. Such a radical change will require patience, steadiness, and purposefulness. A coach cannot turn a team with a losing record around in one season, nor can an orchestral director transform a sloppy and lazy orchestra after a handful of rehearsals. Leaders with clear vision, faith in the power of the gospel, and high standards must take the long view.

We are not alone. The story of early Christianity reminds us of this fact. Faithful Christians—"real disciples," as Ignatius aspired to be—have gone before us, bearing witness to the truth of Christianity, the power of the gospel, and the high calling of discipleship. Calling out across the centuries, they tell us that it is possible now, as it was then, to live as faithful followers of Jesus the Lord in a culture that does not approve of it or reward it. Two millennia ago Jesus Christ—his incarnation, life, death, resurrection, and ascension—set in motion a movement that turned the world upside down. He is the same Lord today. It can happen again.

Annotated Bibliography

Scholars pay close attention to the sources. Their work demands it, and readers depend on it. The literature of early Christianity, however, is massive. Very few have attained the kind of mastery that qualifies them to provide an exhaustive bibliography. If they did, the bibliography would become its own book. I am not qualified, nor inclined, to do so for this short volume. The vast majority of readers would ignore it anyway.

Instead, I wish to provide an annotated bibliography to introduce readers to the most accessible and important sources. These sources will get readers started, like a charcoal sketch that outlines the subject of a future painting. The sketch might not be the finished product, but it gives a good idea of what it will look like.

I have included a brief list of both primary and secondary sources for further reading. These are arranged according to category, and the books within each category are arranged thematically. I have also provided explanations of the categories, as well as brief comments on the books cited.

Primary Sources

Collections

Over the years scholars have compiled collections of primary sources that introduce students to the literature. By far the most extensive collection—nearly exhaustive—is *The Ante-Nicene Fathers* and *The*

Nicene and Post-Nicene Fathers, which run to some three dozen volumes. I have chosen instead to mention a few collections that are more accessible and selective.

Stevenson, J., ed. *A New Eusebius: Documents Illustrating the History of the Church to AD 337*. Revised by W. H. C. Frend. Grand Rapids: Baker Academic, 2013. This collection includes a broad range of sources, both Greco-Roman and Christian, from the beginning of Christianity to the death of Constantine.

Richardson, Cyril C., ed. *Early Christian Fathers*. New York: Touchstone, 1996. This compilation focuses on the major figures and documents of the second century.

Bettenson, Henry, ed. *The Early Christian Fathers: A Selection from the Writings of the Fathers from Clement of Rome to St. Athanasius*. New York: Oxford University Press, 1956. Bettenson organizes this collection according to author, as most collections do. But then he includes long citations from each author according to subject—say, Trinity, atonement, and the church. It is a convenient way to see the diversity of thought from one church father to the next.

Ferguson, Everett. *Early Christians Speak*. 3rd ed. 2 vols. Abilene, TX: Abileen Christian University Press, 1987, 2002. Ferguson has arranged this collection of sources according to topic: war, sacraments, church office, women, and so forth. He also provides extensive notes and commentary. It is invaluable for students who wish to discover the breadth of opinion on any given subject in the early Christian period.

Barrois, Georges, ed. *The Fathers Speak: St. Basil the Great, St. Gregory of Nazianzus, St. Gregory of Nyssa*. Crestwood, NY: St. Vladimir's Seminary Press, 1986. Barrois includes a large sample of letters exchanged among the Cappadocian fathers. He is judicious in his selection. The letters reveal the three Cappadocians as real people. In one letter they argue against the Arians, in the next they complain about the postal service and the weather.

Robinson, James M., ed. *The Nag Hammadi Library: The Definitive Translation of the Gnostic Scriptures Complete in One Volume*. San Francisco: HarperSanFrancisco, 1990. This volume contains the majority of the early Gnostic writings: gospels, letters, acts of the apostles, and apocalyptic literature. The most famous is the Gospel of Thomas.

Early History

Historical writing is not a modern invention. Classical authors, like Tacitus, wrote a number of important histories. Some even mention

Jesus and the early Christian movement. Early Christians, like Eusebius, followed their example and wrote histories, too, focusing on the Christian movement. But their perspective was obviously very different from classical authors, informed as it was by their Christian worldview.

Eusebius. *The History of the Church from Christ to Constantine*. Revised and edited by Andrew Louth. Translated by G. A. Williamson. New York: Penguin, 1989. Living in the early fourth century, Eusebius wrote the first history of the church. He had his biases, of course. But he was surprisingly critical, too, even according to modern standards. This is a priceless source of information on the early church.

Augustine. *The City of God*. Translated by Marcus Dods. Peabody, MA: Hendrickson, 2017. I have included Augustine in this section because this tome, long and detailed, provides readers not only with a vast amount of information but also with a philosophy of history.

Early Letters

We are fortunate to have letters that date to as early as AD 95, just one generation after the apostles. They shed light on the church that the apostles left behind. They are different from the apostolic writings, to be sure; but there is surprising continuity, too. This second generation presided over the transition from Jew to gentile, Hebrew to Greek, rural to urban, apostolic to post-apostolic. Though the Christian movement seemed to hang in the balance, these letters show why and how the movement endured.

Clement. *The First Epistle of Clement to the Corinthians*. In *ANF*, vol. 1. Clement was the bishop of Rome. Writing around the year 95, he addressed the problem of conflict and disunity in the church in Corinth.

Epistles of Ignatius of Antioch. In *ANF*, vol. 1. Ignatius, bishop of Antioch, wrote seven letters to churches and one to a fellow bishop (Polycarp), all the while traveling under guard to face trial in Rome, where he was in all likelihood martyred. These letters provide an unvarnished and unpolished view of the church in the early second century.

The Epistle of Polycarp to the Philippians. In *ANF*, vol. 1. Polycarp served as bishop of Smyrna for many years, perhaps as many as fifty. He died in 155 at the age of eighty-six. He wrote this letter to a sister church. He quoted from a number of books that are now canonical, which illustrates that there was a functional canon long before there was an official one.

Accounts of Martyrdom

Scholars debate what role martyrdom played in early Christianity and how many Christians died. The latter question is simply not possible to answer. It could have been as low as one thousand or as high as ten thousand (or even higher). But it is safe to say that enough Christians died—and died publicly—to shape the life of the early church. The stories of martyrdom became a unique genre of literature. And Christian leaders like Tertullian and Origen wrote essays to the church to prepare people for martyrdom, using the threat of martyrdom as an occasion for instruction in discipleship. Christian martyrs died in the arena as if they were athletes, though spiritual ones. But unlike Roman athletes, their death was deemed a victory, not a defeat.

Eusebius. *The History of the Church*. Revised and edited by Andrew Louth. Translated by G. A. Williamson. New York: Penguin, 1989. I include Eusebius again because his history contains the accounts of a number of famous martyr stories. In fact, Eusebius quotes entire accounts, obviously lifting them from earlier sources.

The Martyrdom of Polycarp. In Richardson, *ECF*. This account includes all the classical elements of early Christian martyr stories. There are false charges, references to Scripture, depiction of a miracle, and description of the execution. But Polycarp was no Jesus. As the testimony states, Polycarp died as a witness to Jesus; Jesus died to save the world from sin.

Musurillo, Herbert, ed. *The Acts of the Christian Martyrs*. Oxford: Clarendon, 1972. Musurillo has compiled most of the early Christian martyr stories, not only in English but also in the ancient languages in which they were written or into which they were translated. It is thorough and useful.

Tertullian. *To the Martyrs*. In *Fathers of the Church*, vol. 10, translated by Rudolph Arbesmann. Washington, DC: Catholic University of America Press, 1959.

Origen. *An Exhortation to Martyrdom*. Translated by Rowan A. Greer. New Mahwah, NJ: Paulist Press, 1979. It seems odd that the early Christian movement produced the kind of genre of literature we see here in Tertullian and Origen. It underscores how real the threat of martyrdom was. Both

Tertullian and Origen, separated by a generation, charged Christians to prepare for possible martyrdom and thus to become disciplined followers of Jesus. Origen actually died as a martyr in 254.

Church Manuals

Even as early as the year AD 100 (or so) Christian leaders were already thinking about how to organize the church, to train people in the faith, to shape liturgy and explain the sacraments, and to establish various church offices and spell out their qualifications and duties. It is surprising how early this process of organization began. It seems the church was in it for the long haul.

Didache. In Richardson, *ECF*. This document reveals how the post-apostolic church was preparing for long-term growth and stability. It was written (or compiled) around the year 100. The church was clearly in transition. Itinerant prophets were still playing a role, to be sure; but presbyters and deacons were starting to exert influence, too. The Lord's Prayer had already become the prayer of the faithful. The Lord's Day was taking the place of the Jewish Sabbath. Baptism and communion functioned as the primary sacraments, which were explained in worship by a rich liturgical language.

Hippolytus. *On the Apostolic Tradition*. Translated by Alistair Stewart-Sykes. Crestwood, NY: St. Vladimir's Seminary Press, 2001. Written (or again, compiled) around the year 200, though not necessarily in the form we have today, this document demonstrates how the church emerged in the second century as an organized and disciplined community. It provides extensive instructions on the catechumenate.

Apologies and Polemics

Known as the Third Way, the Christian movement began as a renewal movement within Judaism but soon expanded into the Roman world. This list of primary sources demonstrates how Christian writers defined and defended Christianity in light of the religious and cultural alternatives.

Early apologies were written to engage Roman officials and the intellectual elite. Most of them set out to prove that Christianity was not a political threat to Rome and to argue that Christianity was both

183

different from and superior to its three major rivals: Judaism, traditional religion, and Greco-Roman philosophy.

Early polemics leveled major criticisms against inside threats to Christianity—that is, movements like Gnosticism and Marcionism that claimed Jesus as their own. Polemics also denounced the Roman lifestyle, labeling it as corrupt. This kind of literature underscores the huge challenge Christians faced in the ancient world: If too accommodating, they would have been absorbed. If too isolated, they would have been ignored.

The So-Called Letter to Diognetus. In Richardson, *ECF*. Written with uncommon polish and beauty, this is most likely the earliest, and certainly the shortest, of the apologies. It is telling that the author cited Christian behavior as an argument for the truth and attractiveness of Christianity.

Martyr, Justin. *The First Apology*. In *ANF*, vol. 1. An adult convert, Justin founded a philosophical academy in Rome. He argued that Christianity is the true philosophy, far superior to the Roman alternatives.

Tertullian. *Apology*. In *ANF*, vol. 3. The first "Latin Father," Tertullian wrote with unusual vigor, passion, and, on occasion, fanaticism. He argued that Christians were being treated unjustly, accused of the crime of a name (being Christian) but not the name of a crime (actual wrongdoing). Christianity, he argued, was different, but not dangerous (as the Romans defined danger).

———. *Against Marcion*. Pickerington, OH: Beloved, 2014. This is a long and sometimes tedious argument against a teacher in Rome who advocated that Christianity sever all ties with ancient Israel, the Old Testament, and every reference to the Old Testament in the books we now call the New Testament. The church excommunicated Marcion. Tertullian shows why.

———. *The Shows*. In *ANF*, vol. 3. This description and criticism of Roman entertainment is sarcastic, incisive, and brutal. It is sobering to read it, because it could apply to modern Western entertainment.

———. *On Prayer*. In *ANF*, vol. 3. This short work demonstrates that towering intellectuals, like Tertullian, cared as much about spiritual practice as they did about Christian doctrine. It is beautiful.

Irenaeus. *Against Heresies*. Rev. ed. Edited by Alexander Roberts and James Donaldson. Translated by Alexander Roberts and William Rambaut. N.p.: Ex Fontibus, 2015. Sometimes referred to as "the heresy hunter," Irenaeus was actually a pastor who simply cared about the people under his charge and therefore took theological threats seriously. He assumed the office of bishop in Lyon around the year 180 after forty-six people had died as martyrs, including the ninety-year-old bishop. Irenaeus took the office of bishop seriously.

Clement of Alexandria. *The Instructor*. In *ANF*, vol. 2. Clement wrote with elegance, insight, and occasional humor as he summoned the faithful to live for Christ. In many ways, this is a kind of manual of discipleship for new Christians.

Theology

The earliest forms of theological writing were apologies and polemics. But over time Christian teachers began to write more formal theology—that is, books organized systematically to address matters pertaining to Christian belief and practice. Many of these books have endured to this day because of their careful argumentation and poetic use of language.

Irenaeus. *On the Apostolic Preaching*. Translated by John Behr. Crestwood, NY: St. Vladimir's Seminary Press, 1997. This is probably the first attempt at writing "biblical theology." It is short and accessible, which suggests that it might have been used for catechetical instruction. It outlines the theological significance of the biblical story of salvation.

Origen. *On First Principles*. Translated by G. W. Butterworth. Notre Dame, IN: Ave Maria Press, 2013. This is probably the first Christian systematic theology. Origen was brilliant. He founded a library and school in Caesarea (Palestine). He was a master teacher, biblical commentator, and textual scholar. His students lauded his godliness of life, too.

Cyprian of Carthage. *The Unity of the Catholic Church*. In *On the Church: Select Treatises*, translated by Allen Brent. Crestwood, NY: St. Vladimir's Seminary Press, 2006. As a bishop, Cyprian was devoted to the unity of the church, which this book explains and defends.

Athanasius. *On the Incarnation*. Crestwood, NY: St. Vladimir's Seminary Press, 1996. Athanasius was a young man when he wrote this short book against his major opponent, Arius, who argued that Jesus Christ was more than human but less than God. Athanasius countered that Jesus was both human and divine. It is obvious, as it is in the case of most of the church fathers, that he received a classical education. His use of rhetoric is magnificent.

Gregory of Nazianzus. *On God and Christ*. Translated by Frederick Williams and Lionel Wickham. Crestwood, NY: St. Vladimir's Seminary Press, 2002.

Nazianzus is known in the Eastern Orthodox Church simply as "the Theologian," largely because of these five essays on the nature of God and Christ. His reputation is well deserved.

Basil of Caesarea. *On the Holy Spirit*. Translated by David Anderson. Crestwood, NY: St. Vladimir's Seminary Press, 1980. Basil explored the identity and role of the Holy Spirit in light of its relative neglect in the Nicene Creed (325). His influence is obvious. The second version of the creed, spelled out in 381, added more substance.

Gregory of Nyssa. *The Life of Moses*. Translated by Abraham J. Malherbe and Everett Ferguson. San Francisco: HarperOne, 2006. I have included this unusual work because it offers a good example of the kind of allegorical reading of the Old Testament that flourished during this period and for many centuries after. Moses climbed Mt. Sinai to receive the Ten Commandments. In the mind of Nyssa, he also ascended into the cloud of unknowing in his encounter with God.

Augustine. *On Christian Teaching*. Translated by R. P. H. Green. New York: Oxford University Press, 1997. Augustine wrote more words than many people will ever read. Much of his writing is lengthy, complex, and demanding. This is Augustine at his accessible and pastoral best. This book is not only about Christianity; it is also about how to teach it.

Lives of Saints

Example has always played an important role in Christianity. Christians discover what discipleship means, promises, and demands by studying the lives of great Christians. The "lives of the saints" became an important genre of literature in early Christianity, and it served as a teaching tool for pastors.

White, Carolinne, ed. *Early Christian Lives*. New York: Penguin, 1998. White has compiled the earliest and best spiritual biographies of the leaders we now know as "saints."

Pontius. *Life of St. Cyprian*. In *Early Christian Biographies*, edited by Roy J. Deferrari. New York: Fathers of the Church, 1952. From an elite background, Cyprian rose rapidly to the office of bishop in the middle of the third century. But he faced criticism when he fled persecution in order to continue his episcopal duties while in hiding. Ironically, he died as a martyr less than a decade later.

Thaumaturgis, Gregory. *The Oration and Panegyric Addressed to Origen*. In *ANF*, vol. 6. Every teacher and professor ought to read this book. Gregory studied under the famous Origen for seven years before assuming the office of bishop in a remote area of Asia Minor. Origen was brilliant as a master teacher; but he was also pastoral. According to Gregory, he modeled the very Christian faith he taught.

Gregory of Nazianzus. *The Panegyric of Saint Basil*. In NPNF², vol. 7. Gregory paid tribute to his best friend and ally, Basil, after his death. Basil was a formidable leader and activist in addition to being a theologian and pastor.

Gregory, Bishop of Nyssa. *The Life of Saint Macrina*. Translated by Kevin Corrigan. Eugene, OR: Wipf & Stock, 2001. Gregory wrote this short piece to honor his sister, Macrina, who founded a monastery; called her brother, Basil, to account for his conceit; and shaped the spiritual life of a generation of Christian leaders in Asia Minor.

Egeria's Travels. Translated by John Wilkinson. 3rd ed. Oxford: Oxbow Books, 1999. This journal, written in the fourth century, tells the story of Egeria's journey from Spain to the Holy Land. It is rich in detail, especially in describing Holy Week in Jerusalem in the 380s.

Augustine. *The Confessions*. Translated by Maria Boulding, OSB. Hyde Park, NY: New City Press, 1997. I include this book here because Augustine set the standard for spiritual autobiography. He reflects honestly and insightfully on his own journey from doubt to faith, rebellion to surrender. It is one of only several books to which I keep returning.

Pastoral Care, Sermons, and Catechetical Instruction

Perhaps the best way to get to know the church fathers is through their preaching, because it made theology accessible to ordinary people. My students comment often that these sermons read as if they could have been delivered last Sunday. As this literature demonstrates, culture may change, but the faith once delivered to the saints does not.

Gregory of Nazianzus. *In Defense of His Flight to Pontus*. In NPNF², vol. 7. Gregory used his avoidance of church office to explore the duties and qualifications of the pastor.

Chrysostom, John. *Six Books on the Priesthood*. Translated by Graham Neville. Crestwood, NY: St. Vladimir's Seminary Press, 2002. Writing about the same time as Nazianzus, John also explored the duties and qualifications of the pastor. Both of these bishops defended a high view of church office.

Basil of Caesarea. *On Social Justice*. Translated by C. Paul Schroeder. Crestwood, NY: St. Vladimir's Seminary Press, 2009. How could a pastor preach sermons like these? But so he did. These sermons call the wealthy to account for their selfishness and abuse of riches.

Gregory of Nyssa. *The Lord's Prayer; The Beatitudes*. Translated by Hilda C. Graef. Mahwah, NY: Paulist Press, 1954. These sermons underscore how important "the obedience of faith" was to these early Christian preachers. They did not separate believing and obeying. They considered them a seamless whole.

Chrysostom, John. *On Marriage and Family Life*. Translated by Catherine P. Roth and David Anderson. Crestwood, NY: St. Vladimir's Seminary Press, 1986.

———. *On Wealth and Poverty*. Translated by Catherine P. Roth. Crestwood, NY: St. Vladimir's Seminary Press, 1981. Chrysostom, actually a nickname, means "golden mouth." These two collections of sermons illustrate why he earned that reputation.

Augustine. *Essential Sermons*. Edited by Boniface Ramsey. Translated by Edmund Hill, OP. Hyde Park, NY: New City Press, 2007. Here is Augustine as preacher. His theology is laced throughout these sermons. Still, the sermons are human, simple, and accessible.

Yarnold, Edward, ed. *The Awe-Inspiring Rites of Initiation: The Origins of the R.C.I.A.* 2nd ed. Edinburgh: T&T Clark, 1994. Yarnold has compiled a number of catechetical sermons from the great bishops of the fourth century. They illustrate how catechetical sermons formed people in the faith. See also John Chrysostom, *Baptismal Instructions*, trans. Paul W. Harkins (Mahway, NJ: Paulist Press, 1963); and Augustine, *The First Catechetical Instruction*, trans. Rev. Joseph P. Christopher (Mahwah, NJ: Paulist Press, 1946). These Chrysostom and Augustine collections only add to Yarnold's rich resource.

Secondary Sources

Greco-Roman Background

There is no end to the sources on the Greco-Roman background to the emergence of Christianity. Mary Beard's *SPQR* is a good place to start. Beard is a master writer. She offers a vivid account of the history of ancient Rome to the year AD 211. She mentions Christianity only on occasion, but each reference is telling. Everett Ferguson has encyclopedic knowledge of the ancient world. His *Backgrounds of Early Christianity* covers most of what a student would want to know about the ancient world: transportation and travel, common occupations, the Roman military, city life, coinage, civic rituals, mystery cults, and so much more. Gregory Aldrete's *Daily Life in the Roman City* describes in detail three ancient cities, which will make most readers glad they live in modern ones. Luke Timothy Johnson explores how Christianity engaged Roman culture, and Robert Louis Wilken shows how several elite Roman intellectuals—Celsus and Galen, for example—understood and criticized Christianity. In my mind no one knows this period better than Peter Brown. He has written many books on Christianity in the ancient world. The one listed here is short, and it includes visuals.

Beard, Mary. *SPQR: A History of Ancient Rome*. New York: Liveright Publishing, 2015.

Ferguson, Everett. *Backgrounds of Early Christianity*. 3rd ed. Grand Rapids: Eerdmans, 2003.

Aldrete, Gregory S. *Daily Life in the Roman City: Rome, Pompeii, and Ostia*. Norman: University of Oklahoma Press, 2008.

Johnson, Luke Timothy. *Among the Gentiles: Greco-Roman Religion and Christianity*. New Haven: Yale University Press, 2009.

Wilken, Robert Louis. *The Christians as the Romans Saw Them*. New Haven: Yale University Press, 1984.

Brown, Peter. *The World of Late Antiquity: A.D. 150–750*. New York: Norton, 1971.

Historical Introductions

For some two hundred years historians have mined primary sources to discover why and how Christianity took root, grew, and flourished in the ancient world, against all odds. As historians, they cannot appeal to God's providence or the work of the Holy Spirit to make their case. Jan Bremmer sums up the arguments of three major thinkers: Edward Gibbon, Adolf von Harnack, and Rodney Stark. Ramsey MacMullen, Robin Lane Fox, and Stephen Benko add their own useful perspectives. Larry Hurtado's books are the most recent and accessible. Both Henry Chadwick and W. H. C. Frend have written standard texts on the period. Henry Chadwick's is the older and shorter. Frend's is exhaustive and long, but also very useful. Michael Kruger focuses exclusively on the importance of the second century. Still young, the church set a trajectory that has endured to this day.

Gibbon, Edward. *The History of the Decline and Fall of the Roman Empire.* New York: Random House, 2003.

Harnack, Adolf von. *The Mission and Expansion of Christianity in the First Three Centuries.* Translated by James Moffatt. 1908. Reprint, San Bernardino, CA: Nabu Public Domain Reprints, 2017.

Nock, A. D. *Conversion: The Old and the New in Religion from Alexander the Great to Augustine of Hippo.* Baltimore: Johns Hopkins University Press, 1933.

Bremmer, Jan. *The Rise of Christianity through the Eyes of Gibbon, Harnack and Rodney Stark.* Groningen: Barkhuis, 2010.

MacMullen, Ramsey. *Christianizing the Roman Empire, A.D. 100–400.* New Haven: Yale University Press, 1984.

Lane Fox, Robin. *Pagans and Christians.* New York: Knopf, 1987.

Benko, Stephen. *Pagan Rome and the Early Christians.* Bloomington: Indiana University Press, 1984.

Hurtado, Larry W. *Why on Earth Did Anyone Become a Christian in the First Three Centuries?* Milwaukee: Marquette University Press, 2016.

———. *Destroyer of the Gods: Early Christian Distinctiveness in the Roman World.* Waco, TX: Baylor University Press, 2016.

Frend, W. H. C. *The Rise of Christianity.* Philadelphia: Fortress, 1984.

Chadwick, Henry. *The Early Church: The Story of Emergent Christianity from the Apostolic Age to the Foundation of the Church of Rome.* New York: Penguin, 1967.

Kruger, Michael J. *Christianity at the Crossroads: How the Second Century Shaped the Future of the Church.* Downers Grove, IL: IVP Academic, 2018.

Early Christian Theology

It is no small task to sum up the theology of the early Christian period, for at least two reasons: first, because theology as a discipline was just emerging and so lacked the categories with which we are now familiar, such as the doctrine of justification; and second, because the power of the Greco-Roman world hovered menacingly in the background. The concerns of the church fathers were different from ours. They focused attention on the nature of Jesus Christ, which we tend to take for granted, and they paid less attention to questions over which we debate so vociferously, like the atonement.

J. N. D. Kelly's and Jaroslav Pelikan's books are classics. But in my mind the best is Robert Louis Wilken's. I have used it in my early Christianity senior seminar. Students rave about it. Christopher Hall has written a series of useful books about the church fathers—how they read Scripture, how they worshiped, and how they thought theologically. His aim is to help readers think *with* the church fathers rather than *about* them. Hans von Campenhausen devotes a chapter each to the major church fathers, both Latin (e.g., Cyprian and Tertullian) and Greek (e.g., Basil and Nyssa). Kavin Rowe's reading of the Acts of the Apostles, the Stoics, and early church fathers demonstrates how unique the Christian movement was in the ancient world. Stoics and Christians might have shared some things in common, but their worldviews were essentially different.

Kelly, J. N. D. *Early Christian Doctrines*. Rev. ed. San Francisco: HarperOne, 1978.

Pelikan, Jaroslav. *The Christian Tradition: A History of the Development of Doctrine*. Vol. 1, *The Emergence of the Catholic Tradition*. Chicago: University of Chicago Press, 1971.

Wilken, Robert Louis. *The Spirit of Early Christian Thought: Seeking the Face of God*. New Haven: Yale University Press, 2003.

Hall, Christopher A. *Learning Theology with the Church Fathers*. Downers Grove, IL: IVP Academic, 2002.

Campenhausen, Hans von. *The Fathers of the Latin Church*. New York: Pantheon, 1960.

Campenhausen, Hans von. *The Fathers of the Greek Church*. New York: Pantheon, 1955.

Rowe, C. Kavin. *One True Life: The Stoics and Early Christians as Rival Traditions*. New Haven: Yale University Press, 2016.

Authority

The foundation of authority in early Christianity was in fact Jesus, which posed all kinds of problems, then as now, chief among them the kind of authority he exercised. He was no Augustus or Socrates or Alexander the Great. His example redefined the nature of authority, for this was God come as a humble human being. Not all Christians back then followed his example, any more than Christians today do. These writings address the question of authority as it applied to church office (bishop), the role of creeds, and the emergence of the canon.

Everett Ferguson's short book explores the origin and use of the "rule of faith." Larry Hurtado shows how the discoveries of various artifacts—say, the codex—have contributed a different kind of evidence to our understanding of early Christian authority. Richard Bauckham defends the reliability of eyewitness testimony, especially in the writing of the Gospels. Bruce Metzger has written the standard book on the process of canonization, and Peter Williams and Michael Kruger have added to and updated his arguments. These texts prove how early in the story of Christianity various books, now canonical, became authoritative, though unofficially. Bart Ehrman suggests that early Christianity produced a wide variety of texts. He argues that there is no reason why only some (the texts that "won") should be privileged over, say, Gnostic texts (the texts that "lost"). Luke Timothy Johnson disagrees, as his book demonstrates. Birger Pearson catalogues and describes the various Gnostic texts and movements. The last four authors or editors—Hans von Campenhausen, Andrea Sterk, Anthony Meredith, and Everett Ferguson—focus on church office and leadership in the early Christian period. Meredith and Sterk in particular offer moving portraits of the skillful and sacrificial leadership of the famous monk-bishops of the fourth century, among them John Chrysostom and Basil of Caesarea. I will address the role of women in Christianity under the category of Christian Life in the World.

Ferguson, Everett. *The Rule of Faith: A Guide.* Eugene, OR: Cascade, 2015.

Hurtado, Larry W. *The Earliest Christian Artifacts: Manuscripts and Christian Origins.* Grand Rapids: Eerdmans, 2006.

Bauckham, Richard. *Jesus and the Eyewitnesses: The Gospels as Eyewitness Testimony.* Grand Rapids: Eerdmans, 2006.

Metzger, Bruce. *The Canon of the New Testament: Its Origins, Development, and Significance.* Oxford: Clarendon, 1987.

Williams, Peter J. *Can We Trust the Gospels?* Wheaton, IL: Crossway, 2018.

Kruger, Michael J. *The Question of Canon: Challenging the Status Quo in the New Testament Debate.* Downers Grove, IL: IVP Academic, 2013.

Ehrman, Bart D. *Lost Christianities: The Battles for Scripture and the Faiths We Never Knew.* New York: Oxford University Press, 2003.

Johnson, Luke Timothy. *The Real Jesus: The Misguided Quest for the Historical Jesus and the Truth of the Traditional Gospels.* San Francisco: HarperSanFrancisco, 1996.

Pearson, Birger A. *Ancient Gnosticism: Traditions and Literature.* Minneapolis: Fortress, 2007.

Campenhausen, Hans von. *Ecclesiastical Authority and Spiritual Power in the Church of the First Three Centuries.* Translated by J. A. Baker. Stanford, CA: Stanford University Press, 1969.

Sterk, Andrea. *Renouncing the World Yet Leading the Church: The Monk-Bishop in Late Antiquity.* Cambridge, MA: Harvard University Press, 2004.

Meredith, Anthony. *The Cappadocians.* Crestwood, NY: St. Vladimir's Seminary Press, 1995.

Ferguson, Everett, ed. *Church, Ministry, and Organization in the Early Church Era.* New York: Garland, 1993.

Worship

How Christians worshiped set them apart in the ancient world. It started with the role of the pastor. David Dunn-Wilson explores how pastors preached, John O'Keefe and R. R. Reno how they interpreted Scripture, and Carl Volz how they shepherded the flock. Andrew Mc-Gowan has written the best introduction to early Christian worship. Harry Gamble shows just how important and useful the biblical text was. Finally, Paul Bradshaw, a prolific scholar of early Christian liturgy, explores the emergence of Christian liturgy; Roy Hammerling concentrates on one aspect of that liturgy, the use of the Lord's Prayer; and John Smith focuses on early Christian music.

Dunn-Wilson, David. *A Mirror for the Church: Preaching in the First Five Centuries.* Grand Rapids: Eerdmans, 2005.

O'Keefe, John J., and R. R. Reno. *Sanctified Vision: An Introduction to Early Christian Interpretation of the Bible.* Baltimore: Johns Hopkins University Press, 2005.

Volz, Carl A. *Pastoral Life and Practice in the Early Church*. Minneapolis: Augsburg, 1990.

McGowan, Andrew B. *Ancient Christian Worship*. Grand Rapids: Baker Academic, 2014.

Hall, Christopher A. *Worshiping with the Church Fathers*. Downers Grove, IL: IVP Academic, 2009.

Bradshaw, Paul F. *Reconstructing Early Christian Worship*. London: SPCK, 2009.

Gamble, Harry Y. *Books and Readers in the Early Christian Church: A History of Christian Texts*. New Haven: Yale University Press, 1995.

Hammerling, Roy. *The Lord's Prayer in the Early Church*. New York: Macmillan, 2010.

Smith, John Arthur. *Music in Ancient Judaism and Early Christianity*. Burlington, VT: Ashgate, 2011.

Christian Life in the World

There has been a proliferation of scholarship in this area, largely because sociologists have provided new tools to discover how Christians lived "on the ground." Michael Green has written the standard text on early Christian evangelism. Alan Kreider demonstrates how the slow, steady, and deliberate growth of the church occurred because Christians refused to accommodate to Rome, and Rowan Greer how the impact of Christianity ("mended lives") was the result of the Christian view of reality ("broken lights"). Wayne Meeks has written on the urban and ethical impact of Christianity in the ancient world. Rodney Stark has contributed to the field by showing the importance of statistics— "counting," as he puts it—in tracing the growth and influence of Christianity in the Roman world. Helen Rhee and Peter Brown explore the Christian impact on social class and wealth, Michael Gehring and Joseph Hellerman on the influence of early house churches, and Cornelia Horn and John Martens as well as Odd Magne Bakke on family life. The subject of women in early Christianity is complex. Generally, the Christian movement was better for women than other ancient religions (with the possible exception of mystery cults). Though attaining spiritual equality, as Patricia Ranft points out, women did not necessarily see this equality play out in ordinary life. Elizabeth Clark's book explores this larger question. Gary Ferngren shows how influential the early Christian movement was on ancient health care. Such practical ministry provides illustrations of the treasure chest of good works that David Batson outlines.

Green, Michael. *Evangelism in the Early Church*. Grand Rapids: Eerdmans, 1970.

Kreider, Alan. *The Patient Ferment of the Early Church: The Improbable Rise of Christianity in the Roman Empire*. Grand Rapids: Baker Academic, 2016.

Greer, Rowan A. *Broken Lights and Mended Lives: Theology and Common Life in the Early Church*. University Park: Pennsylvania State University Press, 1986.

Meeks, Wayne A. *The First Urban Christians: The Social World of the Apostle Paul*. New Haven: Yale University Press, 1983.

———. *The Origins of Christian Morality: The First Two Centuries*. New Haven: Yale University Press, 1993.

Stark, Rodney. *The Rise of Christianity*. Princeton: Princeton University Press, 1996.

———. *Cities of God: The Real Story of How Christianity Became an Urban Movement and Conquered Rome*. San Francisco: HarperCollins, 2006.

Bryan, Christopher. *Render to Caesar: Jesus, the Early Church, and the Roman Superpower*. New York: Oxford University Press, 2005.

Rhee, Helen. *Loving the Poor, Saving the Rich: Wealth, Poverty, and Early Christian Formation*. Grand Rapids: Baker Academic, 2012.

Brown, Peter. *Through the Eye of the Needle*. Princeton: Princeton University Press, 2012.

Gehring, Roger W. *House Church and Mission: The Importance of Household Structures in Early Christianity*. Peabody, MA: Hendrickson, 2004.

Hellerman, Joseph H. *The Ancient Church as Family*. Minneapolis: Fortress, 2001.

Horn, Cornelia B., and John W. Martens. *"Let the Children Come to Me": Childhood and Children in Early Christianity*. Washington, DC: Catholic University of America Press, 2008.

Bakke, Odd Magne. *When Children Became People: The Birth of Childhood in Early Christianity*. Minneapolis: Fortress, 2005.

Clark, Elizabeth A. *Women in Early Christianity*. Wilmington, DE: Michael Glazier, 1983.

Ranft, Patricia. *Women and Spiritual Equality in the Christian Tradition*. New York: St. Martin's Press, 1998.

Batson, David. *The Treasure Chest of the Early Christians: Faith, Care, and Community from the Apostolic Age to Constantine the Great*. Grand Rapids: Eerdmans, 2001.

Ferngren, Gary B. *Medicine and Health Care in Early Christianity*. Baltimore: Johns Hopkins University Press, 2009.

Catechumenate

Christian leaders had to create some kind of bridge to move seekers from the world of Greco-Roman religion to the world of Christianity. This was no easy step. Edward Yarnold explains in detail the formation of the early Christian catechumenate and shows how Catholics have appropriated early Christian practice for the modern church. Michel Dujarier tells the story of how the catechumenate was established and flourished in the ancient world, and Alan Kreider how it changed during the early stages of Christendom. William Harmless shows how Augustine shaped it for the church in North Africa.

Yarnold, Edward, ed. *The Awe-Inspiring Rites of Initiation: The Origins of the R.C.I.A.* 2nd ed. Edinburgh: T&T Clark, 1994.

Dujarier, Michel. *A History of the Catechumenate: The First Six Centuries*. Translated by Edward J. Hassl. New York: Sadlier, 1979.

Kreider, Alan. *The Change of Conversion and the Origin of Christendom*. Eugene, OR: Wipf & Stock, 1999.

Harmless, William. *Augustine and the Catechumenate*. Collegeville, MN: Liturgical Press, 1995.

Notes

Chapter 1 Then and Now

1. Adolf von Harnack devoted a chapter in his book on early Christianity to the linguistic and historical origin of "The Third Race." See *The Mission and Expansion of Christianity in the First Three Centuries*, trans. James Moffatt (1908; repr., San Bernardino, CA: Nabu Public Domains Reprints, 2017), 2:365–81. Both Tertullian and Clement of Alexandria used the phrase, or one similar to it.

2. The language of "third way" has recently surfaced to describe a "middle way" between two extremes—say, when addressing divisive issues like abortion or gay rights. The problem in this case is that this third, or middle, way is perceived as being a compromise, intended somehow to please both sides if they would only be willing to "just all get along." I am not in any way identifying the early Christian Third Way with this modern "middle way." It was not about compromise but about faithful witness to Jesus as the way *to* life and as the way *of* life.

3. *The So-Called Letter to Diognetus* 2.1, in Richardson, *ECF*, 213–14.

4. "The traditional religion of Rome was significantly different from religion as we usually understand it now. So much modern religious vocabulary—including the word 'religion', as well as 'pontiff'—is borrowed from Latin that it tends to obscure some of the major differences between ancient Roman religion and our own. In Rome there was no doctrine as such, no holy book and hardly even what we would call a belief system. Romans *knew* the gods existed; they did not *believe* in them in the internalized sense familiar from most modern world religions. Nor was ancient Roman religion particularly concerned with personal salvation or morality. Instead it mainly focused on the performance of rituals that were intended to keep the relationship between Rome and the gods in good order, and so ensure Roman success and prosperity. . . . In general, it was a religion of doing, not believing." Mary Beard, *SPQR: A History of Ancient Rome* (New York: Liveright Publishing, 2015), 102–3.

5. *The So-Called Letter to Diognetus* 5.1–3, in Richardson, *ECF*, 216.

6. *The So-Called Letter to Diognetus* 5.1–3; 5.5–6; 6.1–2, in Richardson, *ECF*, 216–17.

7. Historians have been debating for nearly two centuries why the early Christian movement succeeded against all odds. Edward Gibbon was the first to make an argument. His monumental *The History of the Decline and Fall of the Roman Empire* laid the theoretical foundation, and early twentieth-century historians like Adolf von Harnack and A. D. Nock

built upon it. Many other historians have contributed their own theories. See Edward Gibbon, *The History of the Decline and Fall of the Roman Empire* (New York: Random House, 2003); Harnack, *The Mission and Expansion of Christianity*; A. D. Nock, *Conversion: The Old and the New in Religion from Alexander the Great to Augustine of Hippo* (Baltimore: Johns Hopkins University Press, 1933), 193–253; Ramsey MacMullen, *Christianizing the Roman Empire, A.D. 100–400* (New Haven: Yale University Press, 1984); Robin Lane Fox, *Pagans and Christians* (New York: Knopf, 1987); E. Glenn Hinson, *The Evangelization of the Roman Empire: Identity and Adaptability* (Macon, GA: Mercer University Press, 1981); Wayne A. Meeks, *The First Urban Christians: The Social World of the Apostle Paul* (New Haven: Yale University Press, 1983); Rodney Stark, *The Rise of Christianity* (Princeton: Princeton University Press, 1996); and Stark, *Cities of God: The Real Story of How Christianity Became an Urban Movement and Conquered Rome* (San Francisco: HarperSanFrancisco, 2006). For a useful summary of the main arguments, see Jan Bremmer, *The Rise of Christianity through the Eyes of Gibbon, Harnack and Rodney Stark* (Groningen, The Netherlands: Barkhuis, 2010), 73.

8. Two relatively recent books, well researched and argued, explore how message and method were seamlessly woven together. See Alan Kreider, *The Patience Ferment of the Early Church: The Improbable Rise of Christianity in the Roman Empire* (Grand Rapids: Baker Academic, 2016); and Rowan A. Greer, *Broken Lights and Mended Lives: Theology and Common Life in the Early Church* (University Park: Pennsylvania State University Press, 1986).

9. The best we can do is estimate. Adolf von Harnack was the first to calculate numbers. He identified the specific cities and towns to which Christianity spread by the year 300 and even tried to count actual numbers of churches. More recently social historians have developed and employed new techniques to count more accurately. For example, they read inscriptions on tombs to see how many make mention, however obliquely, of Christian belief. See Harnack, *The Mission and Expansion of Christianity*; and Rodney Stark, *The Cities of God*.

10. Andrew Walls has identified this adaptive capacity as the "indigenizing" principle of Christianity. He argues that the incarnation itself set the pattern, for God "indigenized" himself by becoming human, though, as Christians believe, he did not in the process become anything less or other than what he already was. See Andrew F. Walls, *The Missionary Movement in Christian History: Studies in the Transmission of Faith* (Maryknoll, NY: Orbis, 1996); see also Lamin Sanneh, *Translating the Message: The Missionary Impact on Culture* (Maryknoll, NY: Orbis, 2004).

11. Alexis de Tocqueville, *Democracy in America*, ed. J. P. Mayer, trans. George Lawrence (New York: Anchor, 1969), 294.

12. Tocqueville, *Democracy in America*, 294.

13. Abraham Lincoln used the phrase in a speech before the New Jersey Statehouse on February 21, 1861. Paul Johnson reflects on this in his essay "The Almost-Chosen People," *First Things*, June 2006, https://www.firstthings.com/article/2006/06/an-almost-chosen-people.

14. G. K. Chesterton, *What I Saw in America*, in *The Collected Works of G. K. Chesterton*, vol. 21 (San Francisco: Ignatius, 1990), 45. See Sidney Mead, "The 'Nation with the Soul of a Church,'" *Church History* 36, no. 3 (September 1967): 262–83.

15. I just discovered that Rod Dreher uses the phrase "cultural memory" too, though I had written this chapter before I read his book. Rod Dreher, *The Benedict Option: A Strategy for Christians in a Post-Christian Nation* (New York: Random House, 2017).

16. David E. Campbell and Robert D. Putnam, *American Grace: How Religion Divides and Unites Us* (New York: Simon & Schuster, 2010). The authors use massive data gathered from the Faith Matters Survey, which was administered in 2005 and again in 2007. That

number, however, is declining. In fact, since 1993 every religious group in America (including mainline Protestant, black Protestant, Roman Catholic, evangelical, and Jewish) has declined to some degree. But the percentage of those who claim no religion at all has risen from 5 percent of the population in 1973 to 23 percent in 2018, according to the massive General Social Survey, a poll that has been conducted biannually for the past forty-six years. See Ryan P. Burge, "Evangelicals Show No Decline, Despite Trump and Nones," *Christianity Today*, March 21, 2019, https://www.christianitytoday.com/news/2019/march/evangelical -nones-mainline-us-general-social-survey-gss.html.

17. John Fea explores the historical roots of the assumption that America is a Christian nation. He does not argue that American history proves it. He suggests instead that it is our *interpretation* of American history that affirms it, however much that interpretation actually plays loose with the facts. See John Fea, *Was America Founded as a Christian Nation? A Historical Introduction* (Louisville: Westminster John Knox, 2011).

18. Will Herberg called the religion of America in the 1950s "the American way of life." See *Protestant-Catholic-Jew: An Essay in American Religious Sociology* (1960; repr., Chicago: University of Chicago Press, 1983).

19. Recent scholarly studies indicate that nominal Christians are declining as a percentage of the population. They are either leaving Christianity altogether or switching to churches that proclaim the Bible as the Word of God, demonstrate greater vitality, and demand more from their members. "Active Christians" are holding their own and, if anything, increasing their "market share" among those who self-identify as Christian. In short, marginal or nominal Christians are shrinking as an aggregate. It appears that being Christian in America is becoming increasingly an "all or nothing" proposition. See Landon Schnabel and Sean Bock, "The Persistent and Exceptional Intensity of American Religion: A Response to Recent Research," *Sociological Science* 4 (November 2017): 686–700.

20. *American Grace* is not the only source for these statistical trends. In addition to the Faith Matters Survey, which Putnam and Campbell conducted and reported on in *American Grace*, there are other equally reliable sources. Pew's Religious Landscape Survey gathered data from thirty-five thousand respondents, and Gallup has conducted its own surveys, too. Perhaps the largest set of data comes from the General Social Survey, which began in 1972 and has continued to this day. The data from these different instruments indicate that Christianity is fading in America, though slowly and unevenly. In 2007, for example, about 16 percent of Americans claimed no religious affiliation, according to the Pew data; in 2015 it was 23 percent. The most religious person in America, statistically speaking, is an older black woman living in the South; the least religious is a young white male living on one of the coasts. Mainline Protestants have suffered the biggest losses. Catholics have, too, except that Catholics have welcomed millions of new immigrants into the fold, mostly from Latin America. Evangelicals have become the largest Christian group in America; moreover, evangelicals demonstrate the highest levels of participation. In 1972, 17.1 percent of Americans identified themselves as evangelical; by 2014 that percentage had grown to 22.7 percent (the peak year, statistically speaking, was 1993, when about 29 percent of the population claimed to be evangelical). Generally speaking, nearly 25 percent of the population are what Ed Stetzer calls "cultural Christians"; another 25 percent "church members," though somewhat nominal; a final 25 percent committed or "convictional" Christians. The last 25 percent would claim no Christian faith at all. See Ed Stetzer, "The State of the Church in America: When Numbers Point to a New Reality, Part 1," http://www.christianitytoday.com/edstetzer/2016 /september/state-of-american-church-when-numbers-point-to-new-reality.html.

21. See George M. Marsden, *The Soul of the American University* (New York: Oxford University Press, 1994).

22. In 1959 T. F. Torrance published the first of two volumes of a work entitled *Conflict and Agreement in the Church* (London: Lutterworth, 1959–60). In it he argued that the "great shame and disorder of the church is that she has collaborated with the disorder of the world and clothed herself with so many of its forms and fashions that so often she is committed to the world and too compromised with it to be able to deliver the revolutionary Word of the Gospel with conviction and power" (1:223). See a summary in Daniel J. Cameron, "Thomas Forsyth Torrance: Ecumenical Theologian," *Christian History*, December 2, 2017, http://www.christianitytoday.com/history/2017/december/thomas-forsyth-tf-torrance.html.

23. A recent Barna report demonstrated that this process of secularization is not occurring at a uniform rate across the country. For example, the twenty most churched cities in America are all Southern and Midwestern, with the exception of Salt Lake City. The twenty most unchurched cities (defined as no participation in organized religious activity over the past six months) are all on the two coasts and in the Southwest, as are the twenty most dechurched cities (defined as no participation in organized religious activity over the past six months after a period of greater participation). People who move from, say, Birmingham to San Francisco would attest to this religious unevenness. See Barna Group, "Church Attendance Trends around the Country," May 26, 2017, https://www.barna.com/themes/barna-cities.

24. Columnist Karl Vaters outlines the assumptions that Christians can no longer make in a post-Christian America, which includes biblical literacy, regular church attendance, consistent giving, predictable political alignment, a recognition of the need for salvation, and so forth. See Karl Vaters, "8 Assumptions Pastors Can't Make in a Post-Christian Culture," *Pivot* (blog), *Christianity Today*, December 6, 2017, https://www.christianitytoday.com/karl-vaters/2017/december/8-assumptions-pastors-cant-make-post-christian-culture.html.

25. In a recent *Atlantic Monthly* article, two modern historians, Graham Allison and Niall Ferguson, use the phrase "applied history" to suggest that history itself provides useful information and analogues that might illumine the present situation and help modern presidents (the very select group to whom they wrote the article) make better decisions. They lament how ignorant of the past most modern leaders, including presidents, are and have been for a long time. I would only add that most modern Christians are ignorant of the past, too. See Graham Allison and Niall Ferguson, "Don't Know Much about History," *Atlantic Monthly*, September 2016, 28–29.

26. Cardinal Ratzinger, who became Pope Benedict XVI, recognized the value of learning from other periods of history but also warned against idealizing them. "Whereas to know how things were at that [previous] time is of invaluable help to us in coping with the problems of our own time, it cannot be simply the standards by which reform is measured. . . . This archaism has often made us close our eyes to the good things which have been evolved in later developments and has caused us to set the taste of one period up on a pedestal." Quoted in Uwe Michael Lang, *Turning towards the Lord: Orientation in Liturgical Prayer* (San Francisco: Ignatius, 2009), 97.

27. A century ago the literary critic and historian Van Wyck Brooks coined the phrase "a usable past" to capture what I have in mind here. He advocated for a critical appraisal of history, not an idealization of it. We can learn from the past, he wrote, but only if we study it carefully. Van Wyck Brooks, "On Creating a Usable Past," *Dial*, April 11, 1918, 337–41.

Chapter 2 Old World and New World

1. See Robert Louis Wilken, "Pliny: A Roman Gentleman," *The Christians as the Romans Saw Them* (New Haven: Yale University Press, 1984), 1–30.

2. Tertullian, *To the Nations* 3.4, in *ANF* 3:111.

3. Pliny the Younger, *Epistles* 10.96, in J. Stevenson, ed., *A New Eusebius: Documents Illustrating the History of the Church to AD 337*, rev. W. H. C. Frend (Grand Rapids: Baker Academic, 2013), 21.

4. Pliny the Younger, *Epistles* 10.96, in Stevenson, *A New Eusebius*, 21.

5. Mary Beard summarizes this concern. "All kinds of mystical movements of enlightenment might attract new worshippers to (say) the religion of Isis. But Christianity was defined entirely by a process of spiritual conversion that was utterly new. What is more, some Christians were preaching values that threatened to overturn some of the most fundamental Greco-Roman assumptions about the nature of the world and of the people within it. . . . All these factors help to explain the worries, confusion and hostility of Pliny and others like him." *SPQR: A History of Ancient Rome* (New York: Liveright Publishing, 2015), 519–20.

6. Pliny the Younger, *Epistles* 10.96, in Stevenson, *A New Eusebius*, 20–21. Recent scholarship has focused on the role martyr accounts played in the early Christian community. See, for example, Daniel Boyarin, *Dying for God: Martyrdom and the Making of Christianity and Judaism* (Stanford, CA: Stanford University Press, 1999); Judith Perkins, *The Suffering Self: Pain and Narrative Representation in the Early Christian Era* (London: Routledge, 1995); Elizabeth A. Castelli, *Martyrdom and Memory: Early Christian Culture Making* (New York: Columbia University Press, 2004); and Robin Darling Young, *In Process before the World: Martyrdom as Public Liturgy in Early Christianity* (Milwaukee: Marquette University Press, 2006).

7. Pliny the Younger, *Epistles* 10.97, in Stevenson, *A New Eusebius*, 23.

8. "The Martyrdom of St. Polycarp, Bishop of Smyrna," in Richardson, *ECF*, 151.

9. Eusebius, *Hist.*, 120.

10. Eusebius, *Hist.*, 119–22. For a scholarly edition of early martyr stories, see Herbert Musurillo, ed., *The Acts of the Christian Martyrs* (Oxford: Clarendon, 1972). Musurillo's book not only provides an English translation of every story but also includes the original ancient language source. It is an invaluable resource. Most of these early stories are short. They contain the facts, but they also provide a kind of spiritual commentary.

11. Richardson, *ECF*, 154, 155. See Gerald L. Sittser, "Witness," chap. 1 in *Water from a Deep Well: Christian Spirituality from Early Martyrs to Modern Missionaries* (Downers Grove, IL: InterVarsity, 2007).

12. Richardson, *ECF*, 153.

13. Everett Ferguson, *Backgrounds of Early Christianity*, 3rd ed. (Grand Rapids: Eerdmans, 2003), 148–300.

14. Ramsey MacMullen, *Christianizing the Roman Empire* (New Haven: Yale University Press, 1984), 16–17. See also Hugo Rahner, *Church and State in Early Christianity*, trans. Leo Donald Davis, SJ (San Francisco: Ignatius, 1992), 1–38.

15. C. Kavin Rowe, *One True Life: The Stoics and Early Christians as Rival Traditions* (New Haven: Yale University Press, 2016). See also Christopher Bryan, *Render to Caesar: Jesus, the Early Church, and the Roman Superpower* (New York: Oxford University Press, 2005), 116–17.

16. Mary Beard devotes a chapter to Augustus in her *SPQR*. She argues that he both appealed to and manipulated the old order to justify and support the dramatic changes that his reign brought about. "The point was that Augustus was cleverly adapting the traditional idioms to serve a new politics, justifying and making comprehensible a new axis of power by systematically reconfiguring an old language." *SPQR*, 369.

17. Suetonius, *Lives of the Caesars*, trans. Catharine Edwards (New York: Oxford University Press, 2000), 58.

18. "The Deeds of the Divine Augustus" (*Res Gestae Divi Augusti*), trans. Thomas Bushnell, http://classics.mit.edu/Augustus/deeds.html.

19. "The Deeds of the Divine Augustus."

20. "The Priene [Calendar] Inscription," Biblical Criticism & History Forum, posted by MrMacSun, June 11, 2017, http://earlywritings.com/forum/viewtopic.php?f=3&t=325 5&p=71360&hilit=priene#p71360.

21. S. R. F. Price, "Rituals and Power," in *Paul and Empire: Religion and Power in Roman Imperial Society*, ed. Richard A. Horsley (Harrisburg, PA: Trinity Press International, 1997), 47–71.

22. James R. Edwards, *The Gospel according to Luke* (Grand Rapids: Eerdmans, 2015), 66–67.

23. Beard, "The Transformations of Augustus," chap. 9 in *SPQR*.

24. Edwards, *Luke*, 68–70.

25. Richard Bauckham has written extensively on the role of eyewitness testimony in telling the story of Jesus.

> I suggest that we need to recover the sense in which the Gospels are testimony. This does not mean that they are testimony *rather than* history. It means that the kind of historiography they are is testimony. An irreducible feature of testimony as a form of human utterance is that it asks to be trusted. This need not mean that it asks to be trusted uncritically, but it does mean that the testimony should not be treated as credible only to the extent that it can be independently verified. There can be good reasons for trusting or distrusting a witness, but these are precisely reasons for trusting or distrusting. Trusting testimony is not an irrational act of faith that leaves critical rationality aside; it is, on the contrary, the rationally appropriate way of responding to authentic testimony. Gospels understood as testimony are the entirely appropriate means of access to the historical reality of Jesus. (*Jesus and the Eyewitnesses: The Gospels as Eyewitness Testimony* [Grand Rapids: Eerdmans, 2006], 5)

26. According to Isaiah, even Cyrus the Persian played a kind of messianic role, because he wielded his substantial earthly power to allow exiles to return to their Jewish homeland and start over. This was the kind of work Messiahs were supposed to do.

27. Again, Richard Bauckham spells out the implications of this kind of testimony. "Eyewitness testimony offers us inside knowledge from involved participants. It also offers us engaged interpretation, for in testimony fact and meaning coinhere, and witnesses who give testimony do so with the conviction of significance that requires to be told. Witnesses of truly significant events speak out of their own ongoing attempts to understand it. . . . The faithful witness, in this sense, is not merely accurate but faithful to the meaning and demands of what is attested. And in the most truly significant cases this is where bearing witness becomes a costly commitment of life." *Jesus and the Eyewitnesses*, 505.

28. "How you loved us, O good Father, who spared not even your only Son, but gave him up for us evil-doers! How you loved us, for whose sake he who deemed it no robbery to be your equal was made subservient even to the point of dying on the cross! Alone of all, he was free among the dead, for he had power to lay down his life and power to retrieve it. For our sake he stood to you as both victor and victim, and victor because victim; for us he stood to you as priest and sacrifice, and priest because sacrifice, making us your children instead of your servants by being born of you in order to serve us." Augustine, *Confessions*, trans. Maria Boulding, OSB (Hyde Park, NY: New City Press, 1997), 282–83.

29. N. T. Wright has written extensively about the victory of Christ in his death and resurrection. He aims to demonstrate that it is not simply about saving us from sin and securing a place in heaven. It is about God's plan to renew and restore the entire created order. For an

introduction to his argument, see *Simply Jesus: A New Vision of Who He Was, What He Did, and Why He Matters* (San Francisco: HarperOne, 2011). For a more extensive work, see *How God Became King: The Forgotten Story of the Gospels* (San Francisco: HarperOne, 2016).

30. Larry Hurtado has devoted his entire career to argue that the undeniable fact of Jesus' death makes the invention of Jesus as the resurrected Lord highly unlikely. If his death had the last word, the disciples would have been incapable of inventing such a tale. See, for example, Larry W. Hurtado, *Lord Jesus Christ: Devotion to Jesus in Earliest Christianity* (Grand Rapids: Eerdmans, 2003).

31. Robert Louis Wilken, *The Christians as the Romans Saw Them* (New Haven: Yale University Press, 1984), 126–63. Augustine devotes many pages to Porphyry in *The City of God*, trans. Marcus Dods (Peabody, MA: Hendrickson, 2017), 297–309.

32. Quoted in Wilken, *The Christians*, 160.

33. Quoted in Wilken, *The Christians*, 162–63. Stephen Benko summarizes: "An irreconcilable difference existed between pagans and Christians on this issue. The pagan took the position that matters pertaining to the divine mystery were obscure and so should be left open to debate. The Christian, however, was convinced that he was in possession of the truth, because Jesus Christ embodied the ultimate revelation about God." *Pagan Rome and the Early Christians* (Bloomington: Indiana University Press, 1984), 59.

34. Jaroslav Pelikan, *Jesus through the Centuries: His Place in the History of Culture* (New Haven: Yale University Press, 1999).

35. Stephen Prothero, *American Jesus: How the Son of God Became a National Icon* (New York: Farrar, Straus & Giroux, 2004). Prothero explores the many versions of Jesus that have won a following in American society. Among them are Jesus as enlightened sage, Jesus as sweet savior, Jesus as manly redeemer, and Jesus as superstar.

36. "These various insights and images attest to one overarching conviction: that the only true power, by which all others—and in all their various forms—must be made critically accountable, is the name, person, and work of Jesus. Powers and authorities stand in no less need of the redeeming and transforming word of the gospel than do the poor, needy and outcast. The gospel of Jesus is the sole authority of the church, to which the resurrected Jesus in this final commandment of the Gospel and the first commandment in the book of Acts enjoins believers." James R. Edwards provides an excellent guide to the various "powers" that Jesus and the apostles faced during their earthly life and ministry. He demonstrates that the New Testament views power very differently. James R. Edwards, "'Public Theology' in Luke and Acts: The Witness of the Gospel to Powers and Authorities," *New Testament Studies* 62, no. 2 (April 2016): 251–52.

37. C. Kavin Rowe writes in his noteworthy book on Acts, "The universal Lordship of God in Jesus leads neither to an apologia to (or for) Rome nor to an anti-Roman polemic. It is simply, but really a different way." *World Upside Down: Reading Acts in the Graeco-Roman Age* (New York: Oxford University Press, 2009), 136.

Chapter 3 Fulfillment

1. Quoted in Robert Louis Wilken, *The Christians as the Romans Saw Them* (New Haven: Yale University Press, 1984), 115.

2. "The Christians had to prove that they were not the upstart superstition that traditionalist members of the society were bound to see in them. For both internal and external reasons, then, it was essential that they find ways to incorporate Israel's story into their own." Wayne A. Meeks, *The Origins of Christian Morality: The First Two Centuries* (New Haven: Yale University Press, 1993), 208.

3. James D. G. Dunn, *The Partings of the Ways: Between Christianity and Judaism and Their Significance for the Character of Christianity* (London: SCM, 1991); and Hershel Shanks, ed., *Christianity and Rabbinic Judaism: A Parallel History of Their Origins and Early Development*, 2nd ed. (Washington, DC: Biblical Archaeological Society, 2011). Early Christians might have parted ways with Judaism, but they claimed to be returning to the ancient faith of Israel.

4. Ignatius of Antioch, *To the Philadelphians* 6, in *ANF* 1:82.

5. *The Epistle of Polycarp to the Philippians*, in *ANF* 1:33–36. By the middle of the second century, twenty-two out of the twenty-seven books of the New Testament had become functionally authoritative.

6. We run into difficulty here in the use of terms. Today scholars refer to the sacred Scriptures of the Jews as the Hebrew Bible. That Bible was translated into Greek before the Christian movement began; this Greek translation is called the Septuagint. Christians adopted the Septuagint as their own, calling it the Old Testament. They believed there was justification in using the term "Old Testament" because Jeremiah announced that God would visit his people and establish a "new covenant" with them, transforming them from within and writing the law on their hearts. Early on, therefore, Christians referred to the apostolic writings as the New Testament and to the Hebrew Bible (the version they used was the Septuagint) as the Old Testament. I will defer to the choice of these early Christians in the language I use.

7. For sources on Marcion, his life and teachings, see Adolf von Harnack, *Marcion: The Gospel of the Alien God* (Durham, NC: Labyrinth Press, 1990); Joseph R. Hoffman, *Marcion, on the Restitution of Christianity: An Essay on the Development of Radical Paulinist Theology in the Second Century* (Chico, CA: Scholars Press, 1984); E. C. Blackman, *Marcion and His Influence* (London: SPCK, 1948); and Alister E. McGrath, *Heresy: A History of Defending the Truth* (New York: HarperOne, 2009).

8. "Marcion cut the bond between the law and the gospel, rejected the Old Testament, attributed it to another God, proclaimed Jesus Christ as the son of an alien God, and denied the birth of Christ and the genuineness of his flesh. No doubt Paul would have turned away in horror from this blasphemous teacher and would have delivered him up to Satan; and certainly he would never have considered even remotely the question whether he himself was not responsible with his own teachings, for these earthshaking errors of Marcion." Harnack, *Marcion*, 124.

9. Tertullian, *Against Marcion* 1.22 (Pickerington, OH: Beloved Publishing, 2014), 30.

10. "Marcion's thinking is superficial; to the deepest things in religion he is insensitive. He is the slave of dualistic presuppositions, seeing everything antithetically, incapable of perceiving the subtleties which are the very essence of human experience and which cannot be pressed into a rigid classification, dualistic or otherwise. His temperament fitted him to be an organizer and a textual critic, but not to be a prophet or pastor or comforter of sin-sick souls." Blackman, *Marcion and His Influence*, 106.

11. Tertullian, *Against Marcion* 4.43, p. 252.

12. Augustine, *The First Catechetical Instruction*, trans. Rev. Joseph P. Christopher (Mahwah, NJ: Paulist Press, 1946), 23.

13. Eusebius spelled out the differences among universally *accepted* books (he called these the "recognized books"), universally *rejected* books (e.g., the Gospel of Thomas), and *disputed* books. The disputed books, he claimed, were familiar to the churches, clearly orthodox and valuable, and widely used, though not necessarily worthy of canonization. Not so the rejected books. "To none of these has any churchman of any generation ever seen fit to refer in his writings. Again, nothing could be farther from apostolic usage than

the type of phraseology employed, while the ideas and implications of their contents are so irreconcilable with true orthodoxy that they stand revealed as the forgeries of heretics." They must therefore be "thrown out as impious and beyond the pale" (Eusebius, *Hist*. 3.25, p. 89). He concludes, "In these pages I have set down all the facts that have come to my knowledge regarding the apostles and the apostolic period; the sacred writings they have left us; the books which though disputed are nevertheless constantly used in very many churches; those that are unmistakingly spurious and foreign to apostolic orthodoxy" (*Hist*. 3.31, p. 94).

14. Eusebius, *Hist*. 3.24, p. 88. Eusebius claimed that the apostle John focused on the divinity of Christ, which evidenced the work of the Holy Spirit.

15. C. E. Hill traces historical evidence to the early part of the second century that proves the church considered all four Gospels as functionally canonical very shortly after they were written. See C. E. Hill, *Who Chose the Gospels? Probing the Great Gospel Conspiracy* (New York: Oxford University Press, 2010). See also Birger Gerhardsson, *The Reliability of the Gospel Tradition* (Grand Rapids: Baker Academic, 2001); and L. M. McDonald and J. A. Sanders, eds., *The Canon Debate* (Peabody, MA: Hendrickson, 2002). The classic books on the process of canonization are Bruce Metzger, *The Canon of the New Testament: Its Origins, Development, and Significance* (Oxford: Clarendon, 1987); and F. F. Bruce, *The Canon of Scripture* (Downers Grove, IL: InterVarsity, 1988).

16. Time and space do not permit an exploration of the various methods of interpretation employed by the church fathers, which tended to follow three basic pathways: literal, moral, and allegorical. See Paul M. Blowers, *The Bible in Greek Christian Antiquity* (Notre Dame, IN: University of Notre Dame Press, 1997); Earle E. Ellis, *The Old Testament in Early Christianity: Canon and Interpretation in the Light of Modern Research* (Tubingen: J. C. B. Mohr, 1991); James L. Kugel and Rowan A. Greer, *Early Biblical Interpretation* (Philadelphia: Westminster, 1986); Donald K. McKim, *Historical Handbook of Major Biblical Interpreters* (Downers Grove, IL: InterVarsity, 1998); Steve Moyise, *Jesus and Scripture: Studying the New Testament Use of the Old Testament* (Grand Rapids: Baker Academic, 2011); and William Yarchin, *History of Biblical Interpretation: A Reader* (Peabody, MA: Hendrickson, 2004).

17. Ignatius, *To the Philadelphians* 8, in *ANF* 1:84.

18. Ignatius, *To the Philadelphians* 9, in *ANF* 1:84.

19. Justin Martyr, *First Apology* 31, in *ANF* 1:173.

20. Irenaeus, *On the Apostolic Preaching*, trans. John Behr (Crestwood, NY: St. Vladimir's Seminary Press, 1997), 68.

21. Irenaeus, *Apostolic Preaching*, 100.

22. Eusebius, *Hist*. 10.9, p. 332.

23. Eusebius, *Hist*. 10.9, pp. 332–33.

24. Augustine, *The City of God*, trans. Marcus Dods (Peabody, MA: Hendrickson, 2017).

25. Augustine, *City of God* 14.28, p. 430.

26. Augustine, *City of God* 19.10, p. 619.

27. Augustine, *City of God* 19.17, p. 628.

28. Augustine, *City of God* 11.24, pp. 331–32.

29. In *The Great Divorce*, C. S. Lewis describes a huge heavenly parade. A tourist from hell assumes that people must be celebrating a person who was famous during her earthly life. The tour guide, George MacDonald, says that she (her name is Sarah Smith, and she hails from Golders Green) was one of the "great ones," not because she was known for her "greatness" on earth but because she lived in a way that made her great from heaven's perspective. *The Great Divorce* (New York: Macmillan, 1946), 106–8.

Chapter 4 Map

1. Wayne A. Meeks, *The First Urban Christians* (New Haven: Yale University Press, 1983).

2. "On the face of it, Christianity had little to commend it. It sprang from an insignificant corner of the Empire, far distant from the capitol city, Rome. Its roots lay in the despised Judaism, and its founder had been executed by that most demeaning of deaths, crucifixion. It had, at least at first, attracted the least influential members of society, and it had been attacked in polemical tracts and held up to ridicule by some of the Empire's best writers. Christians seem to have been persecuted as much by the people among whom they lived as by the imperial authorities." Michael Walsh, *The Triumph of the Meek: Why Early Christianity Succeeded* (San Francisco: Harper & Row, 1986), 11.

3. Ramsey MacMullen, *Christianizing the Roman Empire* (New Haven: Yale University Press, 1984), 37. Origen, a third-century Christian intellectual, wrote a book challenging the arguments of Celsus. See Origen, *Against Celsus*, trans. Rev. Frederick Crombie and Andrew Overett (Savage, MN: Lighthouse, 2016). Scholars have been able to put together much of Celsus's book, though the book itself has been lost. They have done this by piecing together the many quotes we have of it from the church fathers. See Celsus, *On the True Doctrine: A Discourse against the Christians*, trans. R. Joseph Hoffmann (New York: Oxford University Press, 1987), 53–126. For secondary sources on Celsus, see Robert Louis Wilken, *The Christians as the Romans Saw Them* (New Haven: Yale University Press, 1984), 94–125; Stephen Benko, *Pagan Rome and the Early Christians* (Bloomington: Indiana University Press, 1984), 143–56.

4. Quoted in Wilken, *The Christians*, 104–5 (my italics).

5. Quoted in Wilken, *The Christians*, 119 (my italics).

6. Quoted in Wilken, *The Christians*, 102.

7. Quoted in Wilken, *The Christians*, 104.

8. Richard Bauckham has written an entire book refuting just this argument. See *Jesus and the Eyewitnesses: The Gospels as Eyewitness Testimony* (Grand Rapids: Eerdmans, 2006).

9. Quoted in Wilken, *The Christians*, 111.

10. Clement of Rome, *The First Epistle of Clement to the Corinthians* 16, in *ANF* 1:9.

11. Clement, *First Epistle* 36, in *ANF* 1:14.

12. Ignatius, *Epistle of Ignatius to the Trallians* 9, in *ANF* 1:69–70.

13. *The So-Called Letter to Diognetus* 7.3–4, in Richardson, *ECF*, 219.

14. Irenaeus, *Against Heresies* 4.6.5, ed. Alexander Roberts and James Donaldson, trans. Alexander Roberts and William Rambaut, rev. ed. (n.p.: Ex Fontibus, 2015), 376.

15. Irenaeus, *Against Heresies* 3.18.7 (Roberts and Rambaut), p. 331.

16. Tertullian, *On the Flesh of Christ* 4–5, in Bettenson, *ECF*, 126.

17. Origen, *On First Principles* 1.2.7–8, trans. G. W. Butterworth (Notre Dame, IN: Ave Maria Press, 2013), 29.

18. Athanasius, *On the Incarnation* (Crestwood, NY: St. Vladimir's Seminary Press, 1996), 34 (my italics).

19. *The So-Called Letter to Diognetus* 9.2–5, in Richardson, *ECF*, 220–21.

20. Gregory of Nazianzus, *Third Theological Oration*, in *On God and Christ*, trans. Frederick Williams and Lionel Wickham (Crestwood, NY: St. Vladimir's Seminary Press, 2002), 88.

21. For secondary sources to consult on early Christian theology, see Robert Louis Wilken, *The Spirit of Early Christian Thought: Seeking the Face of God* (New Haven: Yale University Press, 2003); Jaroslav Pelikan, *The Christian Tradition: A History of the Development of Doctrine*, vol. 1, *The Emergence of the Catholic Tradition* (Chicago: University of Chicago

Press, 1971); Stephen R. Holmes, *The Quest for the Trinity: The Doctrine of God in Scripture, History and Modernity* (Downers Grove, IL: IVP Academic, 2012); Christopher A. Hall, *Learning Theology with the Church Fathers* (Downers Grove, IL: IVP Academic, 2002); J. N. D. Kelly, *Early Christian Doctrines*, rev. ed. (San Francisco: HarperOne, 1960); and Margaret R. Miles, *The Word Made Flesh: A History of Christian Thought* (Oxford: Blackwell, 2005).

22. Gregory of Nazianzus, *The Second Theological Oration*, in *On God and Christ*, 52.

23. Gregory of Nazianzus, *The Fifth Theological Oration*, in *On God and Christ*, 141.

24. Gregory of Nazianzus, *The Third Theological Oration*, in *On God and Christ*, 86–87.

25. Basil the Great, *On the Holy Spirit*, trans. David Anderson (Crestwood, NY: St. Vladimir's Seminary Press, 1980).

26. Quoted in Wilken, *The Spirit of Early Christian Thought*, 12.

27. Clement of Alexandria, in Bettenson, *ECF*, 174.

28. Irenaeus, *Against Heresies* 5.preface (Roberts and Rambaut), p. 508.

29. Irenaeus, *Against Heresies* 4.20.7 (Roberts and Rambaut), p. 424.

Chapter 5 Authority

1. Rodney Stark, *Cities of God: The Real Story of How Christianity Became an Urban Movement and Conquered Rome* (San Francisco: HarperSanFrancisco, 2006), 26–34. See also John E. Stambaugh, *The Ancient Roman City* (Baltimore: Johns Hopkins University Press, 1988); Wayne A. Meeks, *The First Urban Christians* (New Haven: Yale University Press, 1983); Stark, *The Rise of Christianity* (Princeton: Princeton University Press, 1996); and Peter Brown, *Poverty and Leadership in the Later Roman Empire* (Waltham, MA: Brandeis University Press, 2001).

2. Keith Hopkins, "Murderous Games: Gladiatorial Contests in Ancient Rome," *History Today* 33, no. 6 (June 1983): 1–23. This article tells a gruesome story of how emperors used the Coliseum.

3. Eusebius, *Hist.*, 98.

4. Ignatius, *Epistle to the Romans* 4, in *ANF* 1:75.

5. Ignatius, *Epistle to the Ephesians* 6, in *ANF* 1:51.

6. Ignatius, *Epistle to the Trallians* 2, in *ANF* 1:66–67.

7. Ignatius, *Epistle to the Trallians* 6, in *ANF* 1:68.

8. Sociologists have tried to estimate numbers, using sociological tools to do so. See Stark, *Cities of God*, 25–84. Philip Jenkins tells the story of the growth and spread of these churches in *The Lost History of Christianity: The Thousand-Year Golden Age of the Church in the Middle East, Africa, and Asia—and How It Died* (New York: HarperCollins, 2008).

9. J. Stevenson, ed., *A New Eusebius: Documents Illustrating the History of the Church to AD 337*, rev. W. H. C. Frend (Grand Rapids: Baker Academic, 2013), 2–3.

10. Stevenson, *A New Eusebius*, 7.

11. The study of Gnosticism has created significant controversy among scholars over the last generation. A small group of scholars has advocated that Gnostic Christianity be viewed, even welcomed, as an alternative Christianity. See, for example, Bart D. Ehrman, *Lost Christianities: The Battles for Scripture and the Faiths We Never Knew* (New York: Oxford University Press, 2003); and Elaine Pagels, *Beyond Belief: The Secret Gospel of Thomas* (New York: Vintage, 2003). For rebuttals, see Luke Timothy Johnson, *The Real Jesus: The Misguided Quest for the Historical Jesus and the Truth of the Traditional Gospels* (San Francisco: HarperSanFrancisco, 1996); Darrell L. Bock, *The Missing Gospels: Unearthing the Truth behind Alternative Christianities* (Nashville: Thomas Nelson, 2006); and Craig

A. Evans, *Fabricating Jesus: How Modern Scholars Distort the Gospels* (Downers Grove, IL: InterVarsity, 2006).

12. See Birger A. Pearson, *Ancient Gnosticism: Traditions and Literature* (Minneapolis: Fortress, 2007), 145–89.

13. *The Gospel of Truth*, in *Lost Scriptures: Books That Did Not Make It into the New Testament*, ed. Bart D. Ehrman (New York: Oxford University Press, 2003), 46. See *The Gospel of Truth*, trans. Harold W. Attridge and George W. MacRae, in *The Nag Hammadi Library: The Definitive Translation of the Gnostic Scriptures Complete in One Volume*, ed. James M. Robinson (San Francisco: HarperSanFrancisco, 1990), 38–51.

14. *The Gospel of Truth*, in *Lost Scriptures*, 47.

15. Irenaeus, *Against Heresies* 1.preface, ed. Alexander Roberts and James Donaldson, trans. Alexander Roberts and William Rambaut, rev. ed. (n.p.: Ex Fontibus, 2015), 25.

16. Irenaeus, *Against Heresies* 1.8.1 (Roberts and Rambaut), p. 51.

17. My colleague and friend Jim Edwards put me onto this metaphor.

18. Everett Ferguson, *The Rule of Faith: A Guide* (Eugene, OR: Cascade, 2015).

19. Ignatius, *Epistle to the Ephesians* 7, in *ANF* 1:52.

20. Quoted in Everett Ferguson, ed., *Early Christians Speak: Faith and Life in the First Three Centuries*, 3rd ed. (Abilene, TX: Abileen Christian University Press, 1999), 19.

21. Irenaeus, *Against Heresies* 1.10.1 (Roberts and Rambaut), p. 61.

22. *De Virginibus Velandis*, quoted in Bettenson, *ECF*, 140.

23. Hippolytus, *Ap. Trad.* 21.14, p. 111.

24. Irenaeus, *Against Heresies* 1.10 (Roberts and Rambaut), pp. 61–62.

25. Larry W. Hurtado, *Destroyer of the Gods: Early Christian Distinctives in the Roman World* (Waco, TX: Baylor University Press, 2016), 106–41. See also Hurtado, *The Earliest Christian Artifacts: Manuscripts and Christian Origins* (Grand Rapids: Eerdmans, 2006).

26. Justin Martyr, *First Apology* 67, in *ANF* 1:185–86.

27. Irenaeus, *Against Heresies* 3.11.8, in Richardson, *ECF*, 382.

28. Clement of Rome, *The First Epistle of Clement to the Corinthians* 42, in *ANF* 1:16.

29. Irenaeus, *Against Heresies* 4.33.8 (Roberts and Rambaut), p. 467.

30. Irenaeus, *Against Heresies* 3.3.4 (Roberts and Rambaut), p. 258.

31. Several fourth-century bishops wrote books on pastoral care. See, e.g., John Chrysostom, *Six Books on the Priesthood*, trans. Graham Neville (Crestwood, NY: St. Vladimir's Seminary Press, 2002).

32. Peter Brown writes, "They insisted that Christ's lowly social status had been deliberately chosen by Him, so that no human being should have any doubt as to the direct source of His power. It was an utterly supernatural authority. It owed nothing whatsoever to human structures of power, prestige, or culture. To be born among those who had no such advantages, and to choose his first disciples from among such persons, ensured that the success of His message would be recognized to be utterly miraculous, as patently coming from God alone." *Poverty and Leadership in the Later Roman Empire* (Waltham, MA: Brandeis University Press, 2001), 93.

Chapter 6 Identity and Community

1. Writes Walter Oetting, "This work was done by ordinary Christians. We know of no missionary societies. . . . When the early Christians themselves recount how they learned of the Gospel, they usually confess that their faith was the result of casual contact with the 'way of life.'" *The Church of the Catacombs* (St. Louis: Concordia, 1964), 23–24. For the best studies on evangelism in early Christianity, see Michael Green, *Evangelism in the Early*

Church (Grand Rapids: Eerdmans, 1970); and E. Glenn Hinson, *The Evangelization of the Roman Empire: Identity and Adaptability* (Macon, GA: Mercer University Press, 1981).

2. The City Observatory states that "about one third of Americans say they have never interacted with their neighbors." See Melissa Dahl, "A Third of Americans Have Never Met Their Neighbors," *The Cut*, August 24, 2015, https://www.thecut.com/2015/08/third-of-americans-dont-know-their-neighbors.html.

3. Mary Beard, *SPQR: A History of Ancient Rome* (New York: Liveright Publishing, 2015); Rodney Stark, *Cities of God: The Real Story of How Christianity Became an Urban Movement and Conquered Rome* (San Francisco: HarperSanFrancisco, 2006); and John E. Stambaugh, *The Ancient Roman City* (Baltimore: Johns Hopkins University Press, 1988). Mary Beard estimates Rome's population at about a million, Rodney Stark at 650,000. Beard is probably the more reliable of the two. She has spent her whole career studying Rome and the Roman Empire. After the Roman Empire collapsed in the fifth century, the population of cities dropped precipitously. They did not reach the same size as those ancient cities until the nineteenth century.

4. Gregory S. Aldrete, *Daily Life in the Roman City: Rome, Pompeii, and Ostia* (Norman: University of Oklahoma Press, 2008), 22.

5. Peter Brown writes, "The class of 'middling' persons was more extensive and more differentiated than we had thought. But such persons did not enjoy the autonomy and the protection that we associate with a modern 'middle class.' The powerful and the truly rich remained overbearing presences in a society where so many self-respecting persons lived uncomfortably close to the widespread 'shallow' poverty that had always characterized an ancient society. It was a tense situation. . . . Roman society demanded an uncomfortable mixture of pervasive deference to superiors and openly aggressive brutishness to inferiors." *Poverty and Leadership in the Later Roman Empire* (Waltham, MA: Brandeis University Press, 2001), 49. John M. G. Barclay argues that the competition for honor in the ancient world was fierce, which put the poor at a virtually insurmountable disadvantage. Barclay, *Paul and the Gift* (Grand Rapids: Eerdmans, 2015).

6. John E. Stambaugh writes, "Such subsidies apart, the poor did what they could. Traditionally they became the clients of patrons who provided food or money in exchange for political support or other help. If that did not work—and the sources show that the process could involve an intensely competitive scramble—there was begging, stealing, or starving." *The Ancient Roman City*, 134. See also Helen Rhee, *Loving the Poor, Saving the Rich: Wealth, Poverty, and Early Christian Formation* (Grand Rapids: Baker Academic, 2012); Wayne A. Meeks, *The First Urban Christians*, 2nd ed. (New Haven: Yale University Press, 2003); Karl P. Donfried and Peter Richardson, eds., *Judaism and Christianity in First-Century Rome* (Grand Rapids: Eerdmans, 1998); Mary Beard, *SPQR*, 435–73; Everett Ferguson, *Backgrounds to Early Christianity*, 3rd ed. (Grand Rapids: Eerdmans, 2003), 48–147; and Peter Brown, *Through the Eye of the Needle* (Princeton: Princeton University Press, 2012).

7. Meeks writes, "For a very long time groups of foreigners had gathered in each city: merchants and artisans following the armies or in search of better markets or better access to transportation, persons enslaved and displaced by war or piracy and now set free, political exiles, soldiers of fortune. These noncitizen residents . . . often retained some sense of ethnic identity by establishing local cults of their native gods or by forming a voluntary association, which also had at least the trappings of religion." *The First Urban Christians*, 13.

8. Alan Kreider, *The Patient Ferment of the Early Church: The Improbable Rise of Christianity in the Roman Empire* (Grand Rapids: Baker Academic, 2016).

9. *The So-Called Letter to Diognetus* 5.1–2, in Richardson, *ECF*, 216.

10. *The So-Called Letter to Diognetus* 5.5, in Richardson, *ECF*, 217.

11. David Batson writes, "In linking salvation theology to social cohesion Paul was effectively dismantling barriers between social classes which had existed from time immemorial in Greco-Roman society." *The Treasure Chest of the Early Christians: Faith, Care, and Community from the Apostolic Age to Constantine the Great* (Grand Rapids: Eerdmans, 2001), 49.

12. Clement of Alexandria, *The Instructor* 1.3, in *ANF* 2:211.

13. "The Christian church, by contrast, was a variegated group. In that respect, it was not unlike a miniature version of the new empire. High and low, men and women met as equals because equally subject, now, to the overruling law of one God." Peter Brown, *The Rise of Western Christendom: Triumph and Diversity, A.D. 200–1000*, 3rd ed. (London: Wiley-Blackwell, 2013), 64.

14. *The So-Called Letter to Diognetus* 9.2–6, in Richardson, *ECF*, 221.

15. *The So-Called Letter to Diognetus* 10.3–5, in Richardson, *ECF*, 221.

16. Athenagoras, *A Plea for the Christians* 11, in *ANF* 2:134.

17. Christians requested that authorities turn over Polycarp's body after he was burned at the stake, but they refused, thinking that Christians would abandon Jesus and begin to worship Polycarp. Both pagans and Jews betrayed their own ignorance at this point, for Christians "could never forsake Christ, who suffered for the salvation of the whole world of those who are saved, the faultless for the sinners, nor can we ever worship any other. For we worship this One as Son of God, but we love the martyrs as disciples and imitators of the Lord, deservedly so, because of their unsurpassable devotion to their own King and Teacher." Eusebius, *Hist.*, 122.

18. Origen, *An Exhortation to Martyrdom*, trans. Rowan A. Greer (New York: Paulist Press, 1979), 52.

19. Tertullian, *To the Martyrs* 2.4, in *ANF* 3:693–94.

20. Herbert Musurillo, ed., *The Acts of the Christian Martyrs* (Oxford: Clarendon, 1972), 107–31.

21. Justin Martyr, *First Apology* 14, in *ANF* 1:166.

22. *The So-Called Letter to Diognetus* 5.4, in Richardson, *ECF*, 217.

23. Irenaeus, *Against Heresies* 1.20, ed. Alexander Roberts and James Donaldson, trans. Alexander Roberts and William Rambaut, rev. ed. (n.p.: Ex Fontibus, 2015), 61.

24. Tertullian, *Apology* 23, in *ANF* 3:38.

25. Clement of Alexandria, *Stromateis* 7.16, in Bettenson, *ECF*, 179.

26. St. Cyprian of Carthage, *The Unity of the Catholic Church*, in *On the Church: Select Treatises*, trans. Allen Brent (Crestwood, NY: St. Vladimir's Seminary Press, 2006), 154–55.

27. "House churches," writes Roger Gehring, "served as community centers for the life of the church and as operational bases for missional outreach; as such they were a powerful force for the missional enterprise in all these places." *House Church and Mission: The Importance of Household Structures in Early Christianity* (Peabody, MA: Hendrickson, 2004), 116. See also Wolfgang Simson, *Houses That Change the World: The Return of the House Churches* (Emmelsbull, Germany: C&P Publishing, 1999); Tory K. Baucum, *Evangelical Hospitality: Catechetical Evangelism in the Early Church and Its Recovery for Today* (Toronto: Scarecrow, 2008); and Amy Oden, *And You Welcomed Me: A Sourcebook on Hospitality in Early Christianity* (Nashville: Abingdon, 2001).

28. *The So-Called Letter to Diognetus* 5.6–10, in Richardson, *ECF*, 217.

29. "To the poor, the widows and orphans, Christians gave alms and support, like the synagogue communities, their forerunners. This 'brotherly' love has been minimized as a reason for turning to the Church, as if only those who were members could know of it. In fact, it was widely recognized. . . . Christian 'love' was public knowledge and must have

played its part in drawing outsiders to the faith." Robin Lane Fox, *Pagans and Christians* (New York: Knopf, 1987), 324.

30. Joseph H. Hellerman, *The Ancient Church as Family* (Minneapolis: Fortress, 2001).

31. Most scholars affirm that the early Christian movement served the interests of women, though probably not according to modern standards. For example, women did not serve as bishops. For recent scholarship on the ministry of women in early Christianity, see Kevin Madigan and Carolyn Osiek, eds., *Ordained Women in the Early Church: A Documentary History* (Baltimore: Johns Hopkins University Press, 2005); Margaret Y. MacDonald and Carolyn Osiek with Janet H. Tulloch, *A Woman's Place: House Churches in Earliest Christianity* (Minneapolis: Fortress, 2006); and Beverly Mayne Kienzle and Pamela J. Walker, eds., *Women Preachers and Prophets through Two Millennia of Christianity* (Berkeley: University of California Press, 1998). Wayne Meeks argues, "Both in terms of their position in the larger society and in terms of their participation in the Christian communities, then, a number of women broke through the normal expectations of female roles." *The First Urban Christians*, 71.

32. Meeks, *The First Urban Christians*, 88. See also David L. Balch and Carolyn Osiek, *Family in the New Testament World: Households and House Churches* (Louisville: Westminster John Knox, 1997); Cornelia B. Horn and John W. Martens, *"Let the Children Come to Me": Childhood and Children in Early Christianity* (Washington, DC: Catholic University of America Press, 2008); Odd Magne Bakke, *When Children Became People: The Birth of Childhood in Early Christianity* (Minneapolis: Fortress, 2005); and Rowan A. Greer, *Broken Lights and Mended Lives: Theology and Common Life in the Early Church* (University Park: Pennsylvania State University Press, 1986), 93–140.

33. E. Glenn Hinson writes, "Not merely in theory but in actuality, these initiatory procedures, as gradually developed, assisted new Christians to discern how their participation in the covenant people set them against their former culture and made them a part of the *Militia Christi*, which was charged with the overcoming of the forces of evil, not by physical might but by purity of life and witness. Baptism, as some of the Fathers expressed it, was the layperson's ordination." *The Evangelization of the Roman Empire*, 73.

34. Clement of Alexandria, *The Instructor* 2.1, in *ANF* 2:238.

35. Tertullian, *Apology* 39, in *ANF* 3:46.

36. Tertullian, *Apology* 1, in *ANF* 3:17.

Chapter 7 Worship

1. Since developing this metaphor, I have discovered two other theologians who have also used it: Kevin Vanhoozer and Sam Wells. I can only say that I happened upon it at the Montero concert I attended many years ago, quite independently from these two first-rate Christian thinkers. I assume that neither of them borrowed from each other, either, which tells me that the metaphor of improvisation is a timely one, considering our post-Christendom circumstances. Samuel Wells puts it so well: "The Bible is not so much a script that the church learns and performs as it is a training school that shapes the habits and practices of a community. This community learns to take the right things for granted, and on the basis of this faithfulness, it trusts itself to improvise within its tradition. Improvisation means a community formed in the right habits trusting itself to embody its tradition in new and often challenging circumstances; and this is exactly what the church is called to do." *Improvisation: The Drama of Christian Ethics* (London: SPCK, 2004), 12. See also Kevin J. Vanhoozer, *Faith Seeking Understanding: Performing the Drama of Doctrine* (Louisville: Westminster John Knox, 2014).

2. For several introductory sources on early Christian worship, see Andrew B. McGowan, *Ancient Christian Worship* (Grand Rapids: Baker Academic, 2014); Christopher A. Hall, *Worshiping with the Church Fathers* (Downers Grove, IL: IVP Academic, 2009); Paul F. Bradshaw, *Reconstructing Early Christian Worship* (London: SPCK, 2009); Larry W. Hurtado, *At the Origins of Christian Worship: The Context and Character of Earliest Christian Devotion* (Grand Rapids: Eerdmans, 2000); and Gregory Dix, *The Shape of the Liturgy*, new ed. (London: Continuum, 2005).

3. Quoted in Everett Ferguson, ed., *Early Christians Speak: Faith and Life in the First Three Centuries*, 3rd ed. (Abilene, TX: Abileen Christian Uuniversity Press, 1999), 79.

4. Justin Martyr, *First Apology* 67, in *ANF* 1:186.

5. "Christian worship—the set of communal practices of prayer and ritual characteristics of followers of Jesus—is as fundamental to the church as its doctrine." McGowan, *Ancient Christian Worship*, 1.

6. Richard Bauckham, "The Lord's Day," in *From Sabbath to Lord's Day: A Biblical, Historical, and Theological Investigation*, ed. D. A. Carson (Grand Rapids: Zondervan, 1982), 221–50.

7. Ignatius, *Epistle to the Magnesians* 9, in *ANF* 1:63.

8. Quoted in Ferguson, *Early Christians Speak*, 67.

9. Justin Martyr, *First Apology* 67, in *ANF* 1:186. For texts on "The Eighth Day," see Ferguson, *Early Christians Speak*, 65–66.

10. Paul F. Bradshaw, *Daily Prayer in the Early Church: A Study of the Origin and Early Development of the Divine Office* (London: SPCK, 1981).

11. Didache 8.1–3, in Richardson, *ECF*, 174.

12. Hippolytus, *Ap. Trad.* 41, pp. 164–65.

13. McGowan, *Ancient Christian Worship*, 191–95.

14. Hippolytus, *Ap. Trad.* 41, p. 166.

15. Hippolytus, *Ap. Trad.* 41, p. 164.

16. See Kim Bowes, *Private Worship, Public Values, and Religious Change in Late Antiquity* (New York: Cambridge University Press, 2008); and Allan Doig, *Liturgy and Architecture: From the Early Church to the Middle Ages* (Burlington, VT: Ashgate, 2008).

17. Quoted in Uwe Michael Lang, *Turning towards the Lord: Orientation in Liturgical Prayer* (San Francisco: Ignatius, 2009), 48.

18. Quoted in Lang, *Turning towards the Lord*, 50. Lang concludes, "In private and in liturgical prayer Christians turned, no longer towards the earthly Jerusalem, but towards the new, heavenly Jerusalem; they believed firmly that when the Lord came again in glory to judge the world, he would gather his elect to make up this heavenly city. The rising sun was considered an appropriate expression of this eschatological hope" (45).

19. Hippolytus, *Ap. Trad.* 42, p. 171.

20. Harry Y. Gamble, *Books and Readers in the Early Christian Church: A History of Christian Texts* (New Haven: Yale University Press, 1995).

21. Brian J. Wright, *Communal Reading in the Time of Jesus: A Window into Early Christian Reading Practices* (Minneapolis: Fortress, 2017).

22. Justin Martyr, *First Apology* 67, in *ANF* 1:186 (my italics).

23. Tertullian, *Apology* 39, in *ANF* 3:46. Andrew McGowan comments on how Christians read the Bible in worship, too. "The act of reading itself was typically a performance of a work, the physical text something like a musician's score that invited or demanded not only rendering into voice but an interpretation of sorts by the very act of speaking what had been written." *Ancient Christian Worship*, 79.

24. For the best single volume on the history of preaching, see O. C. Edwards Jr., *A History of Preaching* (Nashville: Abingdon, 2004). He devotes the first section (1–116) to early Christian preaching.

25. Roy Hammerling, *The Lord's Prayer in the Early Church* (New York: Macmillan, 2010), 132. Adds Andrew McGowan, "The first readers of the Gospels did not think of the Lord's Prayer primarily as a model or primer about prayer, although it may have been that too; for them, the first point was actually to *say* it." *Ancient Christian Worship*, 187.

26. Tertullian, *On Prayer* 29, in *ANF* 3:690–91.

27. Clement of Alexandria, "A Hymn to Christ the Savior," *The Instructor* 5.12, in *ANF* 2:295–96.

28. John Arthur Smith, *Music in Ancient Judaism and Early Christianity* (Burlington, VT: Ashgate, 2011). Jeremy Begbie argues that repetition of the Eucharist and repetition in music play a similar role. Thus "every Eucharistic celebration can be seen as a repeated opportunity for time-laden creatures to be incorporated into a temporal environment, established in Christ, in which past, present and future coinhere, in such a way that our identities can be healed, recast and reformed." See his chapter "Repetition and Eucharist," in *Theology, Music, and Time* (New York: Cambridge University Press, 2000). See also Edward Foley, *Foundations of Christian Music* (Piscataway, NJ: Gorgias Press, 2009).

29. Ambrose of Milan, "O Splendor of God's Glory Bright," in *The Presbyterian Hymnal: Hymns, Psalms, and Spiritual Songs* (Louisville: Westminster John Knox, 1990), no. 474.

30. Herbert Musurillo, ed., *The Acts of the Christian Martyrs* (Oxford: Clarendon, 1972), 125–31.

31. McGowan, *Ancient Christian Worship*, 19–20. See also Paul F. Bradshaw and Maxwell E. Johnson, *The Origins of Feasts, Fasts, and Seasons* (Collegeville, MN: Liturgical Press, 2011).

32. For an excellent introduction to the early Christian theology of the sacraments, see Robert Louis Wilken, *The Spirit of Early Christian Thought: Seeking the Face of God* (New Haven: Yale University Press, 2003), 25–49. Kenan B. Osborne, OFM, is one of many modern theologians who explain the meaning of the sacraments by starting with the incarnation. See *Sacramental Theology: A General Introduction* (New York: Paulist Press, 1988), 120. See also Leonard Vander Zee, *Christ, Baptism and the Lord's Supper: Recovering the Sacraments for Evangelical Worship* (Downers Grove, IL: InterVarsity, 2004); and Kevin W. Irwin, *Liturgy, Prayer and Spirituality* (New York: Paulist Press, 1984), 47.

33. Justin Martyr, *First Apology* 61, in *ANF* 1:183.

34. Irenaeus, *Against Heresies* 3.17.2, ed. Alexander Roberts and James Donaldson, trans. Alexander Roberts and William Rambaut, rev. ed. (n.p.: Ex Fontibus, 2015), 324.

35. Clement of Alexandria, *The Instructor* 1.6, in *ANF* 2:215.

36. See Paul F. Bradshaw, *The Search for the Origins of Christian Worship: Sources and Methods for the Study of Early Liturgy* (New York: Oxford University Press, 2002); and Thomas M. Finn, *From Death to Rebirth: Ritual and Conversion in Antiquity* (New York: Paulist Press, 1997).

37. Didache 7.1–2, in Richardson, *ECF*, 174.

38. Justin Martyr, *First Apology* 61, in *ANF* 1:183.

39. Tertullian, *On Baptism* 19, in *ANF* 3:678.

40. Hippolytus, *Ap. Trad.* 21, p. 110.

41. Ignatius, *Epistle to the Ephesians* 20, in *ANF* 1:57.

42. Justin Martyr, *First Apology* 66, in *ANF* 1:185.

43. Irenaeus, *Against Heresies* 5.2.2–3 (Roberts amd Rambaut), p. 512.

44. Wilken, *The Spirit of Early Christian Thought*, 45.

45. See Wayne E. Meeks, *The Origins of Christian Morality: The First Two Centuries* (New Haven: Yale University Press, 1993).

46. Didache 1.1 and 5.1, in Richardson, *ECF*, 171–73. The Epistle of Barnabas and the Shepherd of Hermas also make use of this teaching device.

47. Didache 3.1–6, in Richardson, *ECF*, 172.

48. See Clement of Alexandria, *The Instructor* 2.1, in *ANF* 2:237–42; and Tertullian, *The Shows*, in *ANF* 3:79–91.

49. Tertullian, *The Shows* 15, in *ANF* 3:86.

50. Tertullian, *Apology* 39, in *ANF* 3:46.

51. Clement of Alexandria, *The Instructor* 3.6, in *ANF* 2:280.

52. Justin Martyr, *First Apology* 67, in *ANF* 1:187.

Chapter 8 Life in the World

1. See Robert Louis Wilken, *The Christians as the Romans Saw Them* (New Haven: Yale University Press, 1984), 164–96.

2. Quoted in Wilken, *The Christians*, 174.

3. *Edict to the People of Bostra*, quoted in *Documents of the Christian Church*, ed. Henry Bettenson and Chris Maunder, 4th ed. (New York: Oxford University Press, 2011), 21.

4. Quoted in Wilken, *The Christians*, 181.

5. *Letter to Arsacius, High-priest of Galatia*, in *The Works of the Emperor Julian*, vol. 3, ed. Wilmer Cave Wright (New York: Putnam's Sons, 1923), 67.

6. *Letter to Arsacius*, 67.

7. See Andrea Sterk, *Renouncing the World Yet Leading the Church: The Monk-Bishop in Late Antiquity* (Cambridge, MA: Harvard University Press, 2004), 13–94; Hans von Campenhausen, *The Fathers of the Greek Church* (New York: Pantheon, 1955); and Anthony Meredith, *The Cappadocians* (Crestwood, NY: St. Vladimir's Seminary Press, 1995).

8. Gregory of Nazianzus, *The Panegyric of Saint Basil*, in NPNF[2] 7:411.

9. *The Fathers Speak: St. Basil the Great, St. Gregory of Nazianzus, St. Gregory of Nyssa*, ed. and trans. Georges Barrois (Crestwood, NY: St. Vladimir's Seminary Press, 1986). This book contains many of the letters exchanged among the Cappadocian fathers. On occasion Nazianzus, his best friend, and Nyssa, his younger brother, complained about Basil's calculated moves. It appears that Basil had a larger-than-life personality and ambition, as well as conscience. In his biography of Basil, however, Nazianzus defended him.

10. Gregory, *Panegyric*, 416–17.

11. Basil of Caesarea, *On Social Justice*, trans. C. Paul Schroeder (Crestwood, NY: St. Vladimir's Seminary Press, 2009), 43.

12. See Gary B. Ferngren, *Medicine and Health Care in Early Christianity* (Baltimore: Johns Hopkins University Press, 2009), 113–39; Amanda Porterfield, *Healing in the History of Christianity* (New York: Oxford University Press, 2005); and T. S. Miller, *The Birth of the Hospital in the Byzantine Empire* (Baltimore: Johns Hopkins University Press, 1997). The names of the three major hospitals in Spokane illustrate the point: Sacred Heart, Holy Family, and Deaconess.

13. Basil the Great, letter 94, in *Letters, Volume 1 (1–185)*, ed. Roy Deferrari, trans. Sister Agnes Clare Way, vol. 13 of *Fathers of the Church* (Washington, DC: Catholic University of America Press, 1951).

14. Gregory of Nyssa, *On the Love of the Poor: On the Saying, "Whoever Has Done It to One of These Has Done It to Me,"* in *The Hungry Are Dying: Beggars and Bishops in Roman Cappadocia*, ed. Susan R. Holman (New York: Oxford University Press, 2001), 199–206.

15. Gregory of Nazianzus, *Oration 14: On the Love of the Poor*, in *Gregory of Nazianzus: Early Church Fathers*, ed. Brian E. Daley, SJ (New York: Routledge, 2006), 83.

16. There is scholarly consensus that there *was* impact on the wider culture. As historian Wayne A. Meeks suggests, "Looked at from the perspective of cultural history, what changed was a broad range of sensibilities. There emerged altered convictions about the kinds of behavior that are fitting, right and salutary for human flourishing. A new vocabulary appeared in talk about what one ought to do and why, new senses of the end toward which a virtuous life would strive, new hopes and new fears, new institutions and sanctions come into being, which undertook to direct the formation of character." *The Origins of Christian Morality: The First Two Centuries* (New Haven: Yale University Press, 1993), 2. Larry W. Hurtado argues similarly, "By contrast, the early Christian texts reflect a rather strong effort to promote widely in circles of believers a collective commitment to the strict behavior that these texts advocate. That commitment was laid upon adherents immediately upon their baptism, whatever may have been their consistency in observing it thereafter." *Destroyer of the Gods: Early Christian Distinctiveness in the Roman World* (Waco, TX: Baylor University Press, 2016), 170.

17. Tertullian, *On Idolatry* 18, in *ANF* 3:73.

18. Clement of Alexandria, *Salvation of the Rich Man* 33, in *ANF* 2:600–601.

19. *The So-Called Letter to Diognetus* 10.6, in Richardson, *ECF*, 221.

20. Several historians have tried to show the connection between early Christian theology and practice. See Rowan A. Greer, *Broken Lights and Mended Lives: Theology and Common Life in the Early Church* (University Park: Pennsylvania State University Press, 1986); and Alan Kreider, *The Patient Ferment of the Early Church: The Improbable Rise of Christianity in the Roman Empire* (Grand Rapids: Baker Academic, 2016).

21. Quoted in Wilken, *The Christians*, 97.

22. Quoted in Wilken, *The Christians*, 78.

23. Clement of Rome, *The First Epistle of Clement to the Corinthians* 1, in *ANF* 1:5.

24. Athenagoras, *A Plea Regarding Christians* 34, in *ANF* 2:147.

25. Tertullian, *Apology* 39, in *ANF* 3:46.

26. See Pontius, *Life of St. Cyprian*, in *Early Christian Biographies*, ed. Roy J. Deferrari (New York: Fathers of the Church, 1952); and Gregory Thaumaturgis, *The Oration and Panegyric Addressed to Origen*, in *ANF* 6:21–39.

27. The following section has been adapted from Gerald L. Sittser, *Water from a Deep Well: Christian Spirituality from Early Martyrs to Modern Missionaries* (Downers Grove, IL: InterVarsity, 2007), 63–65.

28. Eusebius, *Hist.*, 237.

29. Pontius, *Life of St. Cyprian*, 9–10.

30. Pontius, *Life of St. Cyprian*, 14. William H. McNeill notes, "Another advantage Christians enjoyed over pagans was that the teaching of their faith made life meaningful even amid sudden and surprising death. . . . Christianity was, therefore, a system of thought and feeling thoroughly adapted to a time of troubles in which hardship, disease, and violent death commonly prevailed." *Plagues and Peoples* (Garden City, NY: Doubleday, 1976), 108.

31. Pontius, *Life of St. Cyprian*, 10.

32. Eusebius, *Hist.*, 237.

33. Eusebius, *Hist.* 7.22, p. 237.

34. Ramsey MacMullen, *Christianizing the Roman Empire: A.D. 100–400* (New Haven: Yale University Press, 1984), 28.

35. Hippolytus, e.g., repeated much of what 1 Timothy outlined. See Hippolytus, *Ap. Trad.* 10, p. 95.

36. Bonnie Bowman Thurston, *The Widows: A Women's Ministry in the Early Church* (Minneapolis: Fortress, 1989); and R. Gryson, *The Ministry of Women in the Early Church*, trans. J. L. Laporte and M. L. Hall (Collegeville, MN: Liturgical Press, 1976).

37. Hippolytus, *Ap. Trad.* 24, p. 131. On the ministry of deacons, see J. M. Barnett, *The Diaconate: A Full and Equal Order*, rev. ed. (New York: Seabury, 1994); J. N. Collins, *Diakonia: Re-Interpreting the Ancient Sources* (New York: Oxford University Press, 1990); and A. G. Martimort, *Deaconess: An Historical Study* (San Francisco: Ignatius, 1986).

38. For the church's ministry to the poor, see Susan Holman, *Wealth and Poverty in the Early Church and Society* (Grand Rapids: Eerdmans, 2008); and Helen Rhee, *Loving the Poor, Saving the Rich: Wealth, Poverty, and Early Christian Formation* (Grand Rapids: Baker Academic, 2012).

39. Quoted in J. G. Davies, "Deacons, Deaconesses and the Minor Orders in the Patristic Period," in *Church, Ministry, and Organization in the Early Church Era*, ed. Everett Ferguson (New York: Garland, 1993), 246.

40. Quoted in MacMullen, *Christianizing the Roman Empire*, 27.

41. See J. G. Davies, "Deacons," 244–46. See also Everett Ferguson, *Demonology of the Early Christian World*, Symposium Series 12 (New York: Edwin Mellen, 1984).

42. D. A. Drake, *Constantine and the Bishops: The Politics of Intolerance* (Baltimore: Johns Hopkins University Press, 2002).

43. *Constitutions of Holy Apostles* 4.1.2, in *ANF* 7:433.

44. John Chrysostom, *Six Books on the Priesthood*, trans. Graham Neville (Crestwood, NY: St. Vladimir's Seminary Press, 2002), 58.

45. Gregory of Nazianzus, *In Defense of His Flight to Pontus*, in *NPNF²* 7:219.

46. Quoted in Carl A. Volv, *Pastoral Life and Practice in the Early Church* (Minneapolis: Augsburg, 1990), 164.

47. Davies, "Deacons," 242.

48. Quoted in Rodney Stark, *The Rise of Christianity* (Princeton: Princeton University Press, 1996), 104.

Chapter 9 Crossing to Safety

1. Material in this chapter has been adapted from Gerald L. Sittser, "The Catechumenate and the Rise of Christianity," *Journal of Spiritual Formation and Soul Care* 6, no. 2 (Fall 2013), 179–203.

2. There is a large body of scholarly literature on the early Christian catechumenate. See, e.g., Edward Yarnold, *The Awe-Inspiring Rites of Initiation: The Origins of the R.I.C.A.*, 2nd ed. (Edinburgh: T&T Clark, 1994); "Catechumenate," *New Catholic Encyclopedia*, 2nd ed. (Washington, DC: Gale, 2003); Aidan Kavanagh, *The Shape of Baptism: The Rite of Christian Initiation* (Collegeville, MN: Liturgical Press, 1991); John H. Westerhoff III and O. C. Edwards Jr., eds., *A Faithful Church: Issues in the History of Catechesis* (Wilton, CT: Morehouse-Barlow, 1981); Michel Dujarier, *A History of the Catechumenate: The First Six Centuries*, trans. Edward J. Haasl (New York: Sadlier, 1979); Robert M. Grant, "Development of the Christian Catechumenate," in *Made, Not Born: New Perspectives on Christian Initiation and the Catechumenate* (Notre Dame: University of Notre Dame Press, 1976), 32–49; Everett Ferguson, "Catechesis and Initiation," in *The Origins of Christendom in the West*, ed. Alan Kreider (New York: T&T Clark, 2001), 229–68; Robert Louis Wilken, "Christian Formation in the Early Church," in *Educating People of Faith: Exploring the History of Jewish and Christian Communities*, ed. John Van Engen (Grand Rapids: Eerdmans, 2004), 48–62; Alan Kreider, *The Change of Conversion and the Origin of Christendom* (Eugene,

OR: Wipf & Stock, 1999); and E. C. Whitaker, *Documents of the Baptismal Liturgy*, rev. ed. Maxwell E. Johnson (Collegeville, MN: Liturgical Press, 2003).

3. Rodney Stark, *The Rise of Christianity: How the Obscure, Marginal Jesus Movement Became the Dominant Religious Force in the Western World in a Few Centuries* (Princeton: Princeton University Press, 1996), 13–21, 191–203.

4. Hermann Beyer, "κατηχέω," in *Theological Dictionary of the New Testament*, vol. 3, ed. Gerhard Kittel, trans. Geoffrey W. Bromily (Grand Rapids: Eerdmans, 1965), 638–40; Horst Bolz and Gerhard Schneider, eds., *Exegetical Dictionary of the New Testament*, vol. 2 (Grand Rapids: Eerdmans, 1991), 273; and Johannes P. Louw and Eugene A. Nida, eds., *Greek-English Lexicon of the New Testament* (New York: United Bible Society, 1988), 414.

5. Eusebius, *The History of the Church from Christ to Constantine* 5.1, trans. G. A. Williamson (New York: Penguin, 1965), 140.

6. Donald G. Kyle, *Sport and Spectacle in the Ancient World* (Malden, MA: Blackwell, 2007); and Victor C. Pfitzner, *Paul and the Agon Motif* (Leiden: Brill, 1967).

7. Tertullian, *To the Martyrs* 1, in *ANF* 3:693.

8. Clement of Alexandria, *The Instructor* 1.13, in *ANF* 2:235.

9. Ambrose of Milan, "Sermons on the Sacraments I," in Yarnold, *The Awe-Inspiring Rites of Initiation*, 102.

10. Quoted in Michel Dujarier, *A History of the Catechumenate*, 96.

11. Didache 1.1–2, in Richardson, *ECF*, 171.

12. Didache 7.1, in Richardson, *ECF*, 174 (my italics).

13. Justin Martyr, *First Apology* 61, in *ANF* 1:183 (my italics).

14. Quoted in Dujarier, *A History of the Catechumenate*, 56.

15. It is natural to ask to what extent a document such as this described what was already widely practiced or prescribed what the author hoped would happen. This problem presents itself when reading any descriptive document from the early Christian period. That it reads as a manual indicates that it probably describes what in fact was practiced, however inadequately and incompletely.

16. Thomas Finn, "Ritual Process and the Survival of Early Christianity: A Study of the Apostolic Tradition of Hippolytus," *Journal of Ritual Studies* 3, no. 1 (1989): 69–89; Robert E. Webber, *Journey to Jesus: The Worship, Evangelism, and Nurture Mission of the Church* (Nashville: Abingdon, 2001), 65–72; and Tory K. Baucum, *Evangelical Hospitality: Catechetical Evangelism in the Early Church and Its Recovery for Today* (Lanham, MD: Scarecrow, 2008).

17. Both Jan Bremmer and Robin Lane Fox argue that we know of few if any professional "evangelists" during this period, except for the wandering "prophets" mentioned in the Didache, implying that the work of evangelism was done by ordinary believers. See Jan Bremmer, *The Rise of Christianity through the Eyes of Gibbon, Harnack and Rodney Stark* (Groningen: Barkhuis, 2010); and Robin Lane Fox, *Pagans and Christians* (New York: Knopf, 1987).

18. Hippolytus, *Ap. Trad*. 15, pp. 97–98.

19. Hippolytus, *Ap. Trad*. 16, pp. 99–100.

20. Hippolytus, *Ap. Trad*. 16, pp. 99–100.

21. Hippolytus, *Ap. Trad*. 18–19, pp. 104–5.

22. Augustine, *The First Catechetical Instruction*, trans. Joseph P. Christopher (New York: Newman, 1946). See also William Harmless, *Augustine and the Catechumenate* (Collegeville, MN: Liturgical Press, 1995); and Thomas M. Finn, "It Happened One Saturday Night: Ritual and Conversion in Augustine's North Africa," *Journal of the American Academy of Religion* 58, no. 4 (Winter 1990): 589–616.

23. Hippolytus, *Ap. Trad.* 20, pp. 105–6.

24. Hippolytus, *Ap. Trad.* 20, pp. 105–6.

25. Hippolytus, *Ap. Trad.* 20, pp. 105–6.

26. Hippolytus, *Ap. Trad.* 21, pp. 110–14.

27. Hippolytus, *Ap. Trad.* 21, pp. 110–14.

28. *Egeria's Travels*, trans. John Wilkinson, 3rd ed. (Oxford: Oxbow Books, 1999).

29. See Yarnold, *The Awe-Inspiring Rites of Initiation*, for examples of these sermons.

30. Quoted in Dujarier, *A History of the Catechumenate*, 82. The following quotes come from a section of primary source quotes addressing the decline of the catechumenate in Dujarier, *A History of the Catechumenate*, 79–100.

31. Quoted in Dujarier, *A History of the Catechumenate*, 82–83.

32. Quoted in Dujarier, *A History of the Catechumenate*, 80.

33. Quoted in Dujarier, *A History of the Catechumenate*, 83.

34. Quoted in Dujarier, *A History of the Catechumenate*, 84.

35. Quoted in Dujarier, *A History of the Catechumenate*, 96.

36. Quoted in Dujarier, *A History of the Catechumenate*, 87.

37. Quoted in Dujarier, *A History of the Catechumenate*, 88.

38. On the end of Christendom in the West see Stuart Murray, *Post-Christendom: Church and Mission in a Strange New World* (Carlisle: Paternoster, 2004); and Douglas John Hall, ed., *The End of Christendom and the Future of Christianity* (Harrisburg, PA: Trinity, 1997).

Conclusion

1. In chap. 4, I quoted Gregory of Nazianzus, who wrote eloquently of the complexity and paradoxes of Jesus as divine and human. A modern author has done the same. *New York Times* columnist and devout Roman Catholic Ross Douthat recently wrote a book about the American church's descent into heresy. He describes Jesus much as Nazianzus did.

> Christianity is a paradoxical religion because the Jew of Nazareth is a paradoxical character. No figure in history or fiction contains as many multitudes as the New Testament's Jesus. He's a celibate ascetic who enjoys dining with publicans and changing water into wine at weddings. He's an apocalyptic prophet one moment, a wise ethicist the next. He's a fierce critic of Jewish religious law who insists that he's actually fulfilling rather than subverting it. He preaches a reversal of every social hierarchy while deliberately avoiding explicitly political claims. He promises to set parents against children then disallows divorce; he consorts with prostitutes while denouncing lustful thoughts. He makes wild claims about his own relationship to God, and perhaps his own divinity, without displaying any of the usual signs of megalomania or madness. He can be egalitarian and hierarchical, gentle and impatient, extraordinarily charitable and extraordinarily judgmental. He sets impossible standards and then forgives the worst of sinners. He blesses the peacemakers and then promises that he's brought not peace but the sword. He's superhuman one moment; the next he's weeping. And of course the accounts of his resurrection only heighten these paradoxes, by introducing a post-crucifixion Jesus who is somehow neither a resuscitated body or a flitting ghost but something even stranger still—a being at once fleshly and supernatural, recognizable and transfigured, bearing the wounds of the crucifixion even as he passes easily through walls. (Ross Douthat, *Bad Religion: How We Became a Nation of Heretics* [New York: Free Press, 2012], 152–53)

I have doubts that anyone, however brilliant, could have invented this Jesus.

Index